Enjoy and
share
the
journey!
love Richard

This. Only This.

This. Only This.

Mindfulness Strategies for Discovering Peace in Every Moment

By

Michael H. Brooks

ZenWhim, Inc.

Mountain View, California

This. Only This.
Mindfulness Strategies for Discovering Peace in Every Moment

Published by ZenWhim, Inc.
650 Castro Street, Suite 120-317
Mountain View, CA 94041

Edited by Jon Hofferman and Catherine Elliott Escobedo

Book cover layout by Sharon Anderson

ISBN: 978-0-9857311-9-9

Library of Congress Control Number: 2012955302

For my Teachers

There is a season for everything, and we do not notice a given phe-
nomenon except at that season, if, indeed, it can be called the same
phenomenon at any other season. There is a time to watch the ripples
on Ripple Lake, to look for arrowheads, to study the rocks and lichens,
a time to walk on sandy deserts; and the observer of nature must im-
prove these seasons as much as the farmer his. So boys fly kites and play
ball or hockey at particular times all over the State. A wise man will
know what game to play to-day, and play it. We must not be governed
by rigid rules, as by the almanac, but let the season rule us. The moods
and thoughts of man are revolving just as steadily and incessantly as
nature's. Nothing must be postponed. Take time by the forelock. Now
or never! **You must live in the present, launch yourself on ev-**
ery wave, find your eternity in each moment. Fools stand
on their island of opportunities and look toward another
land. There is no other land; there is no other life but this,
or the like of this. *Where the good husbandman is, there is the good*
soil. Take any other course, and life will be a succession of regrets. Let
us see vessels sailing prosperously before the wind, and not simply
stranded barks. There is no world for the penitent and regretful.

- The Journal of Henry David Thoreau, April 24, 1859 [i]

TABLE OF CONTENTS

INTRODUCTION

Whether you think you can, or you think you can't, you're right.

- Henry Ford (attrib.) [ii]

THE STATUS QUO

Let's say you love coffee. But not just love it, you live-and-breathe-it LOVE it. While shopping at an outdoor mall, you notice your favorite coffee store across the way and decide you're in the mood for your favorite drink: a triple-shot, sugar-free caramel latte, with a shot of vanilla and a dollop of whipped cream. This drink is your ultimate drink. Giving into temptation, you cross over to the store to purchase one. As you walk across the parking lot, your mind begins a dialogue that sounds something like this:

> Oohhh my goodness, I love this drink. I can't wait to have this drink! When was the last time I had it? It has to have been at least two days ago, but it feels like weeks. It's such a brilliant choice to use that sugar-free caramel; you really can't taste the difference. Oh, I just love this drink. The drink, the drink, the drink! I should ask the store to start advertising the drink so that more

people become aware of this coffee Nirvana. They could call it the "slapshot"! That perfect mixture of "sugar-free" sugar and caffeine wakes you up better than a slap in the face! Oh, finally I'm in the store and... What??? What the heck is with this huge line? Is it National Coffee Day and no one told me? Don't they know I need my drink? Seriously, people, what's with the line? OK, calm down, the drink is worth the wait. Oh man, I can't wait to get this drink. I wonder if I was the first to come up with it? Can I patent it? Come on people, let's move. Are we miming our orders at the counter or what?

Finally, I'm at the counter. Why is he questioning my order? "Thank you." Did he just give me a funny look? Is there something wrong with the drink? Is there something wrong with me? Oh my God, is there something ON me? OK, I'll look down at myself without looking like I'm looking at myself. I don't see anything on me... I really hate these shoes. Oh, whatever, this is stupid. Who cares if I have anything on me? But what if it's a stain in an inappropriate place? Stop it, I'm being ridiculous... I want my drink. I cannot wait! Seriously people, I cannot wait! Let's speed it up, why don't we? Oh, now I'm probably going to be late to pick up Carol. What was I thinking coming in here? Oh, cooooooooomme onnnnnnnnnnnnn...

Is that it being put on the counter? Finally!!! Yes!!! Now that I have the drink there should be a chorus of angels singing... Oh, this is the best! (*sips*) MMMMM, I love that mix of caramel and vanilla... Oh, my life is complete! (*sips again*) So awesome! Yes, yes, yes... so good... (*sips again*) Yum! Now... what's to get for dinner? I know! Chinese food! (*sips*) Ohhh, I LOVE

Chinese food… love, love, love (*sips*) love, love, Chinese food. I love the way they make it with the hot peppers (*sips*)… Right! There was that time we went for Chinese food (*sips*) over there at that new spot in Westside and Tom had that Kung Pao Chicken. That was spectacular! (*Takes the last sip.*) What? It's finished already? Did I order a small-tall by mistake? Did they "short-drinkie" me? Oh, whatever… who was I going to pick up? Why am I at the mall anyway at this hour? What do I want for dinner? Oh right, Mexican food.

WHAT JUST HAPPENED?

Perhaps this inner dialogue seems somewhat manic to some of you, while for others it sounds as if you're listening to an exact recording of yourself. For still others, it might seem like a peaceful mental conversation compared to how your mind normally operates. Regardless, if you step back now and examine what happened objectively, what do you see? First, in this scenario, the imaginary "you" was so focused on your objective—the drink—that your mind dwelled on it incessantly until you actually received it. You got the drink and you relished the taste of it for about two sips before your mind went elsewhere and you completely forgot you were consuming the drink. It's as if you became a machine just taking the coffee in.

What we also see is that while traveling from one side of the mall to the other, you were so focused on the objective of satisfying your craving that you missed experiencing everything that was unfolding around you.

You missed the cool breeze as it ruffled and flowed over your body, the sounds of people talking and laughing with abandon, the way your body felt as it walked out of the cool shade and into the warm sunlight, how the sun felt as it touched your body and caused you to squint. You missed the kaleidoscope of colors of the cars in the parking lot, the shapes of the buildings that make up the mall, the slight pain in your ankle as you stepped off the sidewalk and into the street, the colorful clothes on display in a store window, the aroma of coffee and the subtle wave of humidity that hit you as you walked into the store, the balancing act of the young man on crutches with his coffee and backpack.

And most important of all, after two sips of your drink, you completely stopped tasting the drink. You spent ten minutes focusing on your objective, only to appreciate it for less than thirty seconds before your mind moved to the next craving. You consumed the drink and didn't even realize you had finished it until it was gone.

IS THE RECORD SKIPPING?

How often do we go through exchanges similar to this one in our minds? For many people, it's all day long. Our continually chattering minds provide us a nonstop soundtrack of joy, pain, anguish, guilt, craving, sadness, desire, dislike, and self-elevation, or self-deprecation. DJ Jazzy Chattermind spins the hits of thought hour after hour after hour; sometimes it's death metal, while at other times it's cool, smooth jazz.

If this sounds at all like how your mind often operates, take heart, you're not alone. *(Oh, you're so not alone.)* Almost everyone faces this struggle day in and day out to varying degrees. The thing is, most people accept this as "just the way it is" and don't believe there's anything that can be done about it.

This book will show you that this is not the case. Right now it may seem that your mind controls you like a powerful tyrant, but in time, and with a great deal of practice, patience, and perseverance, you can turn that around so that you have control of your mind.

And just what is this miraculous mindfulness activity, you might ask? *(And thank you for asking. I do welcome questions throughout the course of this book. Just feel free to shout them out when they arise, as that's really what we're doing in our heads anyway. Might as well bring them into the world for others around us to appreciate.)* This will be discussed thoroughly in Chapter One (the definition, not shouting the questions); however, let's get started with a definition that's appropriate for the context of this book. Mindfulness, in brief, is striving to keep your focus on what you are engaged in at the present moment, the experience itself, to the exclusion of all other thought. By engaging in this practice, you learn to examine and ultimately let go of the tyranny of thought which incessantly occupies your mind, keeping you distracted and driving you ever onward.

IT IS AND IT'S NOT

Let me also begin by stating what this book is not: It's not a discourse on an esoteric mystical prophecy, rules about how the universe operates and how to come into alignment with them, or a revolutionary secret that will bring you everything you desire. It is also not a psychological analysis that proposes a method of treatment for a specific condition, either mental or physical. While books on these matters may be fascinating, excellent resources for validation and insight, and appropriate for many audiences, they are not the focus of this book.

Quite simply, this book is a guide for transformation. This book lays out strategies for using mindfulness principles to uncover, understand, and experience firsthand the peace and serenity that already exists inside of you (and inside all of us), independent of the world and all it has to offer. It can help you achieve an inner stillness, a feeling that everything is okay as it is, that can be experienced at any time and in any situation. As transformation involves change, something most people struggle with, we will also address the challenges that change presents.

The techniques in this book can help you make far-reaching shifts in the way you view yourself and the way you view your interpretations of and interactions with the world. For, as many of you have painfully learned over the course of your lives, it's easier to change yourself than it is to change the world.

JUST WHO ARE YOU TO TELL ME?

So just who am I and why am I qualified to write this book? I don't have alphabet soup after my name (PhD, MBA, Dragon Master, or even Senior Member of the High Council of Elders from Krypton), I don't have a degree in psychology, I don't sport an ochre robe as I walk through airports (although I can play a mean tambourine), nor do I live in an ashram hidden away in some exotic country.

I'm qualified because I've done the work. I know firsthand how thoughts and states of mind can be utterly debilitating and can also be completely transformed. Through intensive practice and significant trial and error, I've learned how to experience exquisite peace in the most challenging of situations by putting mindfulness practices into action.

My hunger for peace and balance in my life was driven by the fact that I was looking for something—anything—to blame for the horrible states of mind I would so often experience. Overwhelmingly, anger and irritation defined my consciousness. These emotions and associated states of mind would consume me for days or weeks at a time, while I felt helpless against them and unable to find their cause.

Only rarely would I allow these emotions to manifest outwardly. Out of shame, I hid them well. I'm not the angry tough guy, it's just not my nature. In fact, looking at me, you'd never know such a battle raged inside my mind. *(Not unlike the Incredible Hulk really, though considerably smaller, less dramatic and, uh... not so green.)*

Over time, I came to believe—not simply hope—that there had to be an alternative to this constant battle. I knew there had to be other options. This belief was founded on the fact that at times I would experience feelings of profound peace, balance, and clarity through various meditation practices I engaged in. Afterwards, I could tap into those feelings for the days that followed. Similarly, I had experienced periods of complete peace in a variety of situations in my life. Although the feelings were fleeting, I believed that this did not necessarily have to be the case. I believed it was possible to turn the tide so that peace became the norm and anger was fleeting.

Over the years, I had read a great many spiritual books describing a variety of paths, some "ancient" and some current, and I began to see that many authors and spiritual teachers affirmed this possibility. This strengthened my belief. Now, how to do it? How do I make peace and balance the predominant feelings, while keeping the dark states relatively brief?

Desperate for guidance, I turned to the Buddhist concept of mindfulness, a term I had heard and seen many times, yet had never invested the time to explore. This term was present in many of the spiritual books I had read, although different words had been used to describe the concept.

I was lucky to come across some mindfulness books that weren't specifically associated with Buddhism or any spiritual path, but that spoke to my intellectual nature, and whose teachings I could quickly grasp. Thus began my journey down the rabbit hole. Over the years, I consumed any teachings on the subject I could find—and they would often miraculously appear in the most random of places and situations—and I marveled at the results I saw in both myself and in others who had begun to incorporate mindfulness practices in their lives.

Because of my unabashed love for mindfulness, developed over years of practice, I began teaching these concepts in workshops and classes. Over the years, I have been privileged to witness radical transformations take place in others. In fact, nothing gives me more joy than seeing the eyes of someone in a class as they have a realization, recognition, or epiphany about their mental habits, or when some part of a teaching resonates deep within them.

Gratefully, a number of these students have allowed me to include some of their stories and experiences from their own practice. For the purposes of this book, a number of those stories have been combined or elaborated upon to provide clarity.

SOURCE MATERIAL

The strategies set forth in this book are based on personal explorations that utilize a wide variety of mindfulness approaches, including various spiritually focused teachings, as well as many non-spiritual ones. Additionally, the book includes material used in presentations to, as well as feedback received from, a few hundred very patient and accommodating individuals in classes that I've taught over the years. Lastly, a tremendous amount of personal trial and error rounds out these strategies. *(Graphic images of the carnage left behind have been omitted from the book, in deference to those of you with a more delicate constitution.)*

I have chosen not to take the academic route with this work. However, most of the mindfulness concepts presented here have been researched and proven in numerous psychological and sociological studies during the last thirty years. These studies have provided significant advances in treatment for depression, chronic pain, and bipolar disorders, among others. Mindfulness continues to be an area of great interest to the scientific community, and new findings and results are published and discussed with great regularity. Over the past few years, mindfulness techniques and teachings have found their way into the most unlikely of places, including various military establishments, with very inspiring results.

If any of these areas are of interest to you, I highly recommend that you explore them in greater detail. References can be located easily online, as well as in numerous published works.

Mindfulness teachings have been practiced for thousands of years in many cultures and traditions, and there are many different interpretations and approaches. Many descriptions of mindfulness can be esoteric in nature, but I've done my best to describe them in ways that make them easily understandable to the average reader. While words such as "peace" or "serenity" may not fully do justice to certain profound feelings or experiences, I hope they will serve to convey these inexpressible states to a wide audience.

Finally, this book is not a one-stop shop for mindfulness that will answer all of your questions—there's no way it possibly could be, which is part of the beauty of mindfulness. What it provides is a personal perspective based on years of practical teaching and refinement that I hope will resonate with you.

I OWN, THEREFORE I AM

It's your choice how to engage in your mindfulness practice. Some of you may simply be seeking to understand what mindfulness is all about, while others may be looking to make drastic changes in your perceptions of yourself and the world. Like me for many years, some of you may just take pride in adding another unopened self-improvement book to your bookshelf, in the belief that the accumulated knowledge on that shelf will somehow waft over you as you walk past it. *(From my own experience, I can confirm that this never worked for me, no matter how hard I tried. Even when I went out of my way to walk past that bookshelf, which I believed to be a sign of true dedication, I saw no tangible results. However, I'm always optimistic that it might work for someone.)*

While reading this book will hopefully provide interesting insights and reflections, simply reading it, or any book on mindfulness, is not going to suddenly move you into lasting, peaceful states of mind. This book lays out an approach and provides guidance, but it's up to you to put its teachings into practice. No one else can do it for you. I'm willing to be a cheerleader for anyone seeking greater peace, or wanting to bring more peace into the world (although I draw the line at shaking pom-poms), but it's up to you to do the work.

And I'm also still doing the work. Even after years of practice, teaching, and exploration, I'm still working on myself. I continue to look for new discoveries in science and psychology to gain more insight into human nature and behavior. I continually seek feedback from other people regarding my own struggles, and watch to see how mindfulness is helping them and what I might be able to learn from their experiences.

I constantly marvel at how the feelings of peace and balance continue to deepen, and how mindfulness has brought aspects of the world to light that I would have overlooked in previous years. And from a mindfulness perspective, the world is ever new, ever changing, with more and more to see and experience.

I often feel like Indiana Jones seeking lost treasures (teachings) in the most obscure places. Buddhists often say that you should make your mind like a temple, and in my case, it's often felt like the Temple of Doom (and has been about as disappointing as the movie). However, I'm continually amazed when I see aspects of mindfulness manifest in places I would never have expected to see them, which is part of the joy, and adventure, of this practice.

ABRACADABRA

Lastly, I would be remiss in not calling out perhaps the most amazing, yet subtle, aspect of mindfulness. As the rock band Queen stated so eloquently, "It's a kind of magic." When you are able to reduce the continual battle of thoughts taking place in your mind and learn to hold your mind in a place of quiet, you will begin to see the world in very different and extraordinary ways.

With a quiet mind and calm consciousness, you enter new territory. When you stop trying so hard to figure it all out, things will start to make sense on their own. Insights will come and epiphanies will arise from out of nowhere and you'll know they're not from you. Your effort in becoming quiet is the gesture you make to allow this to happen.

It's not just about striving for feelings of peace and quiet. One might say that a step above feeling serenity is the feeling of being elevated. Here our mundane thoughts and challenges lose their power to weigh us down. We rise above them and, even though we may see the same world and encounter the same challenging situations, we see them in an entirely different light.

AN APPLE A DAY...

Please keep in mind as you explore these pages that mindfulness is a practice. It's not something you read about in order to suddenly find "the answer," or to put an "X" in a checkbox and be done. "Oh yeah, mindfulness, I did that once, but then I got bored with it and moved on to juicing with my inner child." *(No offense to anyone's inner child, unless they're the greedy, tantrumprone ones, in which case I recommend a strict nanny and refraining from bringing them to restaurants.)*

As mindfulness is a practice, it's something you strive to engage in daily, and, as such, you'll have "good" days and "notso-good" days. There's a pattern I've discovered in life, which many of you may be familiar with as well: A good day is always followed at some point by a not-so-good day, which, at another point, is followed by a pretty good day, which, at yet another point, is followed by another not-so-good day... you get the idea. As we'll discuss in greater detail in the book, it's vital to keep perspective.

What you will derive from a diligent practice of mindfulness is an ever-increasing, overall feeling of peace and serenity in your life, and those feelings can continue to extend to depths you didn't even know existed or were possible to experience.

STRUCTURE, STRUCTURE, STRUCTURE

Be happy for this moment, this moment is your life.

- Omar Khayyam [iii]

This book is divided into three main sections:

1) The Basics

2) The Root Cause Analysis

3) Being Present

"The Basics" introduces the concepts of mindfulness in a non-scientific, logical and approachable style. "The Root Cause Analysis" focuses on some of the most common states of mind that we engage in that lead to our feeling mentally conflicted in various ways. Finally, in "Being Present," we will examine how to shift our awareness from constantly engaging with the world to actively engaging in stillness.

Repeated throughout the book are the words "Patience, Practice, and Perseverance," which will be defined and reviewed at length in order to keep perspective and provide guidance. I've found them to be the essential elements in an undertaking such as this, or in any new endeavor.

So as you read this book, I hope you'll exercise patience, since many of these terms and concepts might be new to you, or perhaps different from what you've read in other sources. I encourage you to come back periodically and re-read sections as you're allowing the concepts to sink in.

Within each of the chapters, specific exercises are provided to help bolster the teachings. I encourage you to fully engage with the exercises as they are presented in order to fully grasp the concepts. In reading the material, you'll get a feel for the concepts; however, until you experience them firsthand, this book will be little more than an interesting read (or at least I hope it is).

I highly recommend that you keep track of your observations in a journal, or by taking notes periodically, so that you can begin to notice how the concepts presented in the exercises manifest for you. Highlight text enthusiastically and make notes in the margins if you find that helps you focus on key items. *(Of course, if you've obtained this copy from the library or are looking at it on your e-reader, please just make notes on a separate notepad. I have the utmost appreciation for our libraries and technology and would hate to be the cause of any angst.)*

Look to engage mindfulness whenever and however you can. Really, every moment is an opportunity to practice. And lastly, persevere. If something is unclear or doesn't resonate with you, keep moving forward. The main concepts are explained in a variety of different ways throughout the course of the book.

Seek out knowledge anywhere, everywhere and however you are able.

I wish you the best on your journey.

SECTION ONE: THE BASICS

The journey of a thousand miles begins with a single step.

- Laozi, *Tao Te Ching* [iv]

WE HAVE LIFTOFF

The following three chapters will lay the foundations for a mindfulness practice. First we'll look at and explore just what this mindfulness concept is all about. I will present two main components of mindfulness and provide a number of examples and exercises to get you started.

Next, we'll look at why mindfulness is so important and how it can help you achieve greater levels of peace in your day-to-day life. We will also begin to explore some of the more prevalent mental modes we operate under and why certain things in the world cause us to react in a conflicted manner.

Finally, we'll discuss some of the common challenges we face when attempting to make changes in our lives. Here, we'll create a roadmap for how to get started with a mindfulness practice.

While the concepts presented can be fun to discuss and ponder, their power is found by putting them into action! Otherwise, reading the book would be like reading a guide about how to improve your golf swing, imagining just how great your swing is going to become, and never picking up a club. It doesn't get you very far. Or it would be like reading a book on yoga postures that goes into excruciating detail on how to execute each pose, yet never taking time to get your butt on the mat. Intention only takes you so far. *(You get the point? If not, I can continue: cooking... fishing... origami...)*

CHAPTER ONE: WHAT IS MIND-FULNESS?

Stop the glorification of busy.

- Author Unknown [v]

CLARIFYING MOMENTS AND THINKING CLEARLY

Mindfulness has many definitions, yet can be difficult to comprehend and embrace, since it presents a paradigm shift from how we normally perceive our interactions with the world. Here is my best effort at a way to approach mindfulness: Mindfulness is striving to keep your focus on what you are engaged in at the present moment, the experience itself, to the exclusion of all other thought.

To help clarify this, let me begin by introducing a number of concepts that will be referenced periodically in the book, so that you may fully understand the context in which they are being used.

I will often refer to our unique moods and emotions, which we reside in on a daily, if not hourly, basis, as our state of mind. Our state of mind can also be considered as our unique perspective on the world and the happenings around us at any particular moment. Our state of mind can change over time as our perception of ourselves and the world changes, and events in our lives shape us.

It is through our state of mind that an event in the world can be perceived and experienced in a variety of different ways. Clarity is what we strive for, but confusion is very often where we land. This "confusion vs. clarity" paradigm will be reviewed in great detail in Section Two of the book, "The Root Cause Analysis."

Oftentimes I will use the terms "dark" or "negative" states of mind, and associate them with the concept of suffering. This relation to suffering is based on Buddhist principles and concepts, which teach us that we are living in a state of suffering because of our addictive habits of thought that compel us through life seeking fulfillment of our desires and control of our world. Here I am referring to moods and attitudes we commonly refer to as "negative," such as fear, self-doubt, guilt, depression, anger, jealousy, irritation or hate.

While this terminology is not meant to judge our states of mind, these words convey feelings that we can relate to, and gives us a common language with which to communicate.

Conversely, light, joyful, and happy states of mind will commonly be referred to as "peaceful". I make the assumption that we are all seeking peace in some way, shape, or form. "Peaceful" can be seen as a very generic term that's open to interpretation. For the purposes of this dialogue, let us consider "peaceful" to mean balanced. When we're in a state of balance, we feel no need to change anything; everything is OK as it is.

Being balanced or at peace does not necessarily mean appearing outwardly happy and joyful. When we're at peace or balanced, we're not at odds with ourselves, others, or the world in general. *(Ironically, it's not until people have left their bodies that we convey our hope that they are able to "rest in peace." Yet we often do so little to encourage them to "dwell in peace" during the course of their lives. Descending soapbox now.)*

Additionally, the words "consciousness," "attention," and "mind" will be used throughout the book to refer to our own individual mental structures. These words will be used interchangeably. While there are subtle nuances, for the purposes of this discussion, we'll use them to refer to the same concept.

You'll also come across the words "will" or "willpower," also used interchangeably. These terms relate to our ability to focus our attention and sustain that focus for periods of time, a form of self-control. It is a skill that we all possess; however some have stronger abilities than others. Fortunately, though, from what I have been graced to observe in myself and in others, it is something that can be cultivated and strengthened over time.

LIKE POETRY

There have been many beautiful and evocative approaches to mindfulness put forward over the years by spiritual teachers, scientists, and poets, and I'll be referring to some of them throughout the book. While the definitions may differ somewhat, I believe the essence of the teachings is the same. For example, some refer to it as "living in the present moment with awareness" or "living deliberately."

Jon Kabat-Zinn, the accomplished physician and teacher often credited with introducing mindfulness in the West for use in medical clinics, and later for personal growth, defines it as "moment-to-moment awareness." *vi* The brilliant author of *Walden*, Henry David Thoreau, referred to it eloquently in the following quote: "I went to the woods because I wished to live deliberately, to front only the essential facts of life, and see if I could not learn what it had to teach, and not, when I came to die, discover that I had not lived." *vii*

Mindfulness is completely and fully appreciating the experience of a coffee "slapshot" the entire time you're engaged with it, and not getting carried away in mental chatter or following habitual thought patterns as they wind their way into mindless oblivion.

CURRICULUM VITAE

Some of the earliest writings and teachings on mindfulness can be traced back to Buddhism and Hinduism and the philosophies associated with them. However, it is important to point out that mindfulness is not strictly a religious practice. Unless you choose it to be a part of your spiritual practice, which I personally highly recommend, it can be practiced without any religious associations.

If you do wish to include mindfulness as a part of your spiritual practice, as many do, it will provide tremendous insight into the things that keep you from being at peace with yourself, the world, and Eternity. In time it can foster a feeling of oneness and a connection to the Eternal, which so many of us quietly seek (or loudly seek, if you're a fan of drum circles).

BASIC TRAINING

I consider there to be two main components to mindfulness, which we will explore throughout the course of this book; in fact, the remainder of the book is based on these two components. The first involves learning to pay attention to what you are thinking at any and all times of the day, and thereby start to recognize the trends and patterns of thought that your mind engages in. The second is learning to fight the habit of your mind's continual "doing," and unraveling what it means to "be"—be present, be still inwardly and, ultimately, to be at peace—deliberately.

(By the way, that last paragraph was kind of important. So in case your eyes were just following the letters over the page while you were imagining swimming in a pool full of ice cream, or beer, or both, I recommend you go back and read it again.)

As we observed in our coffee example, all day long our mind provides us with a lovely and insightful commentary about our lives, what's happening around us, and how that impacts us uniquely. Beautifully and colorfully, it critiques the world and the many individuals we interact with. It does a fantastic job of letting us know on a moment-to-moment basis whether we are superstars or slugs, and whether the people around us are superstars or slugs as well.

Our minds may inform us that we are worthless pieces of trash unfit to breathe air, or it may provide us with the profound insight that all beings who have the privilege of being in our presence and basking in our fabulousness should really be bowing to the ground before us in absolute awe as we walk past them.

Above all things, our mind relishes providing a continuous commentary on everything we see and experience, constantly churning along, digesting—or devouring, should we be in a bitter mood—all it sees. It performs seemingly uncontrollable, Olympic-worthy leaps from thought stream to thought stream in an incessantly chatty conversation of one.

Lastly, one of its favorite and most impressive talents is its ability to continuously inform us about what else we should or could be doing besides what we are currently engaged in at this moment: where else we need to be, what we need to do next, or what this experience was like when we did it before, and what it should be like next time. *(It's quite impressive, actually, everything it's able to accomplish in the course of a day.)*

Learning to pay attention to your thoughts will teach you how to objectively observe these habits in action, and then how to counteract their effects. While it may seem difficult to believe, we really do have trends and habits in our ways of thinking. And like all habits, they can be modified or eliminated. But, first, we must recognize them.

COMPONENT ONE - PAYING ATTENTION

As mentioned previously, the first of the two essential components of mindfulness is becoming aware of where your mind is hanging out all day; what are the thoughts that traverse your mind as you make your way through the world? Pay attention to what you're thinking, feeling, and experiencing whenever you can remember to do so. Initially, this means checking in periodically to see what you're thinking about and reflecting back on what you've been thinking about since you last checked in.

Becoming aware of your thoughts does not mean making a judgment about those thoughts or about what kind of person would have those thoughts. This is critical! As well as compounding an already troubling situation, berating ourselves just adds layer on top of layer of mental debris that we'll eventually need to clean up. *(Note: This may be the one area where recycling does more harm than good.)*

Mindfulness does not mean you'll stop thinking altogether, although you can learn to quiet the mind significantly. It means being aware of the thoughts that are traversing your mind as they occur. It's learning how to change what you're thinking about, and how to curtail the constant chatter.

If you learn to do this, then you can begin to choose what you think and when you think it. The mind will become like a tool to use when needed, and not an overbearing parent cruelly forcing vegetables upon you at every meal. *(Oh, the horror!)*

Ideally, you can get to a point where you are focused exclusively on the tasks you engage in throughout the course of a day, whatever they may be—whether walking down the street, having a conversation, or eating a meal. You are experiencing each one of them fully as they are unfolding, and not being endlessly distracted by unrelated thoughts throughout the entire experience.

Paying attention is not always easy, as I think we all can attest to. Unfortunately, we are seldom taught how to cultivate the skills for focus and concentration. The world preaches and continually reinforces living in states of distraction, and as a result, short attention spans flourish. Through the use of quickly changing camera angles, sexual innuendo, and the presentation of images and concepts that appeal to our core human desires, advertisers and the media have mastered the art of capturing our attention; as a result, they have stolen much of our attention span from us.

Because of this conditioning, we find that whenever we're engaged in something we're not particularly interested in—a lecture at school, a meeting at work—our minds will desire to be anywhere but where we are at that moment.

A number of the concepts that follow, which focus on paying attention to your thoughts, will be discussed in greater detail later in the book. Here I just want to introduce them to you so that you can become familiar with them.

The Objective Bystander

In monitoring your thoughts, what you are aiming to do is just to become aware of what your mind is dwelling on. Approach it as if you're watching a movie. Sit back with your bag of popcorn and just observe. What thoughts, ideas, concepts, and images have been passing over the screen of your mind?

When performing this exercise, strive to see yourself as an observer, not as the participant who experiences the thoughts directly. Separate yourself and your emotions from what you're reflecting on, and make every effort not to judge the content of the thoughts. Observe them like a curious scientist examining nature; be an impartial witness. *(But not like a little boy with a magnifying glass playing outside on a hot sunny day… that just spells disaster.)*

Once you begin this activity, in time you may start to notice some interesting patterns and trends in your thought streams. We also have specific emotional states tied to those patterns and trends and there is a tremendous power in understanding the impacts of these relationships. If we can identify and understand those patterns and trends, we can begin to interrupt them when they arise, or as they are being triggered, and avoid certain emotional states. Once they're interrupted, we can then begin the process of proactively changing or eliminating them if warranted.

Does it appear that your mind hangs out at the corner minimart all day, or does it linger in an exclusive department store? Hooters or the Russian Tea Room? Do you find you're thinking about certain friends or loved ones all day? Do you dwell on your neighbor's habit of pushing his yard clippings into the street (and realize that your mind is hanging out in the pro-verbial gutter)? Is your mind focused mainly in the future, when you win the lottery, or in the past, reminiscing about previous relationships? Or are you mentally ambidextrous and spend an equal amount of time in each time zone?

What are your mind's habits? Does it like to tell you that you're not worthy of certain experiences when you're about to engage in a new activity? When you hang out with your attrac-tive best girlfriend / guy friend, does it tell you that you can never be as good looking as they are? Does it get easily riled up when you have conversations with certain family members?

Road Trip

To start with, you want to check in with yourself periodically and reflect on what you've been thinking about. When you first begin, you may find that you can't clearly recall what you've been thinking about since the last time you checked in with yourself. This is not at all unusual and it just takes time and practice to improve this skill. Our ability to focus and concentrate is com-promised by the overwhelming amount of input and distraction we continually encounter in the world.

You may also become aware of the wide swing of thoughts, feelings and emotions you've had over the period between check-ins. Perhaps your mind went from creating a detailed plan for how you'll spend your lottery winnings to dwelling on a long-deceased loved one, including all the emotions and feelings that went with those thoughts—all in just a matter of seconds. *(Our minds do not recognize or honor speed limits. Rebels!)*

You will also come to see that your thoughts, emotions and feelings are all tied together. When you think happy thoughts, you feel happy emotions and feelings, and vice versa. Conversely, when you dwell on sad and disturbing thoughts, your emotions and feelings reflect that as well.

Happy and sad are states of mind and, like all things in life, they're transient, they come and they go. However, it may be the case that some states have more prominence than others. Although they may feel like they're permanent fixtures in our minds as we're experiencing them, especially the challenging ones, in time they'll come and they'll go, and come back again and go again.

We experience many states of mind over the period of a day, or even an hour, though we tend to group them into large-scale categories, or hold onto the ones that have strong emotional connections. If we have a strong connection to a specific state of mind, we often don't realize that we might have left it for a time, then directed ourselves back because for some reason we're more comfortable there, even if it's what we consider to be a challenging state. Oddly enough, it seems that some people are quite happy being miserable.

Like traveling across the country on an extended road trip, you'll pass through many "states" during the journey. Some of the time you'll traverse states that you like, and other times you'll be in states that you don't particularly care for. Some states are bigger and take longer to get through; others can be passed through quite quickly.

Ease of Use

To illustrate the fluidity of our states of mind, consider that when we engage in our favorite hobbies or activities—things we're passionate about—we find that our minds are naturally quieter and less reactive. We pay attention and bring our awareness to what we're engaged in because we enjoy the activity. We wish to experience it fully, and as a result, our mental chatter becomes minimal.

Our minds tend to stay focused in these situations more than at other times. In fact, we may find ourselves longing to participate in those activities because we feel good, and even peaceful, when we're doing them. Be it gardening, hiking, cooking, sewing, photography, sports, or yoga, we all have activities we enjoy that bring us a measure of peace.

When you speak with someone about their favorite hobbies and passions, they "light up" and bring a deeper level of attention to their interaction with you. In fact, they may start to see you in a more favorable light because you show an interest in something about which they're passionate.

EXERCISE: WHAT BRINGS YOU PEACE?

» Consider for a moment the activities you enjoy that make you happy or give you a sense of peace or fulfillment.

- What is it about them that contributes to that feeling?

- What makes them different from other activities you engage in?

- Can you categorize the feelings arising from these activities and see similarities in how they impact your state of mind?

Destination Unknown

It may sound clichéd, but a key concept of mindfulness is: It's the journey, not the destination—because really, in mindfulness and in life, there is no destination. There's just the present moment.

As we'll discuss in great detail in the following chapters, we spend a tremendous amount of time fantasizing about or dreading the future and focusing on results. We begin to believe there is a place we need to get to in life, a place where we will acquire a feeling of completeness or fulfillment. "When I get married or when I get my dream home, when I get my perfect job, when I lose ten pounds, when I get my sexy sports car—then, and only then, will I be truly happy. I will have arrived, my life will be complete, happily ever after begins then."

We're so focused on where we want to be, holding some fictional belief that the future will provide a certain outcome, that we forget where we are now. The truth is, for the majority of us, we will never arrive at fullness and completion because our definition of those concepts, our desired result, will continually change.

Inevitably, when we acquire the thing that we think will make us complete, we'll begin to look for the something else that will provide the next completeness or fulfillment, more complete completeness, even more fulfilling fulfillment. We're running on the proverbial hamster wheel of life.

(And, compassionately, we must consider how hamsters feel about being cast in such a dim light... I'm convinced they're reaching a breaking point and are planning an uprising any day now. I suggest that those of you who have hamsters please take a moment to have a conversation about this with them and show them how their example is actually a benefit to humanity. Catastrophe averted.)

Where we are now, on the other hand, cannot be changed, no matter how hard we may try (and try we do). With a subtle shift in our outlook, we can see that within each and every moment, there is a sense of completeness. Our lives are the sum total of the moments leading up to now, and now itself, aka "the journey." Destination? Unknown, and ultimately, unknowable.

Pump Up the Volume

It may seem that when you begin to pay attention to your thoughts, the amount of chatter in your mind is overwhelming. The truth is, to varying degrees, it has often been that way. You were just unaware of it being so loud because you were accustomed to it. "Chatterbox Central" had become a standard mode of operation for you.

Take heart, you're not at all alone in this. Almost everyone has this experience to some degree, so don't beat yourself up, or feel bad about yourself, or think that you're some lesser being. These kinds of negative reactions defeat the purpose of learning to be mindful. Now, at least, you are starting to understand the playing field.

You may also find that your mind seems even chattier the more aware of your thoughts you become! This is not unusual either. When this happens, more than likely you'll become obsessed with focusing on the amount of chatting going on (chatting about the chattiness). You'll try and focus your attention on anything you can find so that you're not as aware of the constant chatter. It's as though an elephant suddenly appeared, strolling down the middle of your street; you'll be obsessed with that elephant until your mind becomes accustomed to its being there, tires out from exhaustion, or finds relief in another distraction. *(Should you suffer from fear of large elephants, please feel free to substitute. A chinchilla could work as well and is quite an entertaining word to say aloud.)*

Numerous students in my workshops have mentioned experiencing this same phenomenon (the chattier mind, not the fear of elephants). It's almost ironic, since you're actually becoming more aware of what's happening and, as a result, like feeding a habit, there's a part of you that's looking to compensate or cover up this discovery by increasing the volume of thoughts. It's as if they get even louder, more extreme and chatty.

(You're still saying "chinchilla" to yourself, aren't you?)

Patterns

Once you begin paying attention to your thoughts, you may realize that you have numerous different patterns, trends and habits. Here is a list of some common ones. You may find that some of them resonate strongly for you:

- You dwell longingly in the past.

- You are continually planning for events that may or may not occur in the future.

- You have a tremendous number of fearful thoughts.

- You spend what you consider to be an excessive amount of time engaged in sexual fantasy.

- You spend a majority of the day comparing yourself to, and subsequently judging, everyone around you.

- You regularly engage in thoughts of an angry, depressed, or sad nature.

- You alternately love and loathe yourself, sometimes within a matter of seconds.

- You think about certain friends or family members multiple times throughout the day.

Once you spot a trend, check in and ask yourself how you are feeling emotionally and physically when that trend arises. Do you find that when you think of a family member or a particular friend that you become tired, depressed, or agitated? Or, conversely, happy or peaceful when you think of them? Do you find that whenever you have angry thoughts, your body is tense?

The good news about recognizing these trends is that once you are aware of them you can begin to utilize mindfulness to start minimizing their impact.

Source Code

Once you start to see and understand the patterns of thought you engage in, you can begin to look beneath the surface and conduct what's called in the business world a "root cause analysis." Through this analysis, like popping the hood on a car to find the source of that irritating "pathunk" sound, you can begin to look at the sources for your distressed states of mind and subsequently eliminate them.

This activity can take a considerable amount of time, but will evolve the more you engage in the practice. It all comes down to your willingness to look at what's truly happening. What are the underlying reasons for the thoughts you struggle with? Some of these can be spotted quickly, while others—the more difficult ones—may require years of examination and reflection to get to the point where you're honest and open enough to see the source of the issue.

For example, many of your outward and inward reactions of anger may be tied to feelings of fear and a lack of control. By expressing anger, you may feel that you retain a level of control, which you need to make the world around you a livable and stable environment.

Your Receipt for Paying Attention

Becoming aware of what you are thinking, realizing that you traverse many states of mind throughout the day, noticing the speed at which your thoughts jump around, charting the patterns, and understanding that there are things going on underneath the surface, all contribute to laying the groundwork for your foray into mindfulness.

Over time, using the lessons in this book, you can learn to control that runaway train of a mind that you possess. You can learn to stop dwelling on and engaging in thoughts that lead you to negative and disturbing states of mind, and you can learn to pull yourself out of distressing states faster.

You can purposefully choose to stay in agreeable states of mind throughout the day and learn to control your mind, instead of allowing your mind to control you. Ultimately, you can learn how to consciously choose or discard your states of mind at will through mindfulness.

To begin with, I recommend just making a concerted effort to pay attention to your thoughts as often as you can. Through that effort you will begin to see the patterns and trends start to emerge.

COMPONENT TWO - JUST BEING

The second essential component of mindfulness is the concept of being present. By learning to be present, we can cultivate the ability to still our minds and foster feelings of peace because we are not spending our time trying to figure out what to do next, satisfying our desire to have a sense of control over a given situation, or feeding that constant churning of thought that propels us forward in life. This concept will be explored in greater detail in Section Three, "Be... Simply Be." Here again, I just want to introduce you to the concept.

Living with an awareness of the present moment may be drastically different from the way in which we currently live our lives. As such, this concept can be challenging to discuss, since it is difficult to find words that adequately describe the feelings that arise from a practice so different from what we are accustomed to.

Almost constantly, on a moment-to-moment basis, we are driven forward through life, thinking about the next thing we need to do, the next place we need to be, or unconsciously following every whim and distraction that pops up. We don't allow the mental churning to ever stop. We fill up our lives "doing things," complete with a play-by-play analysis, as opposed to willfully stopping and focusing on whatever may be unfolding.

When we are mindfully focused on experiencing and being present, we are not trying to change or evaluate anything. We surrender control and become detached in a way. This does not mean we become cold or unfeeling, we just don't take what's happening personally. We are not trying to control the direction in which things will play out for us. We become absorbed in what's taking place while it's taking place. We are where we are and that is all there is. At such times, you may actually experience more than when you are attached to the idea of feeling something or getting something out of the situation.

And while we may struggle furiously to find peace of mind in the outside world, part of us knows that it can be found within ourselves; we're just having trouble either locating or reading the internal map.

Being (Present)

The following story demonstrates how experiencing stillness can bring about feelings of peace. It shows how, when one focuses on being present in the middle of any common occurrence, the world can be seen in a completely different way than what we are accustomed to. It was related to me by a participant from my workshops who readily embraced the concepts presented and continues to actively work on his practice.

> Recently I was sitting on a bench under a tree at a dog park having a conversation with an acquaintance. We had come to a lull in the conversation and were enjoying the view. I was really focusing on keeping my mind as quiet as possible.
>
> Quite suddenly, the world seemed to soften and my surroundings became somewhat alien, yet pleasant. The sunlight played off of the brown grass. People and dogs of all shapes and sizes were running and playing fetch together. They seemed engaged in absolutely unique and unrepeatable interactions of form.
>
> The whole world seemed to be held in that moment. The feeling then arose that this woman next to me, myself, and this conversation I was engaged in had emerged from stillness/nothingness, would return to

stillness/nothingness, and was currently held by still-
ness/nothingness. It seemed that everything must in
fact be stillness/nothingness, and that many years from
now nothing but stillness/nothingness would ever know
any of it ever existed at all!

It was as if stillness had burped and form had emerged
for a brief moment, held in a moment. How strange,
yet overwhelmingly peaceful, it was! I felt like there was
nothing I needed to do or accomplish during that time.
Everything, including me, was OK as it was.

What's important to call out from this story (aside from the
burping) is that this was just an ordinary moment in the middle
of an ordinary day. It was not some "special occasion" that might
be dependent on a major life occurrence, like a wedding or similar
celebration. It was just a moment, like any other, like all others.

Also important to notice is that our storyteller was not trying
to achieve anything or make anything happen, either mentally
or physically, at the time the experience occurred. Because he
had been working diligently on his practice, he was content to
allow a lull in the conversation and wasn't searching for what to
talk about next in order to fill a void. He could keep his mind
quiet and turn his focus to his surroundings. He was present in
that moment.

I Thought You Said "No Gifts"

While they may be esoteric concepts difficult to verbalize,
we each have an idea of what it means to be still, be present,
and experience an associated level of peacefulness, although the
particulars may look different to each of us.

One way to describe presence might be that in these moments, you forget about "you," your life circumstances, and you simply experience what is unfolding around you. In these moments, "you" have no wants or desires, and even that incessant voice in your head, which is constantly evaluating and seeking feedback from the world, is quelled as you realize that nothing in the moment needs to change.

Typically in these situations, your attention has been captivated by something outside yourself, or by what your body is physically experiencing, which causes you to willingly shut down your internal dialogue long enough to fully take in these sensations.

At these times, you're not "doing" anything or trying to "be" something. You're not trying to accomplish anything or make anything happen. Everything is as it is and there can be a tremendous sense of peace in this.

Seriously, This Is Awkward... I Didn't Get You Anything

Most of us have had moments of being completely present in some way, shape, or form and can recall the peace it fostered, be it momentary or of a longer duration.

For many people, this feeling of being present arises in inspiring situations, such as when they see a beautiful sunset or vista unfold before them, especially when these sights are unexpected. What's interesting to note is that before you see the sunset or vista, your mind is often churning away as it normally would, chewing away on one situation or another. Then, behold, a glorious sunset catches your attention completely, something that's more interesting or beautiful than the thoughts you were engaged in.

The sky in front of you is full of golds, pinks, purples, and reds—a canvas celebrating the sun's glory. The clouds are alive with colors shifting in and out of their folds. You become aware of the temperature getting cooler. You watch as the sun sinks closer to the horizon and the clouds further erupt in a deepening glory of color. You watch in awe as nature performs a dance before your eyes. All the while, your mind is growing gradually more quiet and still—perhaps with intermittent commentary of approval, but overall it is slowing to a crawl.

Again, you've stopped all the doing, all the churning and debate in your head, and you have given yourself fully to that sunset, that moment. You are still. And perhaps, because you are still, you feel a level of peace and contentment. Your body gives a sigh of relief. Then, when motivated or prompted, you are ready to continue along your way.

It's important to recognize that in the moments following this experience of stillness you have a choice: a choice to either pick up all the thoughts that were churning away in your head before you saw that sunset or not. If you do choose to pick them up, perhaps you will have a different perspective on them than you had before.

You might see things differently after a break. You may have a new clarity about what you were thinking, or you might see that your thoughts were not as important as you were making them out to be. You may forget about them altogether; they may have completely lost their importance. Perhaps you even feel rested and revitalized, more optimistic than before you observed the sun's dazzling performance.

Experiential Learning

To further exemplify this idea of being present, reflect back on a time when you were preparing to dive or jump into a pool, lake, or other body of water after not having done so for some time. Unless you were experiencing fear, more than likely you stood there on the edge of the water optimistically preparing yourself for the experience that lay before you.

You wondered if it would be cold and shock your system, or be warm and nurturing? You may have even ventured so far as to dip a toe in as a way of preparing yourself, although you knew it could not completely prepare you for what you would experience when you surrendered your entire body to it. You made the choice to proceed, perhaps with trepidation. And you leapt. At that moment, you stopped the churning of thought. You consciously held your breath in anticipation and experienced flying through the air, allowing gravity to take hold of you, and you eventually embraced the water.

And then you just felt. Time seemed to stop, your senses were in overdrive, and your focus was fully concentrated on your bodily sensations. You were aware of the first moment your skin touched the water, whether on your head, feet, back, or fingers (or in a less pleasant and graceful situation, your stomach).

The temperature of the water and the feeling of wetness collided with your body and you became acutely aware of it all. You had no option but to pay attention. You were aware of your senses as the water enveloped your body, and the change of pressure as you went from a free-fall space to underwater constriction. Your awareness stretched itself to explore the new environment and assess your capabilities.

Regaining your bearings, you willed your body to move upward. You broke the surface and felt a change of temperature again as the air hit your face and the water started to drip down from your head. Opening your mouth to breathe, you encouraged the fresh air to enter your lungs.

Throughout this experience, you were quiet and your mind was still. You were not focusing on what you did earlier in the day, or what you were going to do later. None of your problems mattered. You were completely present, experiencing and being.

Escape from Nowhere

This experience of absorption can also happen when you go to the movies, the theater, or a concert. Even reading a book can induce this feeling of presence, or absence, depending on how you choose to see it.

During these times, you willingly give your attention and focus over to the event unfolding before you. If you buy into the event, then you're captured. You forget about the stories of your own life. You become part of what you are observing.

Have you ever had the experience of someone's cell phone going off, or someone bumping you accidentally, while you're in a movie or engrossed in a book? It's almost as if it shakes you out of a spell. You feel momentarily disoriented, as if you didn't know who or where you are. You're slammed back into this world, this reality of your life. Disappointed or frustrated by this, you want to be pulled into the movie or book again, and so you shift your focus back until, before you know it, you're re-immersed in the story.

What you may also have noticed is that once you came out of the movie or performance, or put down your book, you felt different than you did before you went in or started reading. Again, it's as if you took a vacation from your life's situations. You may now see the issues and problems that were ruminating in your mind much differently. You may also feel more rested and happy, if the show or book was a comedy; or alert, if it was an action adventure; or exhausted, nervous, or frazzled, if it was an emotional drama or work of horror (which can sometimes be one and the same, depending on how bad the book, movie, or performance was).

A Battle of Wills

While you were viewing the sunset, jumping into the water, or watching the performance, you were present. You were 100 percent engaged in what you were experiencing. The thing to note with all of these experiences is that you willfully gave over your attention for a period of time, however brief. The experience was more important to you than the thoughts floating through your mind. After those moments, you may have begun to judge, reflect on and evaluate the experience. But it's the experience itself that we are interested in, not the habitual thought processes that occur afterwards.

There are many situations where you bring a sense of presence to what you are experiencing: a first kiss or engaging in good sex, a meal that overwhelms you with flavors or visual presentation, a challenging, yet invigorating, exercise session where survival is all you are focused on.

Contrast these experiences with a lecture, social engagement, or business meeting you might have endured recently, where you did not want to be there, but attended out of obligation. More than likely, throughout that entire experience you were fantasizing about being somewhere else and what it would be like to be there.

How often have you read a book that you were required to read and realized when you got to the end of a page that you had absolutely no idea what you had just read? So you started again at the top of the page and ended up in a loop of getting lost in distracting thought before you could make it to the end. It became a monumental effort to just make it to the end of the page. Were you fully engaged? Probably not so much.

(And what about now? Are you here now? Pop Quiz! What did that last paragraph say? How many times have you had to read this section?)

When we are willfully focusing on what we are experiencing, we are making a choice to pay attention as best we can and invoking our ability to concentrate. This is very different from what happens when we allow our attention to be lured away. When we give in to distractions, we are not invested in what we are attempting to concentrate on; we believe the thing pulling our attention away will be more interesting or of greater benefit to us than what we are currently engaged in.

More than likely we've learned the hard way—from failed exams, missing important business information, or making critical errors in judgment—that giving into distractions and not paying attention during key moments can cost us greatly in the long run.

In these situations where we try to willfully focus, we may not be interested in the experience in the least; however, our "better judgment" tells us to quiet down the chatter and focus on what's being presented. Or perhaps we feel we are in a dangerous situation and we realize that extraneous chatter can actually be detrimental. Here we understand that we have a choice, and we do whatever it takes to bring our focus, to the extent we are able, to the situation at hand.

In a mindfulness practice, it is important to see that your willingness to focus is a choice. By strengthening your will, your ability to hold your focus and not give in to distraction will increase, regardless of how mundane the situation.

EXERCISE: HOLDING YOUR BREATH

A quick exercise that you can try out right now to focus your attention and bring about a quiet state of mind is to simply hold your breath.

» Take a deep breath and hold it, not until you turn blue and pass out, but just for ten to twenty seconds.

- Now slowly let the breath out. *(Pursing your lips to make a motorboat sound is completely optional.)*

- Did you notice that your mind automatically became quieter when you inhaled?

- Did you find that you intuitively turned your attention to how your body was reacting to this situation, almost as if you were "listening" to your body and not creating or engaging in the typical commentary in your mind?

If this exercise worked for you, congratulations! You can now add one mindfulness trick to your toolkit. If not, don't give up hope, there are many more enthralling exercises ahead.

Environmentally Friendly

For many people, going into nature brings a smile to their faces. And why is that? If you compare the way we feel in nature, physically and mentally, to the way we feel in a crowded mall or event, the difference can be drastic. For the majority of people, even just holding an image in our minds of a beautiful location in nature versus a bustling urban location brings about different emotional reactions.

Interestingly, simply thinking of a beautiful location in nature can cause our bodies to automatically relax, while focusing on a bustling urban location can make our bodies feel tense. Similarly, when we get away from populous areas and into nature, our bodies and minds automatically relax and quiet down.

Our environment has a tremendous influence over how we feel and our levels of energy. This will be discussed in more detail later in the book, but it's something to take notice of now.

In the cities and towns where we live, we have billboards, radios, TVs, 500-plus cable channels, the boundless Internet, magazines, friends, family members, and coworkers all competing for our attention. In nature, it can be easier for us to let go, to get to a state of quiet, to feel present. There's not much else competing for our attention, and the beauty unfolding around us captures our interest.

In nature, there's little or no competition. It's you alone, or with other travel companions. In nature, you can hear yourself think. Your body and mind relax and you can more easily get clarity or a new perspective on challenges you may be facing.

Detractors

There are, of course, times when we resist stillness. We may even know people who are uncomfortable in quiet environments, or we may feel that way ourselves. We can become so accustomed to the activity of the world and our minds that we become anxious or unnerved when experiencing quiet. For who are we if not the chaos in which we dwell?

Additionally, when faced with stillness, we may believe that we have to examine things in our lives that we are not ready to see or are afraid to look at. We push thoughts and feelings to the backs of our mind because we really don't want to deal with them. Then, when we are getting still, they sometimes will creep out of their corners and remind us that they have not gone away; they're just a little more dusty and moldy now.

If you find that this is the case for you, don't let it deter you from your practice. It is just something else to become aware of. As you continue to build up strength through engaging in various mindfulness exercises, and begin to let go of some of the subtle fears you carry, your ability to look at these unpleasant issues will grow.

Mindfulness in Daily Life

Paying attention to one thing at a time does not mean that you cannot mindfully engage in an activity that involves many things happening simultaneously. Take, for example, jogging or running. When you run, you're engaged in numerous activities at the same time: you're shifting the weight of your body, listening to and responding to the sounds you hear around you, using your arms to balance you, and moving your legs in a rhythm.

You're engaged in all of these activities, but you're still only running. And you can pay attention to all of these things individually, shifting between one action of the body and another.

You're not at work, you're not fighting with your spouse or partner, and you're not focusing on the sales call from days ago. You're just running. And if you're really enjoying yourself, you become lost in the experience. Your mind is quiet and you're just experiencing running.

You can apply this same exercise of bringing your awareness fully to what you're engaged in to many other activities, such as taking out the trash, walking the dog, cleaning the bathroom, vacuuming the floors, walking down the street, driving your car, writing an email, brushing your teeth, or going through your activities at work, whatever that might consist of. In fact, you'll come to find that there's nothing you can't do mindfully.

You might be wondering, "If I'm so focused on what I'm experiencing, how do I think about what I need to do next?" Being mindful does not mean that you're a zombie and you can't plan out your day or what you need to do next. When you're planning your next few tasks or your agenda for the day, just stop and take time to focus on planning.

Unfortunately, for many of us, as we plan, we create a full commentary about what we are planning, how we feel about it, and what we expect it will be like, all while multitasking and attending to the endless distractions around us.

So when you plan your day or next activity, stop and just plan out your day. Don't bother with anything else, just stop and plan. More than likely, circumstances will change and you'll need to stop periodically and re-plan. Again, when it's time to re-plan, stop and focus only on re-planning.

Taking It to Extremes

One of the most effective ways to embrace the concept of being present is to focus completely on an individual task and give your full attention to each and every action you engage in as it is being performed. Give yourself completely to what you're doing, even if you don't particularly like what you're engaged in.

A simple exercise to start with is hand-washing the dishes without using a dishwashing machine—the ancient way. *(I can already hear your wails of anguish for being asked to partake in this barbaric activity! So take a deep breath, dismiss your objections, and be open to the opportunity.)*

The details might seem extreme; however, engaging in an activity at an intense level helps to evoke and solidify the concepts you are seeking to understand.

Rising Up

When executing a task one step at a time, you want to focus fully on your senses, engaging in the activity to the exclusion of everything else, especially the overwhelmingly important thoughts about other things you should be doing that are almost guaranteed to arise.

Give all of your focus to the sights, smells, sounds and feelings of the environment around you. Focus also on how your body feels as you engage in the activity. This is where you want to focus your attention, not on the thoughts drifting haphazardly through your mind.

Try not to judge any part of the activity. If a judgment arises, note the judgment and move forward. Don't spend time analyzing the judgment, or yourself for having the judgment, at this time.

You may find that you react to what you're experiencing by smiling or frowning. Again, be aware of the reaction and let that be part of the experience. Notice these responses and feel them fully, but don't create a story, commentary, or explanation around the reaction.

EXERCISE: WASHING THE DISHES

Follow this exercise to the best of your ability, given your current situation; improvise as necessary.

Preparation

Stand in front of the sink with your dirty dishes stacked on the counter. Stop and relax your body and try to quiet your mind. Focus on your breathing. Set your intent by telling yourself that for the next fifteen minutes the only thing you're going to do is wash your dishes. There's nothing else you need to do or accomplish in these fifteen minutes. Nothing else matters except washing the dishes. Nothing!

You're not going to focus on any problem, any future or past event, or any other task for this period of time. You're not going to run to your phone, or to your computer to check for messages.

You may find judgments coming up about washing dishes, as they may be coming up even now reading about this exercise. "There has got to be a much better use of my time." Or "Can't I just 'experience' loading the dishwasher like a sane human being?" Note that these are just judgments and try to set them aside. Be open to the experience because, really, you don't know what this experience, or any experience in life, is going to be like until it happens.

And... Action!

Put all of your focus on your body and your senses. Feel the floor beneath your feet and check in to see how your body is feeling. Are there aches and pains in certain areas? Are your muscles tight in any area? If so, just be mentally aware, take a moment to relax the area, and try not to explore the reasons why the area might be tight; it doesn't matter right now, it's not important, you can figure that out at another time.

Now reach your primary arm out in front of you. Feel that your attention is focused on your hand, lift it up, and guide it toward the faucet. Feel the muscles in your arm stretching as you reach out. Touch the faucet and feel the cold steel of the handle or knob.

Lift or turn the faucet toward the hot setting and feel the muscles on the underside of your arm engage and exert pressure to make the faucet move. Hear and watch the water come out, hit the bottom of the sink, and circle around the drain.

Slowly put your finger into the water coming out of the faucet and feel the temperature and force of the water as it comes in contact with your skin. Feel the temperature of the water as it warms up. Be aware of where the water is hitting your finger and where it might be splashing.

Distraction

You may have a thought come into your mind. "Oh shoot, I've got to pick up my dry cleaning! If I don't pick it up, I won't have anything to wear to work all week. Ugh, I need to get a new wardrobe. All of my clothing is so outdated, but I'd rather endure a night of reality television than go to the mall..." As soon as you realize you're thinking, STOP! Bring yourself back to the present and to the activity of washing dishes.

Remember that all you're doing is washing dishes. You're not doing anything else. When you go to pick up your dry cleaning, you'll pick up your dry cleaning at that time and in those moments. That's a different moment, a future moment that you will experience at a future time; it's not this moment.

There's no need to add commentary about your dislike of buying clothes either; following that train of thought will lead to the frustration depot. So just stop and don't proceed down that path. Go back to the activity of washing dishes and give yourself fully to it.

Your mind may go off on a tangent about your wardrobe and your feelings about shopping for a good ten minutes before you catch that your mind is wandering. This is not at all uncommon. You are so accustomed to your mind being in a wandering state, it's as if it happens automatically. In time, by practicing mindfulness, you will find that this habit decreases drastically.

What's key is to catch it as it's packing up its knapsack to go on a hike and bring it back to the present. Your mind may wander for ten or fifteen minutes, or even hours, before you realize it's on vacation. Don't beat yourself up about this. The key is to just start becoming aware.

In time, you may find that these vacations become more and more abbreviated. You may even get to the point where you feel the urge to go on a mental field trip and you stop yourself before it begins.

Since remembering to pick up your cleaning might be an important task that you prefer not to forget, keep a notepad next to where you're engaging in your mindfulness task. When these "show-stopper" thoughts come up, just pause from your activity and mindfully write down "pick up cleaning," or whatever the show-stopping thought might be, and then come back to the task at hand.

You can assure your mind that the thought is now in a safe place and then proceed with your activity.

Take 2

Come back to washing the dishes. Stretch your arm out to grab the stopper and feel the motion of your body move to accomplish this task. Notice the focus and concentration it takes to guide the stopper directly into the drain. Watch the water as it collects around the drain and starts to fill the sink.

Reach out and take hold of the dish-soap bottle. Feel your hand grasp the bottle, the cool plastic. Lift the bottle and feel the compensation your body makes and which muscles engage to take on this additional weight. Twist the bottle around in your hand and pour it into the water. Watch the line of liquid soap as it leaves the bottle and comes into contact with the water.

See the soap begin to dissipate in the water. Slowly, bubbles begin to form and a rainbow of colors may appear in them as they reflect the light in the room. Another thought arises… "Why don't I live someplace that gets more rain? What did Kermit and the Muppets really mean when they sang about the 'rainbow connection'"?

Recognize this as another thought tangent and drop it as soon as you realize it's occurring. Go back to focusing on the dishes. "This is easy. I can do this. It's not difficult. I'm already a master at mindfulness. I've got this mindfulness mojo down." These too are thought tangents, evaluations, and judgments. Go back to focusing on your senses.

Take 57

More than likely, you'll find your mind will wander and you will have to force yourself back over and over and over and over and over and over again. Don't let this frustrate you. This is not unusual; in fact, it's a completely normal activity for most of us.

The main goal of this activity is to recognize how you're so often pulled into thought tangents when you mean to be focusing. If you can catch yourself thinking, then you're actively being an observer, a scientist. This is success and a very important achievement, as it will become a fundamental practice in your quest to become more and more mindful.

Continue with the task by slowly washing each dish individually. Feel the texture, weight, and shape of each dish. Appreciate the diligence with which some dried foods cling to their containers. Enjoy and explore the various creative ways that your body can manipulate and handle the dishes as you scrub each one. Notice the change of gravity as the dish moves from being submerged underwater to the freedom of air. See the patterns and organization that form as you set the dishes aside to dry.

After you've completed the activity, check in with yourself regarding how you feel. Are you relaxed and calm? Or are you frustrated and anxious? No need to figure out why you feel this way at the moment, it's good just to be aware of how you feel.

(You are now free to go and begin your thesis on the hidden teachings in "The Rainbow Connection," if it's still plaguing you.)

Being present is a concept that will evolve and deepen over time the more you actively engage with it. The greatest hurdle you may face is getting past the incessant churn of living your life in the mode of doing that we've come to accept as the norm. Engaging in tasks in a moment-to-moment and action-to-action manner, such as the exercise above, can help reinforce this concept and break the habits of the doing mind.

Section Three, "Be... Simply Be," will expand on these concepts in more detail.

Bringing It All Together

Component One and Component Two will both take time to get used to. It is critical to remember that this is a practice, and progress will happen by degrees. Ideally, to begin with, you want to strike a balance between the two. Become comfortable monitoring your thoughts and with learning to reside in mental stillness.

After you begin, you will find that you spend the majority of your time commenting on, categorizing and monitoring your thoughts and only a small amount of time actively experiencing stillness. As your practice evolves and you learn to actively influence and control your state of mind, thereby experiencing more stillness more often, the proverbial pendulum will swing in the other direction. You are experiencing more stillness, being present, and there is less need to comment on, categorize, and monitor.

Concluding Components

This concludes the review of the two main concepts of mindfulness: Paying Attention and Just Being. As mentioned, aspects of these two concepts will be discussed in greater detail throughout the remainder of the book. For now, we're setting a common starting point.

DON'T JUST TAKE IT FROM ME

I asked a number of my regular class participants to share what they had noticed about themselves since starting mindfulness practice. A number had only been working on it a few months, while others had been practicing for about a year. Here are some of their responses:

- A few mentioned that their senses seemed to have become more acute. Colors appeared brighter and smells were more pronounced.

- They found that it was easier for them to be around people. They weren't as self-conscious as they had been previously, nor were they as intimidated by others. They were less concerned about how they were perceived by other people.

- In a similar vein, people seemed to engage them more; they appeared more approachable.

- They found that they made more of an effort to pay attention when talking to and listening to other people, as opposed to their previous habit of just "hearing them."

- Some noticed that they had become less anxious about things that had caused them stress in the past. They also seemed to worry less.

- One person in particular mentioned that some of his coworkers had noticed quite a change in him. He was so relaxed lately, they said, that he "almost looked drunk." (Although he assured us that he wasn't.)

You may observe similar results in your own practice. There is no limit to the number and variety of insights and changes possible. It all depends on how willing and open you are to engage your practice.

LET'S GET THIS PARTY STARTED

Here are some exercises you can begin doing immediately to kick off your mindfulness practice. Again, mindfulness is not something that will happen to you, it is something that you must engage in and practice as diligently as you can until it becomes part of your standard operating mode. And please, don't get frustrated if you're not seeing the progress you thought you would see at the rate you thought you would see it. Any specific expectations are detrimental to a practice such as this one.

In fact, check in now and see if you are setting up expectations around your abilities, capabilities, and beliefs about what mindfulness will or won't do for you. As we will discuss in detail in Chapter Seven, "Expectations," it's best to recognize them when they arise and quickly set them aside as best you can, since, more often than not, they will simply lead you to increasingly frustrated states of mind. *(Which is exactly what we're trying to get away from, right? Just wanted to make sure we were on the same page. And does that reference work in this situation, since we literally are on the same page? I mean, this is a book, right? And you're on this page, right? I digress... What am I supposed to be doing now?)*

EXERCISES: OBSERVATIONS

The following tactics can be used continually in your mindfulness practice, not just when you're getting started. These tools of awareness are the basis of this practice.

» To begin with, find ways to remind yourself to check in on your state of mind and what's in your attention throughout the day.

- Perhaps hourly to start with, set some kind of alarm or other mechanism to remind yourself to check in.

» When checking in, ask yourself the following questions:

- What is my current state of mind and how did I arrive here?

- Where has my mind traveled since the last time I checked in with myself?

- What experiences have I been through since then?

- What emotional states have I been processing?

» Notice how much time you spend reminiscing about the past.

- Are there specific events that you go back to frequently?

- If there are a number of events you find you go back to often, are there any similarities among them? For example, were they painful or joyous events?

- Begin to explore why you are drawn to and dwelling on these specific events.

» Notice how much time you spend fantasizing about the future.

- Are there specific scenarios you continuously create and play out in your mind?

- Is there a trend, or multiple trends, in these fantasies? For example, are they aggressive in nature? Do they contain overriding themes of sexuality, romance, power, violence, flattery, or seeking attention?

- Reflecting on these themes, does it seem that these scenarios are in some way compensating for something you're experiencing in your present life with which you're unhappy?

- If a fantasy were to come true, do you believe that you would feel more complete, happy, or more at peace? Do you believe that this relief will be constant and long-term, or only fleeting and temporary?

- How do these feelings about the future correlate with your current situation?

- What events in your current daily life prompt these thoughts?

» Notice whether you're resisting implementing the cultivation of awareness or other new practices in your life.

- Do you have a tendency to resist making changes in your life? Historically, how well have you embraced change?

- Explore what it is about change that upsets you or that you find frightening. Do you believe that it will just be too much effort and it probably won't work, so why bother?

THE END IS IN SIGHT

Congratulations! You just made it through Chapter One!

(Hopefully you're aware at this moment that you are reading a book about mindfulness and have not just spent the past few hours looking at letters on pages while you were actually pondering why celery-flavored pudding never caught on, because, let's face it, we all ponder that at some point in our lives right? Um... don't we?)

KEY POINTS ABOUT MINDFULNESS

- There are two main components to mindfulness that we will reference often in the book, which set a baseline for the practice: 1) Paying Attention and 2) Just Being.

- By Paying Attention, we aim to separate ourselves from the thoughts that traverse our minds throughout the day and start to become aware of the trends and patterns inherent in them. In time we can recognize the ones that lead us to negative states of mind and gradually learn how to handle them more effectively.

- Just Being speaks to the concept of what it feels like to be present, the clarity it can bring, and just how different and peaceful that can feel from our constant "doing" mode. With practice, it's possible to engage these feelings of being, of stillness, at any time.

- Mindfulness is not something that will happen to you; you must learn to engage the practice. Diligently explore the exercises set forth in the chapters and in time you will begin to see results.

CHAPTER TWO: GETTING STARTED

Your living is determined not so much by what life brings to you as by the attitude you bring to life; not so much by what happens to you as by the way your mind looks at what happens.

- Kahil Gibran (attrib.) *viii*

PRIVILEGED

On numerous occasions I've been privileged to witness how a mindfulness and meditation practice can truly touch someone, sparking a change that allows them to break out of states of mind they've been stuck in for a seemingly endless period of time.

One of the most striking examples of this occurred a few months after I started teaching. After a class that focused on the basics of meditation and mindfulness, people were milling around the classroom, visiting and preparing to leave. Quietly, a young college-aged girl pulled me aside and told me that she had been trapped in depression for the previous three months and that the talk I had presented had, in some way, allowed her to break out of it. I could see from the way she was expressing this that she was truly amazed and relieved by what had happened. It had given her a new perspective on her challenges and on the source of those distressing states of mind.

It's important to note that it wasn't anything specific that I did or said during the class that prompted this shift. It may just have been that my approach to the topic touched her and gave her a new way of seeing things. There was no silver bullet. But something allowed her to gain some important insight, make a subtle shift, and step out of a state where she had thought herself endlessly trapped.

She continued to attend my weekly classes for a few months before she had to move back to the East Coast to be closer to her family. Over those weeks, the authentic enthusiasm and interest she brought to the classes helped strengthen and reinforce my own beliefs about how mindfulness can help reshape lives.

WHAT'S BEHIND DOOR NUMBER ONE?

So why choose mindfulness anyway? With a full menu of options available that includes self-help empowerments, New Age secrets, psychological and philosophical theories—not to mention organic and manufactured substances—what advantage does mindfulness bring to the already overcrowded table?

Mindfulness is a way to live purposefully and deliberately. In essence, it's a shift in the way we see ourselves and the way we see and interact with the world around us. It means learning to look at and understand how our minds operate inwardly, how we consider ourselves, and, outwardly, how we consider the world.

With this understanding, we can actively take control of how our thought patterns function, as our minds act and react to the constantly changing world around us. There are no new belief systems to adopt. If anything, it's a letting go of many of our set beliefs.

Through mindfulness you can come to see that, in reality, all of your problems arise from your own mind, from within your own thoughts. For example, you may blame others or the world for your problems, but if you learn to look at a challenge honestly, you'll see that you have a choice in how you respond to it. Blame no longer becomes a way out.

With mindfulness, other people's actions or large-scale actions that occur in the world don't matter so much. You can't control any of that. What is infinitely more advantageous is understanding why you react the way you do to the actions of others, and how those reactions impact your state of mind at every moment. This you can control.

GIVING PEACE A CHANCE

The concept of peace has a multitude of definitions and connotations depending on the context in which it is used. For the purposes of this book, let us think of peace as the feeling that everything is OK with us, and subsequently, with the world with which we interact. It's about letting go of the beliefs we cling to about how the world should be, as well as the things we continually find fault with in ourselves. These beliefs only lead us to live lives of constant conflict. Nothing needs to be different than what it is; not us and not the world. While this may not be a definition worthy of the finest greeting card, it goes to the core of the feeling.

This does not mean that we are apathetic toward the challenges in the world. There are indeed many injustices to be addressed and it's important to help in whatever ways we can—be it financial, giving of our time, or our voice, or our spirit. However, we can see and accept that the world is as it is and as it will be.

Peace, of course, is subjective. To some, striving for this feeling of OK-ness manifests as a desire to gain control in the world, in private relationships or over groups of people. Some even seek control over Mother Nature, Eternity, God, or whatever they see as a force greater than themselves that they wish to conquer. Oftentimes people will resort to violence or repression to obtain a feeling of control. They believe that this will ultimately bring them peace because it gives their view of the world a sense of order.

Other people have the view that peace is somehow going to be bestowed upon them when certain criteria have been met. They live in states of frustration, believing that some day peace will finally arrive and then, and only then, they'll be happy. Their prince, or princess, or both, or neither (we don't judge), will arrive (or leave), and they'll live happily ever after—that is, until they set their sights on the next thing they believe will bring an even deeper, more complete and satisfying state of peace.

Mindfulness challenges us to look at our world—how we perceive it and how we believe we are perceived by it—because these perceptions quietly and continuously contribute to our distressed states of mind. When we are able to see the negative views we hold with clarity and non-judgment, we can then work to change those perceptions to focus on greater levels of, you guessed it, peace and contentment.

IT'S ALL ABOUT THE ACCESSORIES (EVERY WOMAN KNOWS THAT)

One of the most powerful and transformative activities to complement mindfulness is the practice of some kind of formal meditation, something which I will explore more deeply in Chapter Thirteen. The stillness which can be experienced through meditation can be carried over into a moment-to-moment mindfulness practice. What you will find is that stillness doesn't depend on anything external. It's only found internally, yet we constantly look to the world to provide it to us.

I have seen this awakening to stillness demonstrated over and over. New class participants, often skeptical, listen patiently as I explain a meditation technique; then we try it out. Many times you can see the impact just one meditation can have on their perceptions. It's in their eyes: a sense of recognition, and disbelief that they had forgotten what a peaceful state of mind felt like, or that they were even capable of feeling peace again.

In those moments, they realize, and often express in various ways (because I irritatingly request that people talk about their experiences so that others can benefit from their realizations), that they are capable of willfully experiencing moments of peace and stillness. It's so familiar, so close, but it's like they had forgotten how. They get so caught up in the world and their lives that it ceases to be a priority. Then, when they become overly stressed and feel a need for more peace, it almost always feels as if it's out of reach, so far away from where they are in that moment.

In time, they realize that peace is always readily available to them; they just have to stop working so hard to find it in the world or in worldly circumstances. The workshop setting helps; however, they soon understand that they found a level of peace within themselves, by themselves.

I recall one instance in particular when this occurred. It was a small workshop in a wellness center. We had just finished an initial ten-minute meditation and I asked if anyone would like to share what the experience was like for them. One woman commented that it was the most peaceful she had felt in weeks and that she wasn't even aware that it had been so long since she had experienced that feeling, she had been so caught up in her life. Then, very quietly, she said to herself, almost in disbelief, "it's been months."

If you meditate for fifteen minutes a day, striving to keep your mind quiet for that period of time, then that leaves twenty-three hours and forty-five minutes for your mind to go and do whatever the heck it wants to. *(And it typically will do whatever it wants, whether you want it to or not, often resulting in some kind of emotional mental turmoil... The police arrive, there's shouting, someone pulls a knife, a snow globe containing copious amounts of glitter gets broken... it just gets overly dramatic and ugly).*

SO WHAT'S IN IT FOR ME?

The main goal people cite for seeking out meditation and mindfulness is to experience less stress and anxiety in their lives. We collectively struggle with growing amounts of anxiety and stress, which impacts our ability to sleep at night and function well during the day. We spiral down into depression, despair, and other dark states of mind when we feel there is no peace to be had anywhere.

Meditation and mindfulness will help in these areas, but this work can be challenging. This is absolutely not said to discourage you, but only to help you be realistic and dispel any expectations that this practice is simple.

The majority of you reading this book have been viewing and experiencing life though a specific lens for perhaps twenty to sixty years; therefore it's going to take some time to learn how to change that view. So when you start out on your journey of mindfulness and meditation and find it challenging or difficult—take heart! It's difficult for everyone! You're not broken or defective.

Like all things you wish to learn, it takes practice, perseverance, patience, and a healthy dose of self-compassion. These traits are not fostered in the world, and so you'll be swimming upstream. There will be strong currents to contend with; the current of the world promising instant results, and the current of your mind telling you to give up or to stop and go do something else. However, don't use the excuse that it's too difficult in order to stop practicing. Everything in life involves challenges, especially those things worth fighting for. *(Cue the theme from* Rocky *here.)* People adopt different practices at various rates. You can adopt this one at your own rate.

I don't recommend judging your results against others. Certain people have natural proclivities for certain activities, while others seem to struggle endlessly. For example, some people appear to be naturally good at sports, while some of us have trouble just tying our gym shoes. Some are naturally artistic, while others have trouble drawing stick figures. It's not an even playing field, and how could it be?

When you decide to go on a diet, you may gripe and moan or have a full-blown tantrum about how difficult it is. We feel indignation that we cannot eat what we want to eat when we want to eat it. It's as if we're being punished and forced to eat only vegetables. *(And for you strict vegetarians out there, imagine if you were forced to eat drive-thru fast food burgers for every meal. Can you feel our pain?)* But if you persevere and have realistic expectations, after you get over the proverbial hump, you'll see that you feel better and look better, which renews your faith in continuing your diet.

Try not to allow your practice of meditation and mindfulness to fall into that trap of "it's too difficult, so why bother." As they say in Alcoholics Anonymous, "One day at a time." Just focus on getting through the day, this day, mindfully, as best you can. Tomorrow is another day, a different day, a future day, not this day. Tomorrow you will strive to get through that day mindfully, when that day comes. That day is not this day.

There is no end result, no end state, no certificate to be awarded. The goal, if we need to set one, is to be happier or more at peace than you are today, than you are now.

BUT I PLAY ONE ON TV

In addition to experiencing peaceful states of mind, there can be physical and psychological benefits to a mindfulness practice. The psychology community has devoted a significant amount of time and research to this topic in the past few decades. Online searches for the benefits of meditation and mindfulness will bring back page upon page of information.

Here are just a few examples of the known benefits of mindfulness practice:

- Measurable decreased levels of stress

- Improved memory and ability to focus

- Heightened sense of clarity

- Improved ability to communicate and to actively listen

- Greater self-confidence

- Significant improvement for people who are dealing with the following conditions or challenges (among others):

  o ADHD

  o Anxiety

  o Depression

  o Phobias

  o Chronic Pain

  o Chronic Disease

  o High Blood Pressure

  o Sleep Problems

  o Stress Management

Thankfully, research into the benefits of mindfulness continues to expand, and new fields are incorporating mindfulness practice into their existing therapies.

PERSONALLY SPEAKING

Adventures in mindfulness are personal journeys. Each will be unique, but overall they will share some common threads. Here is some feedback from a few folks I have worked with about their experiences with mindfulness over the years:

Meditation and mindfulness opened my eyes and woke me up to a life that I felt I had been missing. It came along at a time in my life when I was experiencing a lot of anxiety and suffering, and it showed me a different way to live.

While my practice is far from perfect, it has started me on a different path, a better one than I was on before.

-Bill

Just being in the moment is such a GIFT to myself [that] I could weep at the thought of people who don't give themselves the gift of stopping and slowing down.

I work with a few troubled people who spend much of their time beating people down in order to feel better about themselves. I try daily to see good in them so I can send them love and peace, although some days I just want to flip them off. So mindfulness and meditation are what I use to get and maintain peace and happiness in my life. I can stop at any moment, good or bad, and find a place to just BE in the moment, and it brings me peace so I can think more clearly before I act.

-Ann

ABSOLUTELY POSITIVELY HAS TO BE THERE, THANK YOU, DRIVE-THRU

Over the past relatively few years, we've come to live in a society focused on immediate turnarounds. We've become accustomed to instant communications that allow for phone conversations and text messages in almost any location, anywhere in the world. As overnight shipping and same-day delivery have become more common and economical, many now expect them as standard operating procedure. We have also come to expect that we can have instant access to unlimited amounts of information via the Internet from almost any location. We throw a meal in the microwave for a few minutes and dinner is served.

As a result of all this efficiency, we've become more and more frustrated when things take time. We want results and we want them now. The concepts of waiting and patience seem outdated. This expectation of immediate results is a particular challenge to the practice of mindfulness.

AUTOPILOT

" I don't think..."

"Then you shouldn't talk," said the Hatter.

- Lewis Carroll, Alice in Wonderland [ix]

Once you start becoming aware of your thoughts, you may find that you've been engaging in a tremendous number of activities throughout the day without really experiencing what is happening at the time. How often do you eat a meal and afterward not really remember what you ate, or the nuances of how it tasted? Have you ended up somewhere in your car and not even remembered the drive there?

There is an apt term for this phenomenon: autopilot. Autopilot means going through the physical motions of an activity while your mind is engaged in a completely different activity. This most often occurs with our routine activities, things we consider to be second nature, like driving a car or cleaning the house, or when we're involved in an activity in which we have no vested interest. Commonly we find that we make mistakes when executing activities while our minds are wandering.

Conversely, when we are engaging in an activity that requires intense focus and concentration, with potentially serious consequences, we actively force our minds to be quiet. We may even encounter fear when our minds are chatty in these situations because we're wondering, "What if I fail?" *(Which so often occurs when we're in situations where we have to cut either the blue wire or the red wire and we forget which one will cause the nuclear device to explode... days like that are simply exhausting.)*

IN THE ZONE OF ZONING OUT... ZONE

Similar to autopilot is the concept of "spacing out" or "zoning out." This occurs when we're bored or tired and have no interest whatsoever in what is happening at the present moment; nothing is catching our attention and we're not engaged in any "meaningful" activity, so we sink into a deep state of daydreaming.

Unlike autopilot, where we're functionally carrying out an action, when we space out, we're typically not involved in any activity. We're slumped down on the couch or in a chair, or perhaps wandering around aimlessly. The lights are on, but no one's home.

Most of us have been in this state ourselves periodically, and probably have had the experience of catching someone else zoning out. If we ask them a question or approach them, they have to shake themselves back into reality, into the present, in order to acknowledge us and respond. *(Hopefully, drooling was not involved, but let's be honest, it happens. Nothing to be ashamed of... we're all friends here.)*

FOCUS, FOCUS, FOCUS

As illustrated above, to be mindful, we need to learn how to focus our minds, instead of dwelling in distraction. The world neither teaches nor fosters the abilities of focus and concentration. In actuality, it teaches us the exact opposite, distraction and fantasy.

A perfect example of this can be seen in the news media. In the late 1990s, cable news programs began running a news ticker at the bottom of the TV screen. As if it weren't enough for us to simply focus on the well-manicured and coiffed news announcer, now we were distracted with additional information running underneath his or her talking head.

We have to wonder what networks were thinking when they introduced this little distraction. It's as if they were saying, "We understand that what this person is speaking about may be putting you to sleep, but look at what else is happening in the world. Whatever you do, kind viewer, please refrain from touching your remote control. We love you, yes, truly love you, and want you to stay with us. Losing you, kind viewer, would emotionally destroy us. Don't... don't go..."

We can see a similar change in movies and television. If we watch a movie or TV program from the '60s or '70s, we may be pained by how little action takes place on screen. The camera lingers on the actors for unimaginable minutes at a time.

In movies today, especially action movies, the camera jumps around quickly, almost erratically, constantly bombarding us with images from every angle imaginable, just to hold our attention. Quick interactions and fast cutting have become the new norm. Directors, producers, advertisers, and networks all know that if they lose your attention for just a few seconds, they've lost a potential or existing customer.

TV screens and video players are standard in many cars today. Until a few years ago, children had to entertain themselves by such low-tech methods as looking out the window. *(And we wonder why our children have trouble paying attention in school?)*

But by knowing what you are up against, the fact that you are continually bombarded with distractions from the world, that you have certain proclivities, and that you struggle with making changes, you can understand the playing field and prepare accordingly. You know where you'll struggle and what obstacles you'll face.

THIS IS SERIOUSLY DULL

In reading this, you might come to believe that mindfulness is "boring," especially if you're accustomed to a fast-paced lifestyle. This is something that you can reflect on. Do you feel you have an entitlement to be entertained by life at all times? What is your perception of boring? How has that perception come about? What habits and beliefs has this created in your life?

Questioning ourselves and reflecting on these ideas helps to challenge the perceptions we've created about ourselves and our interactions with the world.

With mindfulness, you come to see that in being present, your experiences in the world are far from boring. They are actually quite beautiful and endlessly fascinating. You will be amazed at the beauty that can be found in the most simple and mundane experiences, in the world unfolding around you, and the things you overlook and take for granted every day, every moment.

Our society has created a belief that to truly engage and appreciate life, we must be over the top or extreme in our actions; in fact, there are now "extreme" versions of almost every sport and activity. Over-the-top drama sells "reality" television. So why not try extreme stillness and be over the top in your search for peace in the moment?

Soon you may start to see that there is only the present moment. There's only ever this moment, this situation, this experience, this. The distractions of the mind are what pull us from the moment. Within a moment devoid of rambling thought, our minds can be peaceful and calm, regardless of how mundane the task or how chaotic our environment.

And the most wonderful thing about mindfulness is that we can practice it anytime and anywhere, and at no cost. *(What a deal!)*

BABY STEPS: TECHNIQUES

Here are some initial mindfulness techniques and tools that you can practice at any time. The intent of these practices is to help bring you into the present moment by giving your mind something to focus on deliberately, as opposed to having it engage in its typical habit of automatically and incessantly churning away with random thoughts.

By giving your mind a specific focus, something to keep it occupied, you are able to be more mindful about whatever activity you are currently engaged in. Deliberately focusing your mind will eventually allow you to turn your attention outward to the world around you, so that you can be acutely aware of your current experience, not missing what's unfolding around you.

While using any of the following techniques, move part of your attention to your senses and pay attention to what you experience: what you see, smell, hear, taste, or feel. When your mind begins to indulge in mindless chatter, catch yourself, become aware of the fact that you are engaging in random thoughts, and bring your focus back to the technique.

- Focus on your breathing—the flow of the breath in, and the breath out. Just breathe naturally. Don't exaggerate your breathing or you may hyperventilate. *(And that just gets messy and dramatic for everyone around you).*

- Repeat to yourself the activity you're engaged in as you're engaging in it. This may seem quite ridiculous; however, it's an extremely powerful exercise, as it reinforces the idea that you are where you are right now, existing in the present moment.

  For example, if you are walking down a hallway at work, repeat to yourself, "I'm walking down the hallway" the entire time you are walking down that hallway. If you're taking out the garbage, repeat to yourself, "I'm taking out the garbage" the entire time you are engaged in that activity. You can even break it down into more detailed actions: "I'm picking up the garbage bag," "I'm lifting the lid to the garbage can," "I'm placing the bag in the can," and "I'm rolling the can to the curb."

  When that activity changes, begin chanting about your next activity, whether it's walking the dog, preparing food to eat, or eating the food.

KEY POINTS ABOUT GETTING STARTED

- The main result of engaging in mindfulness practice, and one of the main reasons people turn to it, is to experience a greater sense of peace in their lives.

- Mindfulness practice is challenging to almost everyone. It requires a significant amount of practice, patience and perseverance, as well as a healthy dose of self-compassion.

- There is no end result, no end state, no certificate to be awarded. The goal, if we need to set one, is to be happier or more at peace than you are today, than you are now.

- The skills of focus and concentration, which are critical to the practice of mindfulness, are rarely fostered in the world today. With practice and by utilizing the exercises presented in the book, you can increase these skills.

- Learn to recognize when you are operating on autopilot or are simply zoning out. Teach yourself to snap out of those mind states when they arise. These are habits which have been fostered by the world and will limit your ability to be mindful.

- Mindfulness requires focus and concentration, something that is not taught and fostered in the world. But like a muscle, it can be strengthened with regular exercise.

CHAPTER THREE: THE ONLY THING CONSTANT

The world we have created is a product of our thinking; it cannot be changed without changing our thinking.

- Albert Einstein (attrib.) [x]

THAT INEVITABLE STEP: CHANGE

Reading about other people's experiences, such as transformations or achievements, can be motivational and inspiring. Doors of possibility open up that you didn't know even existed. If something about their experience resonates within you, then a spark of hope ignites—you may be able to have the experience as well. You recognize that the possibility exists, and begin to believe that it's available to you too.

Then comes the inevitable step, the decision. Do I proceed down this path and investigate the possibility further, or do I stop and dismiss it as a fleeting whim? We say to ourselves, "What am I thinking, I can't do that." Or: "Well, good for them, but I don't need to have such experiences, I'm fine as I am."

When you look to venture down a new path, you realize that something about you will become different. You compare who you are now to the future possibility and it's just too big. What you may fail to recognize, or don't want to recognize, is that you can become the person who can have that experience... but in order to do so, you must change.

One of the hardest things to do is to believe we are capable of changing. We set our focus on an end result that's so drastically different from where we are now that the entire effort appears insurmountable. In reality, it just takes small changes, one at a time. It may take many small changes to get to a certain point, and that's fine. It does not need to be, and often cannot be, instantaneous. Change takes as long as it takes. We have a bad habit of only wanting to see the "end result."

Sometimes the biggest step might just be making the choice to head down that new path, instead of dismissing it, which may be your normal mode of operation.

CONSTRUCTION AHEAD, PREPARE TO SLOW DOWN

While this is meant to be a motivational book, the truth is... change can be difficult. There. I said it. Don't act like it's a shock. If a tantrum is required, please put down the book and have it in another room. *(It's never good for one's book sales to have people going off on their books in public.)*

While examining your ability to change is not a prerequisite for practicing mindfulness, it's useful to look at your beliefs and feelings about the concept. If you're interested in mindfulness, then more than likely you're interested in getting beyond your status quo. To do that, something must change, and it's important to look at what that something involves. *(See, we're already doing mindfulness work. Who knew?)*

So let's spend some time exploring this concept in order to keep it in perspective and examine our own feelings about facing change. For the majority of us, change is challenging, if not downright seemingly impossible at times. Certain changes can take an incredible amount of work, willpower, and effort.

Dieting is difficult, embarking on an exercise regimen is difficult, starting a new job, getting married, or changing residences can all be difficult, and all involve change. Change means losing the familiar, the comfortable, and venturing into the unknown, the uncomfortable.

In order to change, we have to give up a sense of control by surrendering what's known; this can then lead to fear, which is a feeling that few people enjoy experiencing. However, once a change begins and we start adapting to what becomes the new norm, the feelings of fear gradually subside and begin to lose their hold on us. Furthermore, once we come to accept the change and see that it didn't bring about our worst-case scenarios, we begin to regain a sense of comfort.

Some people can adapt and embrace change more easily than others, and it may be because change is their norm. Perhaps they are comfortable with change because they have experienced a large amount of it in their lives. They see the world as fluid and not as a fixed, quantifiable object.

Regardless of anyone else's norm, we must realize that we each have our own comfort level with change and that we embrace change at our own pace. Until we are willing to buy into a change completely, we encounter inner resistance and turmoil.

Here again is a choice: It is up to us when to make a shift, and we usually won't do it until we are ready.

The world of late-night-TV fitness, self-help and diet gurus tells us (and sells us) that adopting a new routine is easy: Anyone can do it. We may watch these perky infomercial personalities and wish we could just reach through that TV screen and slap them. *(And perhaps with the advent of new technology, one day that may be possible. We can all dream, can't we?)*

Similarly, our friends and family members may tell us that making a specific type of change is easy. Usually, in these cases, they have either fully embraced the change themselves, or the change does not really impact them as it would us, which is why they say it will be so easy. *(Whether to slap them is at your own discretion.)*

Unlike Neo in *The Matrix* [xi], we cannot just plug in and learn jujitsu in a matter of seconds. For us mere mortals, it can take a lifetime to become proficient in such skills.

PACING AND TIMING

Why all this discussion of change? When approaching something new, it's best to level with yourself so that you don't make things more difficult than they need to be. If you look at change objectively, you may note the following:

- Change can be difficult by varying degrees. It depends on the person and the extent of change being made, as well as on their willingness to accept it.

- Your ability to make a change will be dependent on your desire either to make something happen or keep something from happening.

- The potential consequences of implementing or not implementing a change can provide the motivation to put the change in motion. For example, your doctor telling you something catastrophic will happen unless a change is made goes much further than your friends suggesting that you make modifications.

- You will waver until you have completely bought into the change and agree that the change is better than the status quo.

- You will struggle by degrees until you fully embrace the change.

For the majority of us, change in our lives—what is unknown—is not comfortable, and so many of us wish to remain in the comfortable known. Understanding and accepting your own capacity for change is a way of being compassionate and honest with yourself.

Often, when you're struggling with change, you will at some point berate yourself and equate your self-worth to that of slime growing on the slime in the most disgusting of sewers, which not only makes it even more difficult to make a change, but can serve as justification to opt out. Then, not only are you struggling with making a change, you're adding a nice dose of self-loathing on top of it. Helpful? Not so much.

What you may fail to realize initially is that dealing with change is nothing new to you or anyone, there are only varying levels of change. You have encountered and accepted change in the past, for better or worse, but you survived the change. In fact, you are constantly adjusting to change.

Every moment of every day, nature, people, societies, and cultures change and adapt, although we may not recognize that a change took place until we look back and reflect on it. The very nature of the world and our existence is change. Like snowflakes, no two moments are exactly the same (which makes them so gosh-darn cool!). The temperature, the climate, advances in technology, our bodies, politics, common beliefs, and state of mind are always in a state of change.

RISK AVERSION

When we mindfully prepare for change, it's helpful to be aware that we will be faced with a healthy amount of internal, as well as external, resistance (and arming ourselves with deadly ice-cream-sandwich grenades will be of no help here. *In case you were pondering that as a viable option*).

Even changes that we know are good for us, and that could save our lives, can be difficult to put into effect. At some level, old familiar habits and pleasures are going to be threatened.

If your doctor were to tell you that you needed to cut down on your coffee intake or face serious medical issues in the near future, and one of your favorite habits is enjoying a daily cup of coffee with friends at your favorite coffeehouse, then it's going to be a difficult habit to change. Not only will you be fighting the cravings of the body, but you'll also be missing the company of the familiar faces at the coffeehouse. Perhaps you'll have the will-power to continue to go to the coffeehouse and only drink green tea, but the temptation will be strong to indulge in coffee.

Similarly, if your doctor tells you to quit smoking, yet all of your friends and loved ones smoke, not only will you battle the cravings of the body, you'll also be surrounded by people who don't believe they need to quit smoking. You'll constantly be reminded of the comfort and pleasure you find in that activity.

When we embark on moment-to-moment mindfulness practice, the manner in which we habitually live our lives will present many opportunities for resistance. We are accustomed to zoning out as we make our way down the freeway to work, vegging out in front of the TV, or surfing the Internet for hours at a time, just doing what it takes to get through the day and mindlessly going through our routines. We allow media outlets to influence our beliefs and political views, and advertisers to tell us what we should be eating, how we should look, who we should admire, how we should behave, the latest gadget we must own… the list is endless.

While we strive for moment-to-moment awareness, our current condition is likely moment-to-moment unawareness.

BE REALISTIC, REALLY REAL… REALISTIC… LIKE REALITY REAL

As I mentioned in Chapter Two, we live in a guaranteed overnight delivery, drive-thru, instant message world. Tasks that once may have taken days or weeks have become so automated that instant turnaround is becoming the norm. Additionally, technology is not likely to slow down or stop. Therefore, when we mindfully observe ourselves and decide to make changes, we become frustrated when we see that it is going to take an investment of time.

Again, unlike Neo in *The Matrix,* should we choose to become a black-belt martial artist, we cannot just have those techniques and abilities downloaded into our consciousness. We must put in the hours at the dojo.

Notwithstanding that some things come to some people more naturally than others, if we go to the dojo and practice once a month, it's going to take quite some time to achieve that black belt. If we go once a week, then perhaps we'll acquire proficiency in a shorter period of time; if we attend daily, in even less time. The same goes for dieting, stopping smoking, learning to meditate, and practicing mindfulness.

If we want that perfect beach body and only exercise and diet one day each month, should we really be surprised that, come swimsuit season, we're not where we had hoped to be?

So, with regard to mindfulness, know that learning to be present and controlling your thoughts is going to take some time. How long it takes is up to each of us individually. Comparing ourselves to others is pointless and simply a distraction.

GAINING BUY IN

How poor are they that have not patience! What wound did ever heal but by degrees?

- William Shakespeare, *Othello* [xii]

In beginning any new practice, it's a great advantage if we believe that the change we are embarking on will benefit us in some way—that is, we are not happy with our as-is state and long for a to-be state, something different from where we are today.

Unfortunately, that road to the to-be state can be long, trying, and frequently discouraging. We need reminders and motivators to help foster patience, which is one reason why Weight Watchers, Alcoholics Anonymous, and similar programs are successful; with group meetings and support structures firmly in place, they make it easier to achieve a goal than going it alone. They incorporate reminder mechanisms that tell us we're still on track—or if we've veered off the path, they tell us how to turn the steering wheel to get back to the road.

We must also foster a belief that the change we wish to bring about is possible to achieve. In terms of mindfulness and meditation, if you've experienced just a moment of stillness and peace at some point in your life, then who's to say you can't experience more moments for longer and longer periods of time? The doors of possibility are endless in number; it's our minds that close and lock them up, telling us that we are unworthy or incapable.

If you can read a magazine article, then you can read a book. If you can talk in front of five people, then you can talk in front of fifty. If you can hold your mind still for a moment and stop the constant churning of thought, then who's to say you can't do it for two moments, for a minute, for five minutes, for ten, an hour, a day? It comes down to patience, practice, and perseverance.

Just keep trying. To start down the road of making any kind of change, we must have patience and compassion for ourselves. We must be realistic, know our strengths and weaknesses, and be OK with them. This is itself mindfulness awareness! We also may need a swift kick in the butt to get motivated at times! *(And if you know that this is the case for you, then I implore you to seek out that thing that will provide you with that kick in the butt! However, I don't encourage you to seek it through personal ads, as that could lead down a road of major distraction.)*

As mentioned earlier, the point is to not berate ourselves when we encounter internal opposition or resistance. We must look at our perceived weaknesses, acknowledge them, and move on. The truth is, we'll continue to buy into resistance and opposition until we're fed up with it and decide to change, whatever form that change may take.

Unfortunately, with mindfulness training, there are not as many formal support structures in place to help foster this practice; however, here are some ideas that might help support you in your practice:

- **Notes:** Use sticky note reminders. You will want to keep your practice in the forefront of your thoughts because it's our thoughts themselves we are trying to change. By putting up motivational quotes or reminder words on sticky notes around your home or office space, you can remind yourself to be in the present moment.

  Be careful though. Within a few days the notes will begin to blend in with the wallpaper, so move them around every few days or create new ones. Write things on them that help evoke strong reactions or that deeply motivate you.

- **Alarms:** Create alarms on your phone calendar program. Smartphones and apps make it easy to set up an alarm or chime to go off at specified intervals.

  When they alert you, check in with yourself and reflect on your level of mindfulness between the intervals. Compare your present state of mind to what it was at the last interval. Ask yourself what happened to shift you into the state you're in now.

- **Intent:** Set your intent every morning to be more mindful than the day before. Write out a declaration document which inspires, encourages, and reminds you why you are taking on this change in your life.

  For example, write out, with as much detail as you possibly can, your as-is state, including what is motivating you to make these changes. Next, write out all the things you find beautiful or motivating about living mindfully, your to-be state. Hold that to-be state in your attention with as much strength as you can throughout the day.

Have faith that you can make the changes you wish to make. Once you're able to make small changes, with tools you'll learn in the following chapters, you'll then know that greater, larger changes are possible. Faith changes to belief over time. Remember to keep your perspective though—some changes are just going to take more time and effort than others.

- **Be realistic:** Set realistic goals and milestones for yourself along your journey. If you're unsuccessful in reaching them, then stop and review what happened and re-plan. It's good to stretch ourselves beyond our perceived capabilities, but, unlike the Buddha, we must crawl before we walk.

We may have high hopes and ambitions, but when it comes down to it, we can only control ourselves (which is the point of this book). The world, on the other hand, often has plans of its own, which may interfere with those hopes and ambitions.

- **Community:** Find others who are also interested in learning and practicing mindfulness. Seek out local meditation or yoga groups that incorporate mindfulness in their practice. Being able to talk about these topics with others can be motivating, insightful and reassuring.

- **Remember:** Remind yourself daily of what you're doing and why you're doing it. If you're struggling with motivation, reconnect to moments of determination you experienced in the past and remember what those feelings were like. Make this as visceral as possible.

- **Journal:** Write out the beautiful realizations and experiences you encounter through your mindfulness practice as it evolves. Write these out with as much detail and clarity as you possibly can. Really strive to capture the essence of them. Write them for yourself as if you're writing in a diary; don't hold back, no one else needs to or should read them.

Then, if you start to feel that you've lost touch with your practice or you're going through a particularly difficult struggle, go back and read these entries. If you've done a good job capturing the essence of the experiences, then you'll be able to take yourself back to those states of mind and remind yourself that those experiences were real. You can experience the beauty of them again, and motivate yourself to move forward and continue with your practice.

KEY POINTS ABOUT CHANGE

- Mindfulness is about change, and ultimately, transformation. It requires us to do something different than what we are doing today. Don't focus on a final result, as that can make the effort seem insurmountable.

- Change is a process and will take as long as it takes. The amount of time it takes us to make changes in our lives is different for each of us.

SECTION TWO: THE ROOT CAUSE ANALYSIS

It is the function of art to renew our perception. What we are familiar with we cease to see. The writer shakes up the familiar scene, and, as if by magic, we see a new meaning in it.

- Anaïs Nin [xiii]

The intent of this next section is to review and dissect some of the most common states of mind we engage in during our day-to-day lives, and the resulting moods and emotions associated with each. These are the concepts that were identified in "Component One - Paying Attention" in Chapter One.

Buddhists state that there are 10,000 states of mind, and while that might be fascinating to diagram out, for the sake of simplicity, time, and sanity, we'll look at just a handful, ones to which most of us can easily relate.

When they arise, many of these states can lead us down a path of feeling conflicted, often ending in a seemingly stagnant pool of mental suffering. Other states allow us to feel varying depths of comfort and peace. All of them, however, are transient; they come and they go. Nothing is permanent.

By stepping back and objectively looking at them, we can examine, understand, and begin to recognize subtle inherent patterns, behaviors, and outcomes associated with each. If a particular state causes us to experience negative feelings, through examination, we can diagram out the mechanics involved and begin to see how it leads us toward the undesired reactions. With this knowledge, we can gradually create strategies that will allow us to divorce ourselves from those states of mind, and the toll they take on our emotional well-being.

Alternatively, if a particular state shifts us in the opposite direction, toward peace and contentment, we can learn how to more actively engage that state at will, or use it to rescue us from the depths of a negative state.

In the chapters that follow, we'll examine these concepts in detail:

- **Chapter Four: Understanding the Playing Field** - Just what is it your mind is doing all day?

- **Chapter Five: Perceptions** - Learn to examine and question your perceptions of the world, understand how and why they arise, and, if warranted, what you can do to change them.

- **Chapter Six: Under the Influence** - Review how judgmental thinking clouds your view of the world and impacts your state of mind.

- **Chapter Seven: Expectations** - Establishing expecta- tions limits your ability to experience situations as they are unfolding naturally. Learn to recognize how they lock us into all-or-nothing thinking, leaving little room for us to be open to new possibilities.

- **Chapter Eight: Stories** - What are the stories you have created about yourself and your place in the world? Identify how those stories are shaped by others and why we find it so challenging to change them.

- **Chapter Nine: Projections and Reflections** - Discover how and why you are dependent on feedback from others. Become conscious of how this limits your ability to remain in peaceful states of mind.

- **Chapter Ten: Clarity** - Recognize how, and to what degree, your state of mind is influenced by your environment, and develop plans for how to lessen its impact.

- **Chapter Eleven: Happiness and Gratitude** - Explore your ideas about what constitutes happiness. Learn how focusing on the concept of gratitude will allow you to shift your attention away from what you don't have, the things that you believe will bring you feelings of peace, to what you already have, and the peace that is present because of them.

In connection with each of these concepts, we'll also review the triggers that start us moving into distressed states of mind. So put on your lab coat, because, just like in biology class, we're going to turn on the spotlight, grab a scalpel, and begin to dissect and explore (but without the mess and smell of formaldehyde).

A few disclaimers before we jump in. As mentioned previously, this is not a medical or psychological examination or evaluation of mental states. It is rather a logical examination of common mental habits and their resulting impacts.

Also, a number of behaviors will be reviewed that can often lead to negative states of mind. These should not be seen as a personal critique of anyone's behavior. They are being brought up in order for us to examine why we may see them as beneficial and why we choose to engage in them.

In a way, this is self-discovery. You are trying to look at yourself objectively without evaluating or judging. You are working to get a clear picture and understanding of who you are and how you operate.

In some chapters, the information presented may sound esoteric or New-Agey. Language is a challenge when discussing these kinds of concepts. I ask that you set judgments aside, allow the concepts to play out as presented, and see if you don't gain at least some level of insight. You may be surprised.

CHAPTER FOUR: UNDERSTANDING THE PLAYING FIELD

There can be only one permanent revolution — a moral one; the regeneration of the inner man. How is this revolution to take place? Nobody knows how it will take place in humanity, but every man feels it clearly in himself. And yet in our world everybody thinks of changing humanity, and nobody thinks of changing himself.

- Leo Tolstoy [xiv]

IT'S ONLY IN YOUR MIND

"But... there is no mind." This comment stopped me dead in my tracks, which was kind of tricky at the time, since I was pulling onto a busy freeway with cars queued up behind me.

My traveling companion and I had just departed a meditation retreat weekend, and I was discussing the numerous emotional challenges I was experiencing as a result of participating. Due to my over-analytical nature, I was struggling to find explanations for these challenges, but could find none.

Amused, yet also somewhat annoyed by my quest for rational answers, my companion looked me straight in the eyes when she delivered that line, and instantly my chatty mind was like the black-and-white static of a television screen that's not receiving a signal. I struggled for a rational retort, but alas, I had none. *(I believe my intelligent response was something along the lines of "W... w... what?")*

Later, my analytical nature would go crazy puzzling over the idea that there is no mind. There had to be a mind, I reasoned, because there must be a functioning mass of intelligence in my head that contained some kind of anomaly that was the source of my unpleasant emotions. If there is no mind, what causes us to experience negative and positive thoughts, and challenging mental states? Toiling over this question, seeking some rational answer from science, metaphysics, spirituality, and even Bugs Bunny to help me disprove this concept, I exhausted myself trying to figure out what made up the mind.

Was it thoughts, electrons, neurons and neural networks, "dark matter," DNA... or maybe alien implants? Often I would find solace by embracing the ultimate logic that could only be found at the bottom of the dish of my current favorite flavor of ice cream.

As mentioned at the beginning of the book, at one time I consistently dwelled in very negative states of mind. Sadly, these moods were so pervasive that I didn't realize how much they ruled my outlook on life until I became mindful of them. I also had no idea that there was even an option to completely change my perspective to one where peace and balance were the pervasive states. I felt like I was addicted to these negative moods and to try and combat them only made them more prevalent and all-consuming. I would have brief periods of living in peaceful states (sobriety), but would eventually be pulled back in and feel powerless against the negativity.

I was so ashamed of these mental attitudes that I did everything I could to hide them. The face I showed the world was one of peace, charm, and charisma. After all, I meditated daily and dutifully devoted myself to my personal spiritual practices. Surely, I believed, the source of my internal conflict couldn't be within me. That's ridiculous because, you see, I'm perfect. It had to be something in the world that was the culprit.

Alas, when I was introduced to the idea that there may be no mind, my fallback excuse—"something in the world is at fault for causing my mind to experience the negativity I experience, such as the influence of other people or world events"—was just ripped away. That one line resonated as so truthful within me that, at my core, I could not deny or fight it.

If there really is no mind, then there are only thoughts, which are things that I know from my meditation practices can be controlled and quelled. Perhaps, because I allowed myself to experience negative states of mind, I was not in control of my thoughts and wasn't perfect after all. OK, so maybe I was not as perfect as I thought I was. *(After all, there's no reason to get extreme about the whole matter.)* The next step had to be to learn to control my thoughts and understand what shapes and influences them.

Oddly enough, to this day, my travel companion has no recollection of making that statement to me in the car. Which begs me to ask the question, "Perhaps it was only in my mind?"

COMMON THOUGHT

Despite the doubts raised by the above story, for this book and for the sake of having a common language with which to communicate, we will continue to refer to the conglomeration of thoughts, the lens through which we experience the world and our associated identity, as the mind. Or, as we also called it in Chapter One, our attention or consciousness.

CHECK THE INGREDIENTS

Something that might be useful as you begin to embrace mindfulness is to shift your perspective to see what it is you're actually at odds with. Have you ever asked yourself (and perhaps even answered yourself) what a thought actually is?

If we reflect on the things that challenge us in our lives, we'll typically point to people or situations or bodily issues—things that physically exist in the material world that we interact with on a physical level. Thoughts, on the other hand, are not physical or tangible. Our only interaction with them is in our own minds. *(Which doesn't even exist, remember?)*

Simplistically speaking, we're doing battle with ourselves. Either we are mentally pointing to something outside of ourselves as the source of our troubles or we're creating a negative commentary on our own character. So, to take it a step further, it's through our thoughts, and the emotions that arise from them, that we create our conflicts with the physical world, as well as with ourselves.

If you reflect on the nature of a thought, how would you describe it? If you're very visual, it may be like a movie clip passing in front of the projector of your mind. Or perhaps you experience a thought like a brief bit of dialogue, a voice in your head speaking to you, telling you how wonderful and horrible you are, in between telling you that you need to make sure you don't forget to pick up peanut butter from the store on the way home. Upon examination, there's nothing tangible about a thought, yet it can wield the power to make or break our day.

In the Harry Potter books and movies [xv], they use a clever device to represent memories and thoughts from the past: Memories are extracted from one's head with the pull of a magic wand and emerge as a whiff of smoke that can be inserted and stored in a glass vial. They can then be reviewed in a device that allows others to watch the memories play out as if they were actually present when the memory took place.

There's no judgment on the part of the viewer. The memories are just historical references to an event that was recorded through the eyes of the person who experienced it, and it's much like a news clip on television. The memories in the vials can be taken out, viewed, learned from, and then put away until they're needed again.

The thoughts don't jump up and demand to be reviewed, the characters choose when they wish to review them and then decide how to act on what they viewed if they choose.

Realistically, we can't contain or capture thoughts. (They have minds of their own.) When scientists study the brain, they don't see the actual thoughts, images, and emotions that we experience. They see areas of activity light up in reaction to certain stimuli. They can see that certain areas are associated with certain emotions and responses and that specific areas light up when different behaviors are enacted.

When it comes to the idea that we can change the way that we think, there are no hard-and-fast rules to tell us what is and what is not possible. Anything is possible. The only limitations are those that we ourselves put in place and adhere to.

We are welcome to become free thinkers or free non-thinkers, as the case may be, so get out your best revolutionary garb and prepare to engage. *(And, yes, if you're more at home in your* Star Trek *costume than in your Gettysburg revolutionary outfit, that will work just fine.)*

WHAT'S ON YOUR MIND?

Throughout the day we spend a significant portion of our time engaged in "daydreaming," which is an interesting expression, since the word "dream" implies an experience of non-reality. Yet, when we engage in daydreaming, it shapes our state of mind and affects our emotions and how we perceive our current reality.

For example, when you're sitting in traffic, uninterested in the radio and the world around you, you escape into the world of daydreams. Here you are more mentally engaged, you experience having a greater sense of control, and you are not hindered by the miles of cars ahead of you keeping you trapped in your current location.

In this daydream reality, anything is possible and you have unlimited power. With that unlimited power, you become a superhero, you're royalty, rich, popular, a rock star, or a sexually irresistible model, and all of these elaborate "realities" are created within the comfortable confines of your little car (and it can become quite crowded in there, especially if you drive a subcompact).

Similarly, our unguarded thoughts in this daydreaming state can drive us into agitated, sad, and frustrated states of mind should our temperament lean in this direction. Here we alone engage in one-way battles and arguments with friends, family, coworkers, politicians, or the unsuspecting radio announcer.

As mentioned in Chapter One, this is suffering because, when we are addicted to thought and the associated states of mind that result from uncontrolled thought, we are seldom ever at peace with ourselves and the world. Freedom from suffering can be seen as freedom from the addiction of thought.

Therefore, in order to understand the individual playing field we each have to work with, we must begin to understand the thoughts that fill our consciousness day in and day out. It is imperative to understand the nature of our thoughts, since they ultimately control our states of mind, emotions, feelings, and outlook on, and experience of, the world. By engaging in this examination and practicing the strategies of mindfulness—**learning to control our minds instead of allowing our minds to control us, understanding why we think what we think, and ultimately learning to change the way we think**—we can change our habits of thought and learn to keep our minds in a quiet and controlled state.

(Note: That was a pretty important paragraph and quite key to the book. So in case your eyes were just wandering over the letters on the page while your thoughts were engaged in planning your house made entirely of pizza and nachos, I highly recommend reading it at least one more time.)

SEPARATION ANXIETY

As touched on in Chapter One, you can begin paying attention to your thoughts by imagining that a part of you is stepping back and watching them as they float through your consciousness. Like watching a movie, you want to become aware of the thoughts as they crisscross your consciousness like images projected on a screen.

Or you might envision your mind as a section of clear blue sky and the thoughts like clouds that you observe passing by. A day with a cloudless sky would be the ideal; however, more often than not, clouds of varying density and size will drift in and out. Some days will consist of periodic, light, effervescent clouds that dissipate before your eyes, other days consist of full, thick cloud cover accentuated by periodic loud thunderclaps.

But even on those dark days, you can be comforted in knowing that, above the dark thunder clouds, perfect blue sky is there waiting. It just needs a little help blowing the clouds away so that it may shine through.

When engaging in this practice, imagine that "you" are the being witnessing the thoughts, unattached to and disassociated from what they are or what they may mean; you are just witnessing. Try and separate yourself, much as you watch TV or movies. You are not the movie. Although you can easily get caught up in it and have emotional reactions to what you see, you maintain a sense of separation. You don't own what you see on the screen. When you learn to witness your thoughts, you can reflect on what you are seeing and experiencing from an objective standpoint.

It's challenging, but the goal is to try not to get too emotionally involved with the thoughts when witnessing them. You may find that you begin critiquing yourself for what you are thinking. While you eventually will begin to look at why you were thinking what you were thinking and when you thought it, you first just want to become comfortable with the concept of paying attention to your thoughts.

REMINDERS

Reminding ourselves to monitor our thoughts can be a big challenge when we first start practicing. Because we are so often victims of random thought tangents and have our attention pulled in a million different directions over the course of a day, or even just an hour, we must find every way possible to create reminders for ourselves. Essentially, we need to create a habit of reminding ourselves to just pay attention.

To assist with this practice of monitoring your thoughts and identifying the trends and patterns that emerge, keep a notebook, journal, or diary with you and periodically make notes about what you notice. You may want to record the day of the week, time of day, and the general situation if you find that helpful. Be as detailed as you like, or just keep it at a very general level. *(If people are nosy and ask what you're writing about, just tell them that you're tracking irregularities in your digestive cycles and, more than likely, you won't be asked again.)*

Also, I recommend the reminder devices that were presented in Chapter Three, such as leaving sticky notes for yourself and setting alarms. These reminders interrupt your routine of indulging in random thought, and prompt you to be mindful of what is unfolding in the present moment. This moment.

THE 10,000-FOOT VIEW

When practicing this activity, you want to remain as objective as possible. Again, the intent of this exercise is not to judge yourself, something that just leads to stressful states of mind. This is just a discovery phase, where you are beginning to see what's going on in there and are becoming accustomed to the concept of paying attention to your thoughts.

In time, you'll begin to see what trends of thought are present in your consciousness, which ones are pervasive thought patterns and which ones seem random. You can even begin to create different categories for your thoughts.

For example, you may find that you have many thoughts throughout the day that you categorize as having an angry nature, or perhaps a self-deprecating nature. You may notice that you're actually quite content and happy in certain situations. Perhaps you find that you have many thoughts of a jealous nature. Or you may find that you are continually anxious about where you need to be next.

Do you create many what-if scenarios? Do you spend much of your day fantasizing about being somewhere else, anywhere else than where you are at that moment? Do you spend a good portion of the day reliving experiences, both happy and not so happy, from days gone by? Are your thoughts in the morning drastically different than they are in the afternoon and in the evening? What's your state of mind on the weekends, compared to during the week? Do you obsess about sex or food, or both (because really, at times, what's the difference?), at the same time every day or in specific situations?

After just a few days or a week, you may begin to see some surprising trends in the thoughts that roam through your attention. You may find that you spend a large amount of time dwelling on the good old days or fantasizing about the lives of celebrities. You may find that you think self-deprecating thoughts many times over the course of a day and many of them in the late afternoon. You may find that you think irritated or jealous thoughts more often than you were aware.

Often, some thoughts are so ingrained in your nature that you're not even aware you are thinking them throughout the day. Again, you don't want to judge yourself for the types of thoughts you're thinking, as that can just make a challenging situation worse. You really just want to become aware of where your mind hangs out during the day.

Understandably, each day brings new experiences, and there are many factors involved in what you may be feeling or thinking at any particular time. But by practicing the act of monitoring your thoughts as often as you can, you begin to get an overall sense of what your predominant thought patterns are. Gradually, over time, the more you practice, become aware, and are willing to look, the patterns and cause-and-effect situations will begin to emerge.

CAUSE-AND-EFFECT

Recognizing the cause-and-effect situations is critical. Spotting a trend in the way you react in specific situations allows you to discover specific factors that lead you to certain states of mind. You now have the power to take action and change the dynamics of those relationships, if warranted.

This is the same sort of procedure you would use to remedy a physical problem. For example, say you realize one day that you've been having a more difficult time with allergies recently. Since you don't enjoy this feeling, you decide to investigate why this seems to be happening. By paying close attention to when they begin to act up, you soon notice that every time you spend time in your garage, the reactions kick in. You look around the vicinity of your garage and notice that your neighbor has planted some new flowers along the side wall. You take a sample of the flower to your allergist, who tests you and confirms that you are indeed allergic to the flower. Mystery solved.

In the same way, we can determine what situations lead us to have emotional allergic reactions. These can include positive and negative reactions we have to people we encounter in our lives, as well as reactions we have to certain locations, activities, or tasks. Granted, this kind of detective work can be more difficult than identifying the source of a physical allergic reaction.

BREAKING IT DOWN

Once you become aware of some of the main themes in your thoughts, and the challenges they provoke, you can purposefully take this awareness down to a deeper level and ask yourself what's really going on underneath the surface. "Why does this cause a reaction to arise in me?" "Why does this upset me?"

For example, in many situations, our troubling states of mind are a result of our own fears and our desire for control in order to combat those fears. Often, it can take a while before we are able, or willing, to understand just what's happening in these situations and how different flavors of fear and control can manifest.

A common reaction is that we begin to judge ourselves for feeling the things that we feel, which not only is futile, but causes even more internal conflict, and can defeat the entire purpose of the examination.

Once we understand our motivations and the root causes for our reactions, we can catch when we are beginning to indulge in certain behaviors and, over time, put an end to these habits. In time, our big issues begin to dissipate in intensity and eventually become non-issues.

Sometimes, talking over the profound challenges with a counselor or therapist, or even an objective friend, will allow us to gain insight into ourselves that we may not be able, or may not be willing, to recognize through our own efforts. Typically a counselor will prove more beneficial than a friend, since friends may be concerned about upsetting or offending us.

PLAY-BY-PLAY

For example, while monitoring your thoughts, you may notice that you experience twinges of irritation every time you speak with a friend we'll call Bob. Even though you really like Bob, and nothing appears to have changed about him recently, you feel irritated around him, which causes a state of confusion. If you can step back and objectively look at what's happening, you can start to find the cause for these feelings of irritation.

If you allow yourself to really explore the emotions you're experiencing, you may see that underlying the irritation is a subtle feeling of jealousy. You can then ask yourself, "So why in the world am I jealous of Bob?" Then you may notice that you've become increasingly aware that Bob possesses things in life that you wish you possessed as well. Bob has a very lucrative career that has given him a very nice standard of living. Thus every time you speak to Bob, you are reminded that he possesses material items that you think you would like to possess, and this makes you feel unworthy or bad about yourself.

So you can ask yourself, why is it that you don't have what Bob has? And you may come to see that Bob spent years working tirelessly, and always enjoyed excelling in his career and climbing the corporate ladder, while you were not inclined to do that. You shunned corporate life in order to work in environments where you could be more relaxed and work at your own pace. Lately you've questioned that decision, or are feeling resentful that your career of choice has not provided as much of a financial reward as Bob's has for him.

Now you must ask yourself why you react with irritation. And you realize that instead of feeling bad about yourself when the triggering interactions take place—which none of us enjoys—you automatically resort to feelings of irritation, which gives you a sense of control and justification. The truth is that you're jealous of Bob's situation, but you have no issue with him, since you find him to be a great guy. From this realization, you can compose a strategy for counteracting those feelings when they arise.

Spend time evaluating if you would be happy in a similar work environment. Think about whether the material rewards would really make you feel better. Would it be worth the trade-off? Do you really believe material things are a sign of success?

If you feel bad about yourself for having this conflict, you can cultivate the humility to know that at least you are trying to work through your emotions around this issue, which perhaps will start to dissipate your self-judgment. Even more significantly, you can immediately notice the irritation arising when you're interacting with Bob and remind yourself of your internal struggle and the work you are engaged in around it, which will ideally diffuse the irritation.

Your new understanding becomes more powerful if you can see how this is a common pattern for you; that the same emotional state arises with regard to other people you know in similar situations. Over time, and by mindfully working on the issue using the exercises in the book, you can reach the point where the irritation, or other negative emotion, stops manifesting altogether. The situation becomes a non-issue.

Looking even deeper, you might spot feelings revolving around your own perceived inadequacies. Again, these realizations can be difficult to look at, and you will develop the willingness to deal with them at your own pace. However, once you can spot the source of the itch, the frustration can be alleviated by degrees.

CUTTING YOUR LIFE SHORT

"I could tell you my adventures—beginning from this morning," said Alice a little timidly: "but it's no use going back to yesterday, because I was a different person then."

- Lewis Carroll, *Alice's Adventures in Wonderland* [xvi]

One thing that is quickly noticeable when we begin to pay attention to our thoughts is that, in general, we spend a tremendous amount of time focusing on events that occurred in the past or those we believe or hope will occur in the future. Thus we spend very little time focused on what's going on right now, right here, in this moment... the present.

And even when we are focused on the present, often we're judging, ranking, or evaluating what's unfolding, or creating stories about what's happening between us and the situation we're experiencing. Thus we are not experiencing the moment as it is. We are focusing on what we want it to be.

In a way, by living in the past or the future, and thereby being absent from the present moment, we are cutting our lives short. We may not like to acknowledge it, but we each have a set amount of time to live our lives. Only Eternity knows when it will be time for us to move on. If we are absent from the current moment, we are essentially avoiding living this life we have been given. We are too busy living in memories of the past or fantasies of the future, neither of which are really our lives, they're only a circus of ideas and thoughts. As you will discover in the coming chapters, so much of this is time wasted.

We only have this moment, and we so often fill it with absent-minded emptiness. There is a certain irony to this paradigm. We live in a world so focused on youth and beauty and we do all we can to look and feel young, yet we're not there to really experience it. We are trying so hard to be so much instead of just being with what is, as it is.

DAYS GONE BY

When we dwell on events from the past, the scenario playing out in our consciousness could be something that happened five seconds ago, five minutes ago, hours ago, days ago, weeks ago, or years ago. In these situations, there are numerous things we're doing: we're reminiscing about experiences, good or bad; we're trying to recapture the feeling of something that brought us a level of satisfaction, or we're tormenting ourselves with past regrets and perceived failures; we're trying to gain perspective on why something unfolded the way it did; and/or we're comparing what's happening currently to something that occurred in the past.

What's interesting is that when we dwell on a memory of an event that happened in the past, many of the associated emotions that we experienced at the time are experienced all over again; they all come rushing back to the present moment.

So if we dwell on a particularly frustrating or upsetting event from the past, we'll begin to experience frustrating or upsetting states of mind in the present moment. Similarly, if we focus on a beautiful, happy time that occurred in the past, the emotions we associate with that time will come back to us as well. It's as if our minds actually can't tell the difference between what they are experiencing now and what they experienced in the past.

When we engage in this behavior, our feelings or emotions rarely reflect anything that's actually occurring in the present moment because we're really not here, we're living in the past.

TOMORROWWORLD (WHERE ALL OF YOUR DREAMS COME TRUE)

The future depends on what we do in the present.

- Mahatma Gandhi (attrib.) [xvii]

On the flip side, we also spend a tremendous amount of time engaging in thoughts about the future. Perhaps we're fantasizing about how we're going to spend our time once we retire or how fabulous our future wife or husband is going to be. We can get so carried away in fantasy that it's as if we've created an actual movie in our minds, complete with wardrobe, lighting, and a most attractive cast of scandalous characters.

We also spend time worrying about the future, creating endless what-if scenarios about a presentation at work we're nervous about, an exam we feel ill-prepared for, an upcoming first date and the fear of rejection, a pending interview, or a trip to the doctor or dentist. We wonder "What's going to happen if…?" or "What will happen when…?" All of these scenarios can incite feelings of anxiety or dread in very subtle ways.

We also create subtle levels of stress in the current moment around things we're looking forward to because we're not there now: the fabulous vacation we have coming up, the day off from work, a date with that special someone we're falling for, attending an event with good friends or family that we've been looking forward to for weeks, and on and on and on... We are resentful because we are not in the future moment, which we perceive as better than the one we are currently in.

In all of these situations, we devalue the present and bypass most of the experiences unfolding around us because our minds have placed so much emphasis on the future event—an event we believe nothing in the present can match in terms of importance or significance.

When our thoughts stray from the present moment, we respond emotionally as if the future event were happening right now. We actually create emotional responses for something that hasn't even happened and, more often than not, won't happen the way we think it will; but we experience all the projected emotions as if they were happening right now, we pull them into this moment.

When we focus on a to-be experience, one that has us anxious, nervous, or upset, we may find that our shoulders slowly rise up toward our ears and our bodies become tense. If this is a common mental state for you, and you experience physical discomfort as a result of it, it's something to pay attention to.

We let these thoughts run rampant in our consciousness when we're not paying attention to what we're doing. For many of us, this situation occurs often and we are completely unaware of it. In time we may notice that our shoulders hurt or our stomach is in knots, and we don't realize why our bodies are in so much pain.

Just consider the power of this for a moment: You are actually creating a fictional state of mind right now, on your own, in this moment, complete with emotional feelings and reactions, through the power of your own thoughts, which you ultimately control. The problem is that you're out of control in being able to control them!

Now consider this: If you're able to manufacture anxiety and stress on your own, just imagine the feelings of peace and tranquility you can manufacture for yourself using the same behaviors. Peace and tranquility don't arrive when a certain set of outward experiences comes into alignment, they are always there beneath the surface. We just create mental chaos in our lives to cover them up.

We may engage in this kind of future-focused thought in order to escape a current unpleasant or boring situation. We'll create scenarios in our minds in order to be anywhere other than where we currently are. If we lose interest in what we're engaged in—a meeting at work or a lecture at school—how quickly our minds jump away to another place and time. We may even walk out of the meeting not having a clue about what was discussed or agreed upon.

The future events will happen when the future events happen. Despite what we wish to believe, there is nothing we can do to control the future. Perhaps a better use of time is to be present where you are, and allow the moments to unfold as they will, and experience them as they do.

THE PRESENT

Remember, no matter where you go, there you are.

- Confucius (attrib.) [xviii]

When you're somewhere else in your mind, then you're not experiencing what you're currently engaged in. We can only truly experience this current moment. We can only do what we are doing in this moment. We can't do something in the future or past. Logically this makes sense to us, but our minds will continually pull us away into dreams of the past or to the fictional future.

We typically find that we are easily in the present moment when we're engaged or interested in what's happening. Because we have an interest in it, we find it easy to pay attention. We're there until we become uninterested. If we're avid sports fans, while we're at the game of our favorite team, we're wrapped up in what's unfolding, reacting to the game as it plays out before us until the final buzzer rings.

Unfortunately, much of the time when we are trying to focus on what's unfolding in the present moment, we're judging or evaluating what's unfolding around us, or we're creating stories about the relationship between ourselves and what we are experiencing.

Do we like what's happening? Are we engaged in an internal constant commentary about what we are hearing or seeing? Are we comparing everything we're experiencing against our own beliefs, likes, dislikes, and preferences? Are we weaving what we are experiencing into a story with regard to how the information we are receiving may be beneficial or detrimental to us? Are we narrating the experience to ourselves: "It's too hot/cold in here." "Why aren't they watching the game? Who cares about the news?" "They're serving raspberry tea? That's so 2006."

All of this internal commentary separates us from the experience at hand. We are more concerned about how the event affects us, what our opinion of it is, or how the outcome will impact us, than we are in experiencing the event itself.

When our minds are still and quiet, focused on the present moment unfolding, we have a level of mental peace and calm. As soon as we begin to focus on a time or place other than where we are at this moment, we invite that other reality into our minds and we then experience the emotions, feelings, and perceptions associated with that other time and place. *(I highly recommend enforcing a cover charge as it becomes popular and the crowds grow. The extra income never hurts.)*

VENTURING FORWARD

As you begin to see the landscape unfold and you take a few steps forward, you will start to make your own discoveries about your mental operating system. Moreover, your interactions with the world may begin to change. Part of the magic of mindfulness is discovering that it's not so difficult to change your perspective, and that what you believed were hard-and-fast rules governing how things work in the world are more flexible than you thought.

Following are some observations, techniques and tools which might help to get and keep you moving forward.

THE JOYS OF OWNERSHIP

One of the first things you might observe is that you have a difficult time letting go of certain thoughts. It may seem as if you are so connected to a thought at times that you can't get rid of it. It feels like you have an obligation to see a thought through to an end, as if, if you didn't, you would be abandoning it. If it is a future-based thought, do you feel the need to create a happy resolution so that you can experience a feeling of accomplishment?

As mentioned earlier, the more you go to the proverbial dojo to practice mental martial arts, the more control you gain over your thoughts and the faster you can spot and recognize random daydreamy thoughts. Then, by shifting your attention, you can drop the random thoughts and stay in more quiet, still, and peaceful states of mind.

SWEET DREAMS

Another interesting area to investigate is your relationship with your dreams. For the majority of us, when we're dreaming, it's as though what we're experiencing in the dream is actually happening. It's no different than an experience that is happening in the "real" world. If we have a nightmare, we may wake up in a panic with our heart beating rapidly. While we were having the dream, it was reality to us, no different than our experiences throughout the day.

This is a good example of a shift in perspective. Have you ever noticed that sometimes you go to bed completely happy, then you wake up in the morning agitated and upset? Well, what happened between going to sleep and waking up? While your body rested, your mind and emotions continued to interact within your dreams.

You may wake up in the morning in a grumpy state of mind and not recall that you were happy when you went to sleep. That grumpy feeling may remain until something happens to shift you into a different state of mind. If you notice this happening, what you could do is ask yourself, "Hey Mr. or Ms. Grumpy Face (it's best if you can do this in a Smokey the Bear voice), why am I in the state of mind I'm in this morning? What did I dream about last night? What was I thinking about in the shower, as I made coffee, as I was getting dressed?" Try not to accept the state you're in at face value. See if you can discover how it may have shifted.

If a particularly disturbing dream wakes you up in the middle of the night, you awake upset, but then calm yourself down by telling yourself that it was only a dream, it wasn't real. The reality is that you're lying in your bed resting and you are not being eaten by your boss, who somehow has grown eight heads and is in the process of roasting you in an open fire pit with a side dish of macaroni and cheese! The associated disturbing emotions may linger awhile, but you rationalize away the experience and often will soon forget about it altogether (although you may find yourself looking at your boss a little differently the next day. *And*

*wondering why you're best served with mac and cheese instead of a
sensible salad).*

A BATTLE OF WILLS

Like going on a strict diet and making a conscious effort not
to stray, the pursuit of mindfulness requires willpower, something
we all possess to varying degrees and engage in proportion to our
vested interest in the specific situation at hand.

For many of us, if we decide we want to just lose a few extra
pounds, we may pay somewhat greater attention to what we eat,
but we'll allow ourselves to stray periodically, since there is no
burning need driving us to action. However, should we receive
bad news from our physician, or if our perceived immortality is
otherwise challenged as a result of our diet, our mustering of willpower to drastically alter what we eat may be much more extreme.

Our will is tied to our emotional investment in wanting to
change something or to bring about a desired result, and the
belief that we can bring about that desired change. For some,
their willpower is strong and the pursuit of their goals appears
to be effortless. For others, the concept of changing something,
even something minor in their lives, seems overwhelming and far
beyond their capabilities.

The beautiful thing is that willpower can be cultivated; we
can practice improving the strength of our will. For example,
we can start by making a choice to stop engaging in a particular
habit or behavior to which we have a minor emotional attach-
ment, since this will be relatively easy to change (e.g., we can
get out of bed when the alarm goes off, instead of snoozing for
multiple fifteen-minute increments). Once we gain the confidence, strength, and belief in our abilities, we can begin to attack

the more challenging habits in our lives that we wish to change, such as smoking.

You will find that on some days it's easy to keep your will focused and stay on course. On other days, it's the complete opposite. If you can retain a strong commitment to the end result, then on the difficult days you won't give up the effort altogether, but will weather the difficult times to the best of your ability, then try again the next day.

WHY IS THIS IMPORTANT?

The same is true with regard to mindfulness. You focus your will as intensely as you can on keeping your mind from straying into random past and future thoughts throughout the day. When you find that you've gone off course, you recognize what has happened, and, as best as you can, come back to focusing on the present. This is key! If you can recognize that your mind is straying, then mindfulness is already starting to work for you.

A fellow teaching acquaintance of mine came up with a brilliant technique for this concept, similar to how we teach children to respond to a fire: Just Stop, Drop, and Roll!

> **Stop!** Realize that your mind is wandering on a tangent.

> **Drop!** Immediately and ruthlessly drop the thoughts from your mind. Understand that there is no need to hold on to them.

> **Roll!** Roll back to focus on being present again and reaffirm your intent to focus on the moment. If you have suffered negative emotions from the tangent, then purposefully focus on happy or uplifting thoughts and allow them to roll around in your consciousness until

the negative emotions have been quelled and you return to a state of equilibrium.

Do not beat yourself up when you become aware of your mind wandering! Do not berate or insult yourself. That kind of internal dialogue will only make things worse for you. Remember that a mindfulness practice can be extremely challenging to engage in, but at least you're trying. Keep some perspective. You're trying to undo many years of conditioning. It's going to take time.

THINGS TO KEEP IN THE BACK OF YOUR MIND

Our thoughts are fluid and our states of mind change constantly; however, we may find that we have a habit of consolidating our feelings, like "I'm sad," or "I'm depressed," or "I'm in a funk," and because of that we believe we are stuck with no end in sight, adrift in a sea of bad drama. Here are some pointers for starting your practice:

- **Keep perspective:** Nothing is permanent. Know that things will change—this is the (permanent) nature of the world. All things are subject to change at all times, regardless of how much we want things to stay the same.

  For most people, if we look back over the course of our lives, we've had good times and not-so-good times. We've had good days and not-so-good (aka "bad") days. Good followed by not good, which is followed by good, which is followed by not good, which is followed by good, and on and on... (you get the point). It's a cycle.

  When we're in good phases, we're content. When we're in not-so-good phases, our states of mind seem as if they will never end and we want to be anywhere but where we are, in the middle of them.

- **Dropping thoughts:** Understand that you can drop a thought at any moment, even mid-thought. Interrupt yourself. When you find yourself daydreaming, catch yourself and just immediately drop that dream. Focus all of your attention back on the present moment, wherever you may be.

  Similarly, if you realize that you're focusing on something upsetting or negative, stop and shift your focus to something positive. Find something, anything, to shift your attention to. Remember: Stop, Drop, and Roll!

- **Oscillations in thought:** The way we experience the world is very much based on our state of mind at any given moment. Depending on our mood, one situation can have very different outcomes.

  If we're in a negative state, the situation can seem horrible. If we're in a peaceful state, the things we don't enjoy about the situation may just roll off of us.

  Have you ever tried to go back and physically re-create a situation that at one time brought you peace, but doesn't now? We can come to know that our experiences are not completely a result of external circumstances, although they can influence it.

  A beautiful setting can have an impact on our state of mind, but we may find that we can be in a negative state of mind in a beautiful setting and a peaceful state of mind in a disruptive setting. Understand your state of mind at this current time and know that, unguarded, it is subject to change at a moment's notice.

- **Not real:** Understand that a thought is just a thought. It's not reality nor is it the absolute truth. Typically, it's just an interpretation or evaluation of an event occurring in the world.

TRICKS OF THE TRADE

The following practices can be of benefit in your efforts to remain purposefully mindful and present.

- **Journal:** As I mentioned earlier, in order to become aware of some of the trends and patterns of thought that you engage in, keeping a notebook, journal, or diary with you so you can quickly and easily make notes about your states of mind or of your thought patterns can be quite beneficial. Review it periodically and see if you can begin to identify any trends.

- **Keep it in your attention:** Remind yourself as often as you can that you are working on your mindfulness practice. Whenever you realize that your mind is wandering, remind yourself to come back and focus on the present moment to the best of your ability. Engage in this effort over and over again until it becomes a habit.

- **Chants:** Chanting is an extremely powerful tool that can be used at any time and it does not require any spiritual associations, unless you choose to make them. Silently chanting a reminder to yourself to be present will remind you to stay focused, and help bring your attention to the present moment.

Here are some examples of chants you might find beneficial: "There is only this moment." "Be here." "There is nothing but this." "Now, Now, Now." "Focus on this moment."

Additionally, inspirational or uplifting chants can help to shift your mood while keeping you focused on the present: "I am at peace," "Life is amazing and beautiful," and "I can stay mindful."

If you take the time to engage in chanting in this manner, you'll soon find that certain words resonate with you and you'll begin to employ them more often, sometimes automatically.

- **Take charge:** Consciously seek out ways to shift and lighten your mood. If you're in a negative state of mind, then watch ten to fifteen minutes of your favorite funny movie. Actively seek out things on the Internet that will make you laugh. Pay attention to how your state of mind shifts during this activity.

I DON'T HAVE TIME FOR PATIENCE!

The truth is rarely pure and never simple.

- Oscar Wilde [xix]

As discussed previously, one thing that the majority of us lack is patience. We live in a drive-thru, guaranteed-overnight-delivery, watch-on-demand, walk-out-the-door-with-it, augment-it-with-surgery-if-it-doesn't-look-the-way-you-want-naturally society. To have to wait is an inconvenience and a chore. Convenience is a commodity.

When embarking on a journey of mindfulness, results cannot be guaranteed to be as quick as sending a package overnight or just turning off a switch, unfortunately. Often people will attend a beginner yoga or meditation class in hope of acquiring a quick fix that will bring them peace and serenity in their lives when they're in the midst of crisis. Once they come to see that both meditation and yoga entail a tremendous amount of work and effort, they can become frustrated and despondent.

This situation leads them into conflict because they've been influenced by pictures or advertisements of people in yoga poses or sitting in a meditation pose with giant smiles on their faces, emanating a sense of joy and peace. Perhaps they go in thinking, "Oh, if I can just drive thru and pick up one of those meditation moods, I'll feel better; all of my problems will be solved."

Like the majority of activities in life, becoming skilled requires practice and patience. Take, for example, learning to play a musical instrument, excelling at a specific sport, learning a new language, or grasping the concepts of physics. We all start at different places; some people have natural talents and proclivities and progress quickly, while others struggle with the basics for years.

It is essential to foster patience within yourself, as well as to keep a realistic perspective and know that change takes time. It will take as long as it takes. What can be helpful is to periodically look for results. Objectively look to see where you've been able to make subtle shifts in your patterns of thought or attitudes. You're simply looking for some small wins. They will give you the confidence to keep moving forward.

LOST AND FOUND

And let's not forget the magic I mentioned before. As you begin to pay attention to your thoughts and your interactions with the world, be sure to leave some room for the brilliance of life to surprise you. When you change the way you interact with your thoughts, you change the way you interact with the world—and the world just may change the way it interacts with you.

For example, shortly after moving to a new city for a job, I decided it would be fun to teach meditation classes again. As I began searching for a venue, I had the idea that "just the right place" was out there waiting for me. After a few days of looking and not finding anything, I became frustrated. Then I had the intuition to stop trying so hard and see if I could let a place find me. I put away my map and just started to drive.

This became a bit of a game. At first, I made random turns at will: "Let's see where this leads," "what if I turn here," etc. Soon, though, I wondered whether I could quiet down and feel where the right place to turn would be. Gradually I started to trust my intuition and turn when it felt like the right thing to do.

As I drove through the city, I gazed at the buildings to see if anything popped out at me. I passed numerous potential locations, such as yoga studios, martial arts studios, and gyms, but none of them felt like the "right" place.

This went on for a couple of hours. I found myself taking unfamiliar freeways, seeing areas and landmarks I had no idea existed. Through it all, I held on to the belief that I would locate the space, or rather, as stated above, that it would find me. Finally, at a certain point, I exited a freeway and arrived in an area of town that for some reason I just liked. I couldn't put my finger on it, but there was something about it that felt comforting. Then, as I wound through the streets, I felt an urge to stop the car. Looking around, I saw a small private gym with an adjoining yoga studio. I parked and walked over to take a look.

Unfortunately it was closed, but when I peered through the window, it looked perfect. When I called the owner the next day, he told me that he had been trying to think of something he could offer the community, and free meditation classes fit the bill perfectly. (*Magic.*)

I taught there for several years and had the opportunity to meet some amazing individuals. It was also in these classes that I started to compile and share some of my early teachings on mindfulness.

CRYSTAL BALL

"I know who I WAS when I got up this morning, but I think I must have been changed several times since then."

- Alice's Adventures in Wonderland [xx]

The subsequent chapters in this section will look at a few specific mental structures that we create and engage in that can bring about distressed states of mind and how to work to remedy those situations—our Root Cause Analysis.

If you are actively working on mindfulness, then periodically compare your overall state of mind to where you were when you began your journey, and then at various intervals going forward. "Am I happier now than I was six weeks ago?" and so on. While realistically knowing that you will have good days and not-so-good (aka "bad") days, or weeks, what you are looking for is a general sense of your state of mind.

Some of the thought patterns you engage in will be relatively easy to change, while others, the showstoppers, are going to take more time to work your way through. Some showstoppers have significantly more emotional connections and may take years to work through. Understandably, they are the things you wish to overcome the most and, subsequently, you'll have the least amount of patience with them.

Again, this is where patience and perspective are critical. As in yoga class, for many of us, sitting in half lotus can be achieved in a relatively short amount of time; full lotus (the complete pretzel) takes significantly longer.

KEY POINTS TO UNDERSTANDING THE PLAYING FIELD

- First, become aware of your thought trends and patterns by stepping back and trying to witness them objectively.

- Once you begin to recognize the trends and patterns, you can begin to look at the cause-and-effect relationships that bring them into being. What events and experiences bring about certain states of mind?

- Upon examining your thoughts, you may see that you spend a tremendous amount of time dwelling in the past. Since the mind doesn't differentiate between past and present emotional states, if you focus on upsetting events that occurred in the past, you will experience the emotional reactions you had at that time in the present moment.

- Similarly, we spend a significant amount of time in the fictional future creating anticipated states of mind. Again, we will experience those planned-for emotions in the present moment, even though we really have no idea what the future holds.

- In both situations, our minds pull us away from focusing on and experiencing the only thing that's real, this moment, now.

- When we are focused on the present, we may be spending much of the time evaluating and comparing our current situation with other situations. We may spend time engaging in judgments about what is unfolding and how it pertains to us personally. Unchecked, these habits may also lead to distressed states of mind in the current moment.

- Invoking your willpower to keep your mind calm and clear, focused and concentrated, will result in your feeling more peaceful in the current moment.

CHAPTER FIVE: PERCEPTIONS

It is in thy power absolutely to exclude all manner of conceit and opinion, as concerning this matter; and by the same means, to exclude all grief and sorrow from thy soul. For as for the things and objects themselves, they of themselves have no such power, whereby to beget and force upon us any opinion at all.

- Marcus Aurelius, *Meditations* [xxi]

TAPESTRIES

Perceptions are the means through which we interpret what we observe from the world around us and how it relates to us specifically. Our perceptions are based on experiences we are directly involved in, experiences we observe as bystanders, and experiences we see and hear about through various media outlets or from our peers.

The impact of an experience on our consciousness can be seen as a thread. In time, all of these threads are woven together, creating a tapestry that reflects our view of, and relationship with, the world. As you may imagine, these threads come in different shades and colors, as various as all the experiences that are possible. At this moment, and all moments in time, we are the sum total of all of our experiences. How we integrate them gives rise to each of our unique tapestries.

Additionally, each of us is born possessing our own proclivities: activities and situations we are innately drawn to, or attitudes found in the "fabric" of our beings. Because of this, we may automatically reject things that do not resonate with us or quickly accept things that do. For example, for some, science is the only truth; for others, religious faith or spirituality is what matters.

Our individual proclivities and experiences combine to define who we believe ourselves to be and how we perceive the world. This is what makes each of us unique and why no two tapestries look the same. Even two people brought up in identical circumstances will interpret experiences differently and, accordingly, their tapestries will differ in appearance.

Our tapestries become the foundation for how we see and relate to the world. Every new experience is matched against our tapestries and it either blends in, or clashes and is rejected.

Taking time to examine and question your perceptions allows you to see the structures and limitations that have been instituted in your life, either by yourself or by others. Questioning the source of your perceptions can free you from blinders that may be constricting your view and open you up to endless opportunities to expand your experience of the world, of other people, and ultimately, of yourself.

JAILBREAK

When you're a child, the world is explained to you by your society, parents, and peers, and its operating principles are laid out so you can understand how to adequately function within the agreed-upon rules. As you grow, you develop a prescription for how to see and interact with the world, and your appropriate place in it. You also create a story about how it all works in relation to you, in order to get what you want from it and navigate through it with the least amount of resistance.

After a time, as you grow and evolve, you may find that you must question all or part of the story that has been created by you or dictated to you by society. Certain aspects that may have resonated with you in the past are no longer acceptable. You may find that you can no longer operate within the familiar paradigm.

The challenge lies in how open you are to making modifications, and your willingness to question your perceptions of the world in order to change your prescription, and incorporate a swatch of new colors in your tapestry.

GLOBAL IMPACTS

The outside world can cause a shift in perspective. For example, the events of 9/11 altered the perceptions of most Americans. Our sense of security was challenged as never before. A forced change such as this challenges our sense of control, which makes us feel safe and defines our place in the world.

Major world events have an impact on people's perspectives. We like to believe that we are the ones in control of our lives and our surroundings, but natural disasters such as earthquakes, tornados, and hurricanes, or political upheavals, including wars and revolutions, can shatter our sense of control in an instant. After these events take place, we seek to understand and find meaning in what occurred in order to put our picture of the world back together and feel a sense of control once again.

It can be advantageous to reflect upon your reactions to events that impact you directly and personally. Typically these are on a smaller scale—for example, an unfortunate accident, a debilitating illness or loss of a loved one—yet they impact your life in dramatic ways. When they occur, do you seek to blame others, even God, for the tragedies that befall you and dwell endlessly in misery? Or do you accept them, adapt to the new reality, and do your best to move on?

EXERCISE: ADAPTATION

Without judging yourself or getting caught up in emotion (again, this is about self-discovery), try to reflect upon some of the major events that have occurred in your life that have had an impact on you. These would be moments that you've bookmarked in your consciousness.

» Like an objective scientist, analyze the situation and consider the following:

- How was your perception of the world challenged by this event?

- Did it break apart some of your strongly held beliefs? What were they?

- What was your reaction to the challenge? Was it anger, anguish, denial, surprise, confusion?

- How long did it take for you to "recover" (if you did)?

- Can you identify what shift occurred that allowed you to "recover" and how your perception changed? Was the new perception emotionally more positive or negative?

- It can also be beneficial to notice if there are any themes in these bookmarked moments. Do you focus more on positive or negative experiences when you reflect back?

CHANGE MISMANAGEMENT

As reviewed in Chapter Three, for most people, the idea of change arouses feelings of fear, because by nature change involves moving from the known, the comfortable, to the unknown and uncomfortable.

Change that takes place over time is usually not as unsettling as sudden and dramatic change. Gradual change can be integrated at an acceptable pace. Sudden change makes us feel that we are being challenged, that something is being forced upon us against our will and that is beyond our control.

While we would like the world to change to fit our desires, the truth is that, if we're not happy with our lives and our experience, then we must change ourselves—because as we all painfully come to learn, changing the world to fit our personal preferences is beyond most people's capabilities.

You may think, "If only such and such a person would stop doing that thing they do, my life would be so much better." Or, "If only such and such societal revolution would happen, I would be so much happier." "If only people would recognize my innate brilliance and build me a castle." "If only..."

In these examples, you are not only living in the fictional future, but also ceding all of your personal power to another entity. You've rendered yourself helpless by creating a situation where your state of mind is dependent on the actions or feedback of others.

Changing ourselves does not require a drastic shift in the way we operate in the world (although that can sometimes be beneficial). But change can come about with just a slight, subtle shift in perspective. We may find that a small shift in the way we see one thing can have an impact on the way we see things in other parts of our lives. It can have a crossover effect.

TAKING A STEP BACK

As mentioned, changing your perspective requires that you look at a situation as objectively as possible. To do this, we must separate ourselves from our emotions and our personal invest-ment in the situation. This is especially true if we feel we have been wronged in some way.

Again, it helps to review the situation as if you were watch-ing a movie. Attempt to look at it from every angle you can imagine. Remove yourself, your emotions, your personality, and your self-interest. Take yourself out of the picture by substituting an anonymous figure in the role you played.

Consider the intents, wants, desires, motivations, and fears of all the parties involved, including your own. Be careful not to judge the other people, just observe what is taking place. Try to understand the other players' points of view. Also be careful not to judge yourself; but at the same time be willing to see where your actions might be causing other people difficulty.

This kind of exercise can be tremendously helpful in developing compassion for others, as well as for ourselves. As we'll see in greater detail later in the chapter, compassion can help provide different perspectives on situations and provide clarity to our sometimes clouded view.

The following story demonstrates how, when you step outside of the picture and look at a situation objectively, a simple realization can spark a sudden change in perspective, which can quickly alter a troubling mind state and bring clarity out of confusion.

CYCLES

A student in one of my workshops was actively working on mindfulness to help him with numerous difficult states of mind. Over time, he had come to realize that there was an immense amount of frustration towards the world inherent in his day-to-day thought patterns. This frustration would cloud his outlook on life and inhibit his ability to hold on to peaceful states of mind. His story is a good example of how a subtle realization around a certain conditional state of mind can cause a shift in perspective that can carry over into many other areas of one's life:

> I had gone on an early morning nature hike one Saturday in a nearby nature preserve. I had found these times in nature to be tremendously soothing and helped me to clear my head after a long and stressful week at work. The area where I like to hike is up at the top of a mountain and at that time in the morning the road is often full of serious cyclists looking to get in a good workout before the weekend traffic becomes too congested for them to move about as they like.
>
> As I was driving back down the mountain after my hike, I came to a particularly challenging intersection

where the road I was on merged into another road in which it was difficult to see oncoming traffic coming from both directions. As I was waiting at the stop sign, peering around to ensure there was no oncoming traffic, I took my foot off the brake and started to inch out onto the road to make a left turn. Seemingly out of nowhere, one of the cyclists sped by my right side onto the merging road, essentially cutting me off.

At first I was surprised because I thought it was a car that I had not seen on the intersecting road. Then it turned to shock as I realized this cyclist came out of nowhere and that I could have easily hit him. Then I got pissed off because he had startled me, cut me off, and hadn't even bothered to stop at the stop sign. It's as if he had mentally flipped me off for being in my car and driving cautiously Then I got even more upset because I felt like all the peace I had found from my beautiful hike, which I hoped was going to carry over into my weekend, and possibly into the upcoming week, had now been lost.

I drove along for about fifteen minutes fuming over this experience and seething in frustration. I kept thinking, "How could he have done that to me? Why was he such an asshole? What did I ever do to him, he doesn't even know me?" And on and on... Then it hit me: The words I was using. That cyclist didn't do anything to ME; he would have done it to any car that happened to be in that exact spot at that exact moment. It had absolutely nothing whatever to do with my character or me in general. I just happened to be at that spot, at that moment, and it interfered with what he wanted to do.

Suddenly the anger lessened and I was slowly able to let go of it as this new perception started to sink in. Then I started to reflect on how often I engaged in that habit of thought—that people, strangers, were doing things to me, when really their actions had nothing to do with me. I just happened to be in a particular spot at a particular moment, which just happened to interfere with what they desired to do.

How much time had I wasted in anger and frustration over situations just like this? I had a perception that these were always personal attacks on my nature or judgments against me in some way. I repeatedly allowed myself to believe I was a victim.

Later, when situations like this would arise, I would feel that habit of reacting in anger start to rise up, recognize what was happening, then would talk myself out of it by recalling this story and reiterating to myself that there's no need for me to dwell in anger over this kind of situation. Over time, this previously automatic reaction disappeared altogether.

In this example, you can see how the student had created a pervasive perception in his life that he was a victim. As he notes, this mental pattern would arise periodically and was a common theme in how he viewed his relationship to the world.

Stepping outside of the picture allowed him to view the situation from an entirely different viewpoint. He was then able to see how that theme had been manifested in many other circumstances in his life. Recognizing this, he could then take an active role in modifying those reactions when they arose in the future.

If he chose to take it even further, he could also look at why he tended to assume that role as a victim and respond with anger.

Did that response afford him a perception of control or authority in the world? If so, why did he believe the response was necessary?

We may resist looking at these kinds of situations where we have negative reactions because we perceive that we are "wrong" or "bad" for responding this way, and we feel a sense of shame. Instead, perhaps we can view them as occasions where we didn't see a complete picture, as in the example above, and remove the burden of guilt. It is only when we are willing to look at these disagreeable aspects of ourselves that we will be able to alter them.

This story exemplifies the steps that make up mindfulness practice: Pay attention to your thoughts, begin to recognize trends or patterns in your behavior, then analyze and take action to change them if warranted. Yes, making the changes can be difficult; however, recognizing the pattern can provide the push required to begin working on the change.

EXERCISE: STEPPING BACK

We often create perceptions in our minds based on a one-sided view of a situation. Stepping back and looking at a situation objectively (stepping outside of the picture) can change our state of mind significantly.

» As in the example of the driver encountering the cyclist, can you identify specific situations that trigger emotional responses in you? These may include interactions with close friends, family members or coworkers, watching media personalities, or any situation involving other people in the world.

• Remove yourself from that situation, step outside of the picture, and see if you can specify your role in the situation, like the driver being singled out for abuse by the cyclist.

- Next, try to observe the situation from a different standpoint. What might be the perceptions of the other parties involved? For example, the cyclist, absorbed in his morning adventure, is frustrated by the presence of automobiles and refuses to let them get in the way of his fun.

- While it may not change the situation itself, it can change your perception of it. Now at least you have more insight into what is taking place holistically and may be able to drop some of your automatic emotional responses.

SELF-REFLECTION AND COMPASSION

When you wake up in the morning, tell yourself: The people I deal with today will be meddling, ungrateful, arrogant, dishonest, jealous, and surly. They are like this because they can't tell good from evil. But I have seen the beauty of good, and the ugliness of evil, and have recognized that the wrongdoer has a nature related to my own—not of the same blood or birth, but the same mind, and possessing a share of the divine.

- Marcus Aurelius, *Meditations* [xxii]

Two of our most powerful allies in working with and challenging our perceptions of the world are compassion and self-reflection. While different, there are numerous instances when one blends into the other.

Compassion can be defined as the ability to see ourselves in others, without judging, understanding that all beings suffer in some way until they can find and sustain peaceful states of mind. By understanding that we are all works in progress, we can remove the pressure that comes from believing that we and others should be perfect. In doing so, we allow ourselves and also (let's be completely honest, shall we, we're all friends) those who have the pleasure of interacting with us to reside in more peaceful states of mind.

Self-reflection is the ability to objectively look at ourselves and the perceptions we hold. And, with a hefty dose of self-compassion, we may do so without berating ourselves for what we see.

COMPASSION FOR OTHERS

This man beside us also has a hard fight with an unfavouring world, with strong temptations, with doubts and fears, with wounds of the past which have skinned over, but which smart when they are touched. It is a fact, however surprising. And when this occurs to us we are moved to deal kindly with him, to bid him be of good cheer, to let him understand that we are also fighting a battle; we are bound not to irritate him, nor press hardly upon him nor help his lower self.

- John Watson, *The Homely Virtues* [xxiii]

While it may seem obvious, realizing and accepting that everyone's tapestry, or perception of the world, is different is essential. One perception is not better than another, they're just different.

We all experience the world through our own prescriptions for living. Thus there is no way that we can fully understand the motivations and points of view of everyone in the world, or even fully understand the points of view of our closest friends and family members.

This being the case, it is futile to compare ourselves to others. And while we may not agree with others' behavior or opinions, we can have compassion, knowing that they too struggle in their own ways. Their actions, however opposed to ours they may be, are their means for trying to achieve peace and find order in their lives. When you start to react negatively, or to judge others' actions, catch yourself and say to yourself, "Like me, they are doing the best they can with what they have."

It's also important to realize that everyone feels justified in their own actions and beliefs. Even the harshest of dictators feels justified in his beliefs and his actions against others.

Something that may seem like simple common sense to us may be a completely foreign concept to another. Again, this will depend on their experience and upbringing. Unless it's pointed out to them, or until they have the realization on their own, they may have no idea what the impact of their actions (or inactions) is.

However, if you are compelled to point something out to another person, make sure you are not coming from an authoritative or egoistic standpoint, where you feel that you know more, or know better, than others do. Otherwise, you create a divide based on how right you are and how wrong others are. *(Tricky, tricky, tricky.)*

It's also good to remember that a cultural norm in one society may have no bearing in another. Encountering situations where extremely different cultural norms prevail can seem baffling, almost frightening. When you find yourself evaluating the actions of others, it is beneficial to take this into consideration.

EXERCISE: AWKWARD

A good exercise that I highly encourage you to try is to purposefully put yourself in just such a situation, one in which the cultural norms are drastically different than what you are accustomed to, and observe how you react.

» This could be something along the lines of:

- Attending a festival at a cultural center for a culture other than your own.

- Visiting a drastically different country and attending some local events.

- Attending a religious service or ceremony of a different faith.

- Attending an event held by one of the subcultures in your, or a neighboring, city.

This can be quite eye-opening (not to mention highly amusing for onlookers).

(Note: Please ensure that you are inserting yourself into a safe environment, e.g., one in which no human sacrifices are required.)

» Notice how this situation has an impact on your perceptions.

- How comfortable are you initially? Do you feel fearful, or are you open to whatever may unfold?

- Does your comfort level increase or decrease during the event? What is causing this to happen?

- Can you imagine what your life would be like if this were your cultural norm? How might that impact your view of the world?

- Do you find yourself judging the experience the entire time you're there in an attempt to make yourself feel more comfortable?

- If there are changes in your perception or you have any revelations, take time to examine how they may impact other perceptions in your life.

ON PARADE

What people in the world think of you is really none of your business.

- Martha Graham [xxiv]

We may also believe that other people have it better than we do in some way. The media, which continually flaunt the lives of celebrities for the viewing public, perpetuate this perception. We see celebrities and other public figures on display and, often unconsciously, engage in the habit of comparing ourselves to them.

We may believe, for example, that their lives are more exciting and more fulfilling than ours. Again, this is a perception, and in many cases may be far from the truth. Celebrities suffer the same mental conflicts as everyone else, perhaps even more so, since they may suffer from delusions of grandeur from the constant stream of flattery and approval from those who surround them.

Similarly, advertising agencies want us to identify with the people in their ads. They want us to believe that if we use the same products as the models or actors in the advertisements, we too can be as fulfilled, satisfied, sexy, and happy as they appear to be.

By focusing on people's insecurities and appealing to our desire to be popular, appreciated, admired, or even to just fit in, advertisers create a perception of the world based on the belief that, if we possess product *x*, *y*, or *z*, we will find greater satisfaction in our lives. *(If only...)*

We also habitually compare ourselves to our social environment and those around us. These subtle evaluations can cause us to feel that we should be different, something other than what we are. If we feel inadequate by comparison, we may begin to berate ourselves.

People often have a perception that their self-worth is defined by the material objects they possess. They take pride in what they own and like to show off their things. Be it a new or expensive car or home, clothing, or accessories, some people like to make sure that everyone around them is aware of their possessions.

By winning approval in this way, they elevate themselves in their minds to a place of stature and power, a place of greater control. What they may fail to ask is, "Am I happy? Am I at peace? Am I just projecting confidence in an attempt to hide insecurities? Would I really care what anyone else thought about me if I were truly happy or at peace? Would I need to impress others if I were completely at peace with who I am?"

EXERCISE: GLOBAL VIEWS

» Explore your perceptions of people who are prominently featured in the media, especially if you believe that their lives are better than yours.

- Is there some way you can prove those perceptions are true? What are you using to gauge your assumptions?

- Where did these perceptions come from? Were they in fact fostered by the media?

» Explore perceptions you may have about other social groups, countries, cultures, or spiritual communities— anything different than your own.

- What influences have shaped your perspectives? How did they originate? How do you know they are valid? Can you see where they might restrict your view of the world?

- Do you find you quickly judge others based on your perceptions?

- Do you generalize all people who are part of these or other groups?

OPEN YOUR EYES

As mentioned, reflecting on our own perceptions can take courage and patience. To do this, we have to ask ourselves why we believe what we believe and how we came to believe it. Typically the willingness to engage in this kind of examination can take some time.

We often do not want to look at things that we consider "bad" parts of our personality, as if we are ashamed of them in some way. Self-reflection requires that we have an immense amount of compassion for ourselves and, ultimately, a willingness to look.

We want to become aware of all aspects of ourselves, not just what we consider "good" or "bad," but the complete picture. Beating ourselves up for our perceived faults will only make things harder for us.

If you find that you are continually or often in conflict with the world in your day-to-day affairs, and if you are completely honest with yourself, do you really feel you are in a position to judge anyone or anything? Have you ever made the mistakes that you see others making? If someone cuts you off while driving, you can ask yourself, "Have I ever cut anyone off, although perhaps inadvertently?" Perhaps the person driving like a maniac has a pregnant woman in the car who's in the throes of labor, or has someone with them who needs to get to an emergency room. You don't know, but you like to presume you do, since this makes us feel justified in our opinions and reactions.

Have you ever misjudged what another person was doing because of your own assumptions? After learning the truth, did you acknowledge the lesson and evaluate why you made such assumptions, or did you try to justify your assumptions to cover your embarrassment?

There is an honesty and bravery in seeing and acknowledging these aspects of ourselves. Ultimately, if we have an aversion to exploring something, we will be unable to change it.

BLAME 2.0

During our investigations we may find that we're quick to point to other people, or the world in general, as the root cause of our problems. "It was because of them that I'm in the mood I'm in and I reacted as I did," or "It was because of this or that event in the world that I'm in a bad mood—it's their fault."

While it's true that the actions of other people have an impact in our lives, when engaged in mindfulness examinations, it's important not to point to the actions of others as the reason for your problems. As has been mentioned previously, we are limited in our abilities to change other people and the world (what with that blasted free will that they possess). However, we have complete control of our ability to change ourselves.

When a situation arises in which your interaction with another person throws you into a challenging state of mind, it's important to look at why you react in the manner that you do. How or why they did what they did does not matter; your reaction is the only thing that matters. Assigning blame is an easy out and will give you a feeling of justification, but it will not free you from your troubled state of mind. It can be helpful to understand their perspective, but more important is to understand your reaction.

In the case of the driver and the cyclist, letting go of blame and understanding why he reacted the way he did, and seeing how that crossed over into other areas of his life, was ultimately what freed him from it.

While it may be appropriate to respond to someone who is out of line, especially in an abusive situation, it's holding on to your emotional reactions that becomes the issue. And in fact, the more you understand why someone is acting the way they are, the better able you may be to help them deal with their troubled state of mind.

EXERCISE: A WILLINGNESS TO LOOK

Many of our perceptions are built upon unclear or incomplete understandings of ourselves and the world, and are often generalizations.

» Reflect upon perceptions you've held about yourself, such as that you're smarter or dumber than other people, or feelings you've had about the opposite, or the same, gender, or beliefs about other cultures and societies.

  • Were there times in the past when you questioned those perceptions? What prompted you to challenge them? Was it a particular situation that was very dramatic or traumatic, or something very subtle?

  • Did you allow those perceptions to cross over into other areas of your life and affect other perceptions you held—perhaps judgments of yourself or others?

» Do you find that when you've had perceptions or made assumptions that turn out to be incorrect you try to gloss over them, or cover them up with some excuse, in order to hide your embarrassment or to continue to feel justified in your attitude?

  • Did you honestly look at why you made the assumption in the first place?

  • Can you look at why you refused to let go of that perception?

» Explore perceptions you have about acquaintances with whom you have contentious relationships.

- Imagine what their lives might be like. What are their specific situations? What are their goals? What do they want from life? What is their perception of peace and happiness? How does their view differ from yours and what might have been involved in forming their outlook?

- As disheartening as it might be to recognize, do you see any similarities between the two of you?

- If you look at yourself honestly, can you see where you may have made the same mistakes as others whom you judge negatively?

REWEAVING

All of this investigation into perceptions is important to mindfulness because it's not until you are willing to examine and question your perceptions that you will begin to see how they have created limitations in your life. Again, be careful these examinations do not become exercises in beating yourself up or making you feel bad about yourself; it's simply an investigation.

Seeing yourself in a negative light is also a perception. While you may feel bad about recognizing certain confused perceptions within yourself, this recognition is the first step in moving toward greater clarity, both with regard to yourself and the world.

Once you give yourself permission to explore the possibility of seeing something in a different light, you break the limitations imposed by your perceptions and loosen your self-imposed constraints. You then gain the confidence to look for more opportunities to challenge yourself. Similarly, as you begin to see more opportunities, your willingness and strength to embrace change also grows.

Over the long term, the more you can open yourself to observing the perceptions that lock you into seeing the world in a specific way, the more the world will open up, magically becoming ever-changing and ever-new.

Only you have the ability to remove the threads you no longer wish to be part of your tapestry. Remove the loose threads and create an entirely different image, if you so choose.

KEY POINTS ABOUT PERCEPTIONS

- Taking time to examine and question your perceptions allows you to clearly see the limitations that have been constructed in your life, either by yourself or by others. Questioning deeply the source of your perceptions can free you from the blinders that constrict your view and open you up to endless opportunities to expand your view of the world, of other people, and ultimately, of yourself.

- It's important to understand the sources of our perceptions. How have our family, society, peer group, and the media influenced our perception of the world?

- Stepping back and removing ourselves from a situation in order to see things more clearly can provide tremendous insight into why we react to certain situations in the manner that we do. By observing how certain reactions come about, we can sometimes see how those states of mind cross over into other areas of our lives.

- Compassion for others, as well as ourselves, is important when trying to understand a situation from other perspectives. Realizing that, like ourselves, everyone is

doing the best they can with what they have can alleviate the desire to assign blame in order to make ourselves
feel better.

CHAPTER SIX: UNDER THE INFLUENCE

For there is nothing either good or bad, but thinking makes it so.

- William Shakespeare, *Hamlet* [xxv]

UNADULTERATED

One of the most subtle activities our minds engage in is comparing our view of ourselves, our beliefs, ideas and self-image to what we are currently perceiving in the world. Though subtle, these comparisons are among the most detrimental to our state of mind, and they are happening incessantly. These comparisons are what we commonly refer to as judgments. *(Enter dramatic and ominous music here.)*

If your perspective is the view of the world you create for yourself, then judgments are your comparisons of that view to everything else. The results of these comparisons manifest somewhere along a spectrum of perceived opposites: good and bad, right and wrong, acceptable and inappropriate, beneficial and harmful, moral and immoral, righteous and sinful. The trouble is, everyone wants their view to be on the positive side in order to sustain their perceptions. Or, if they believe their view falls on the negative side, they may still try to make a positive out of that. *(That's right, I'm bad. Don't mess with me, man.)* For clarity and as will be discussed later in the chapter, judgments should not be considered the same as preferences.

So, when executing a judgment against something in the world, we are, in our own view, striving to be on the positive side of that judgment. We are in the right and the object of the judgment is in the wrong. Conversely, we also tend to execute judgments against ourselves—we see ourselves on the negative side and inferior to something else—which results in unproductive guilt.

Casting judgments is like holding up a mirror wherever we go and comparing ourselves to what we see. We compare our beliefs, values, or self-image to the object we perceive and determine where we rank in relation to it: superior, equal or beneath. These outcomes will then provide validation for our actions and beliefs. If we rank ourselves as superior or beneath, we respond with some type of emotional reaction. If we deem ourselves to be equal, little or no emotion results; however it can act as a reinforcement of our belief.

FOUL! BLOCKING... FIVE YARD PENALTY

There are a number of ways in which judgmental thinking presents challenges for being mindful and maintaining peaceful states of mind. First, there is a purity to life and its experiences that judgmental thinking corrupts. When we allow judgmental thinking to dominate our minds, it clouds our vision and we miss out on the authenticity of the moment as it is actually unfolding.

We add a filter by inserting our perspective into the experience and that's all we allow ourselves to see. Further, we may begin to see the world in generalizations and miss out on the uniqueness of every moment.

We are so busy constructing and holding on to our vision of the world, seeing it the way we wish to see it, that we continually create mental evaluations to reinforce our vision. In doing so, we close the door on possibility, causing us to miss out on the endless opportunities for discovery and growth.

For example, you may be very proud of your ability to cook lasagna. You have spent years honing your craft and consider yourself an expert, and you are often told as much. You accept an invitation to attend a class with some friends and discover that the entire class is devoted to the proper way to cook lasagna. Since you consider yourself an expert, you spend the whole class comparing their methods to your own. You're so set on being the expert that you add a filter to everything they say, or you don't even listen. You consider everything they recommend to be beneath your expert abilities. Of course, what you may miss are some tips or nuances that might actually improve your skills. If you were open, you might even get an entirely new approach to cooking; you may see certain aspects you had missed on your own, which then might allow you to entirely redefine and enhance your approach.

Things in the world simply are, and they'll continue to be that way without our constant evaluations. I'm not implying that you should be apathetic towards life. If something is truly causing harm, especially harm to other beings, then evaluation and action are warranted and necessary.

YOU'RE ALL RIGHT WITH ME

The second, and most detrimental, way in which judgments challenge mindfulness and a peaceful consciousness is through their effect on our own attention and state of mind.

When we believe that we are in the right, we have created a belief that elevates us to a place of authority. We feel we know better and thus are in a more suitable position to evaluate a situation. "They," the people who don't agree with our view, do not have the clarity that we do and thus "they" are mistaken. Our opinion has greater merit than theirs; we are, in fact, entitled to it. Thus our egos thrive and flourish.

In actuality, no one has authority, each of us only has a different perspective. I think we can all agree that throughout human history, no one human ego "gets it." Hitler's armies in WWII, the Khmer Rouge in Cambodia, the Crusades in the Middle Ages—even serial killers believe they are justified in their actions, based on their judgments against others. Their view of the world is superior.

If we believe and continually act as though we are an authority in a particular area, this attitude will inevitably bleed over into other areas of our lives. If we perceive ourselves to be an authority on one thing, then why shouldn't we be an authority on all things? We become fixed in our thought patterns and start to believe that only we know the rules for how the world should operate, constantly evaluating everything we encounter.

It is especially dangerous if other people continually validate our beliefs and attitudes, becoming our own personal "yes-men (or women)." A righteous attitude can then become an addiction, and as it increases, we will begin to feel a greater sense of power. Like any addiction, we will then have a dependency, and spiral into frustrated states of mind when we don't receive our fix or our authority is challenged. It may become increasingly difficult for us to become flexible with our thought patterns and attitudes because we have constantly closed doors of possibility and perspective.

Conversely, if we are on the receiving end of a negative judgment made by others, we may react in a variety of ways, based on our level of clarity and temperament. If we buy into what the other party is saying because we believe them to be an authority, then we will feel bad about ourselves and descend into negative states of mind, spurring reactions of depression and self-hatred. Should we violently disagree with the charge made by the judging party, then we will react with anger and disdain.

The other option, when being judged, is to take a mindful approach to the situation. Understand the intent and motivation of the judging party. Take a neutral and detached stance, one where your emotions are completely in check. Then reflect upon the charge. If it resonates with you, then look into it further and explore options to change, instead of dwelling on how horrible you are because of it. If it doesn't resonate, realize that it is only the other person's opinion and their own issue to work out. They believe they are seeing clearly. In this situation, if there is a way to correct them in an egoless manner, then showing them where they are unclear might be beneficial. *(However, your odds of winning at poker in Vegas are better than the chance that someone will appreciate being corrected.)*

IT'S ALL YOU, MAN

If thou art pained by any external thing, it is not this that disturbs thee, but thy own judgment about it. And it is in thy power to wipe out this judgment now.

- Marcus Aurelius, *Meditations* [xxvi]

When we evaluate something as having a "bad" or negative nature, it lowers our consciousness, because inwardly, and sometimes outwardly, we are shunning the object of our judgment. Internally we begin to criticize the recipient. *("People who like baseball are ignorant and personally I only want to be surrounded by evolved people like myself, thank you very much.")* We make a mental list in an attempt to rationalize our negative evaluation. *("Football is a real sport, with faster action, more coordination, and better teamwork.")* We may even begin an internal imaginary argument in order to provide the justification we need to validate our feelings. *("And what the heck is with soccer anyway, that's just as inferior as baseball.")* Through association, we may then begin to focus our negative emotions on other things in the world. *("Small trucks are ridiculous too. Seriously, what's the point of owning one? I bet they're driven by people who are into baseball and soccer.")*

Again, when we evaluate something as good or of a positive nature, it strengthens and tightens our definitions of the world and how we believe it should operate. *("People who practice yoga are more evolved and healthy than people who don't. Schools should adopt teaching yoga and drop dangerous, primal, and aggressive sports like football.")* We feel proud and validated in our stance. In both instances, positive and negative, these opinions lock us into a particular view of the world and limit our ability to broaden our perspectives.

These reactions can be momentary in nature or last for significant periods of time depending on how passionate we are about the subject; sometimes they last an entire lifetime. *("People who get tattoos have no respect for their bodies and I want nothing to do with them. And don't even get me started on piercings that are not in the ears. Uncivilized heathens!")*

DUDE, YOU MISSED IT

The one thing we are not doing when we are engaging in these internal debates is being mindful of the world unfolding around us in the current moment. Instead, we are either reflecting on a past time when the judgment originated or was reinforced, or we are creating a tremendous amount of one-way dialog in our minds in an attempt to justify our views.

When the urge to judge arises, strive for neutrality of mind. If you are compelled to evaluate something, then focus on: "Will this mental interaction bring me closer to, or further away from, a sustainable, peaceful state of mind?" If you feel the urge to pass judgment, catch yourself and ask, "Why does passing this judgment really matter to me? Will it make me feel better or worse about myself? How did it originate?" This line of questioning can help diffuse your judgmental reactions and allow you to remain impartial and non-reactive.

IN THIS CORNER

When we judge something, it is because our beliefs, views, or self-image are being challenged. Even just observing things that are different from what we believe can pose a threat. Judgments, by their nature, give us a feeling of control by telling us where we fit in. They justify our actions, from mild to extreme, and create a sense of belonging, or membership, in a society.

Through judgments, we can define our place in the world by constantly making comparisons. We compare ourselves to other people around us, or we compare the places and things we know and are comfortable with to the place where we currently happen to be. Judgments make the world okay for us and provide comfort because they allow us to be the authority (the "judge" part of "judg-ment") and, thereby, maintain a sense of control.

If our judgments are questioned, then our okay-ness with the world is challenged. Typically we resist or fight these challenges because we don't want to believe that our perceptions of the world are incorrect or that we're not fitting in with whichever societal group we identify with.

Often judgments are based on mutual moral and ethical agreements about right and wrong, or good and bad, among small or large groups of people in an effort to bring about a sense of order, control, and community. In both personal and societal contexts, they help to create mental structures through which we feel we can operate successfully.

If you step back and look at them objectively, in their pure form, judgments are essentially comparisons of illusions. They are illusions because they are only ideas, which are simply creations of the mind; they are entirely subjective, not reality or fact.

(And, personally, for the record, just between you and me, I've got nothing against these judgmental people. I just don't appreciate how bold and authoritative they are with their statements. Who do they think they are really? I tell ya' what. They could stand to cash in a reality check, if you ask me.)

THE VERDICT IS OUT

We may see a parallel between judgments in our personal lives and judgments rendered in a judicial system. Once the judgment or comparison is enacted—innocent/positive or guilty/negative—a sentence will follow, which will be based on the severity of that judgment.

Judgments follow the paradigm of "if, then." If [judgment] is true, then [follow with this course of action (typically an emotional response)]; if [judgment] is false, then [follow with this course of action (typically a different emotional response)].

The emotional response will reflect either an affirmation of, or a threat to, one's sense of control or level of comfort, which are often one and the same. Similarly, legal judgments consist of a specific situation being compared to the "letter of the law." A comparison is made between what has been agreed upon by society as a proper way to conduct oneself and one's behavior in a specific situation. Based on that comparison, a verdict is reached, and at a later point, the consequences of that comparison are assigned.

As we move through the world, we will encounter situations in which our minds feel the need to make a comparison, typically, "How does this situation relate to me specifically?"

For example, you may be out running errands and see someone whose skin is decorated with a variety of tattoos and piercings in multiple visible locations. Your mind will immediately kick in and execute a comparison. You will compare your personal feelings about tattoos and piercings—which have been formed by all of your previous experiences with people with tattoos and piercings, or what you have been told about people with tattoos and piercings—to the object of your judgment, the person before you. You will then project these feelings onto this person with whom you have never interacted and who you honestly know nothing about.

Again, based on your history, your verdict may range anywhere from "This person is a menace, flee the vicinity immediately!" to "This person is so amazingly cool. They must be so brave and rebellious and shun society's norms and not care what anyone thinks." But both conclusions are made without interacting with this person; you completely manufacture the reaction.

What also occurs, beneath the surface, is that we make a comparison between the definitions and beliefs we hold about ourselves—who we are and our value as a person—and the object of our judgment, which is based solely on previous experiences and what we have been told about this type of person or situation. We may devalue ourselves if we think we are inferior to the object and begin to dwell in negative states of mind. Or, if we believe ourselves to be superior, our ego may be inflated and we may develop a self-righteous attitude. We will then begin to justify our response by engaging in particular thought patterns to back up our case. None of these activities leave us with any semblance of a peaceful state of mind. If we were peaceful, we really wouldn't care either way.

24 / 7 / 365

In our day-to-day lives, these judgments occur constantly and incessantly, and so automatically that we are completely unaware that they are taking place. They are knee-jerk reactions to the situations we encounter. They are the things we like or dislike, agree with or not, find appropriate or inappropriate, see as beneficial or detrimental, find attractive or unattractive.

As mentioned earlier, each evaluation has the power to produce an emotional reaction. If we are constantly making these judgments, unaware of what we are doing, then we are creating wave after wave of emotions, either self-affirming or self-deprecating, and allowing them to wash over us. If we are not mindful, and don't recognize what is taking place as it is taking place, we will simply ride the waves of associated emotions until we are completely swept away.

EXERCISE: NOTICING JUDGMENTS

Remember, judgments are just comparisons that your mind makes in order for you to maintain control in your life and provide a comfortable context for seeing the world.

» With regard to mindfulness, the goal is: the instant you find yourself in a judgmental state of mind, stop and reflect on what's happening.

» Ask yourself:

- What am I comparing the object of the judgment against?

- What is the source of this determination? What is it based on and how did it evolve?

- Am I making a comparison against myself and how I view myself?

- Is the comparison revolving around my perceived view of the world, my beliefs, opinions, or values?

- What is the emotional response the comparison elicits?

- In what other scenarios in my life could this same type of judgmental comparison be playing out?

US AGAINST THEM

One of the most common, programmed reactions we engage in is our evaluation of physical traits in both others and ourselves.

This often-automatic reaction occurs constantly as we encounter people in the world.

In this process people are held up and compared against our personal standards for physical appearance, which can include weight, height, age, skin color and tone, level of fitness, body shape, perceived care of body, perceived level of attractiveness, and perceived aberrations. We may have different beliefs and stereotypes about these different traits.

Upon encountering others, we will make a judgment based on our beliefs about these traits, ranging from very favorable to very unfavorable, attractive to unattractive, saintly person to serial killer. These evaluations will lead us to feel either better or worse about our own physical appearance. How do we measure up to him or her? Or how attracted are we to his or her characteristics?

Consider the many verdicts we pass on others through these judgments. What are your own beliefs about weight and age? Do you attribute a sense of worth to an individual based on those beliefs, and elevate or devalue your own worth against them?

If you notice someone overweight and young, do you believe that they are reckless or unhealthy, or were poorly raised, and that they should do something about it? If you see someone older who appears to have a very fit body, do you mentally accuse them of having had plastic surgery because you believe it would not be physically possible for you to have the same body at that age? Do you feel better about yourself if you can believe these ideas? *(Damn right I do, because they're a mess compared to me!)*

If you visit a country that you haven't been to before, do you continually compare its residents' living standard against your own and judge it accordingly? Do you believe these foreigners have it better or worse than you do based solely on what you observe? Do you form general opinions of the population as a whole based on your evaluation of the surroundings? "They must be so happy because they live in this beautiful, scenic place," or "They must be so unhappy because this place is so primitive. It's almost barbaric, there are no malls."

If you visit the home of a new friend or one of your child's friends, do you create a story about the lifestyle of the family based on their environment? If the home is messy, do you instant- ly judge the person and value or devalue yourself, based on how you keep your own home? Do you elevate or degrade your own worth based on the possessions you observe in the person's home?

When you hear about other faiths or religions, do you in- stantly question them or believe they are inferior to yours? Since religious beliefs are so fundamental to our ideas about right and wrong, it is understandable that religion is the cause of so many conflicts in the world.

But how can we possibly know what's best for others or which religion is supreme, or even claim that one is "better" than another? How much time do people really spend trying to understand another religion or spiritual path? Or do we just automatically dismiss it because it is different than our own or because others have told us it is inferior?

Again, judgments serve to reinforce a structure for the world. While they may comfort us because we believe we know what is right and wrong and our place in the middle of it all, they constrict our ability to experience the world as it is and allow moments to unfold organically, possibly teaching us new things we couldn't conceive of on our own.

The world is okay while our structure is in place. If that structure is disturbed, the world, and subsequently we ourselves, may no longer be okay. If we are willing to break judgments apart, we can see that we live under illusions of control, which inevitably create more mental suffering than peace.

EXERCISE: LOOKING AROUND

Consider the following situations and examine how your judgments may play a role in each:

» Pay attention to the judgments you make about physical traits, with regard to both sexes.

  • How often do you find yourself judging the attractiveness of members of the opposite, or same, sex?

  • If you don't find them attractive, what is your reaction and what are the subsequent thoughts that arise? What makes you qualified to judge?

  • If you do find them attractive, what is your reaction and what are the subsequent thoughts that arise? What makes you qualified to judge?

  • How often do you find yourself judging your own perceived level of attractiveness and stature against members of the same sex?

» Pay attention to judgments that arise when you enter a new place or when you meet new people for the first time.

  • How do those judgments make you feel? More or less comfortable?

> » When you travel, do you spend time comparing and evaluating the new location and your experiences to those that you know and are comfortable with?
>
> » What judgments do you base on your religious beliefs? Are these things that you have researched objectively, or are you only believing what you've heard or been told?

WHY? BECAUSE I SAID SO

Our beliefs are initially taught and then continually reinforced by our parents and our peers. More often than not, we are taught other people's beliefs without being given the opportunity to discover, explore, and eventually devise our own beliefs. Later, if these learned judgments are justifiably contradicted, we are thrown into a state of confusion until we can come to terms with the contradiction.

Over the course of our lives we will also create judgments based on our personal experiences. We may like cold weather and dislike warm weather because of how our bodies react. We may hate vegetables because of how they were prepared for us as children. When we share this information with others, we begin to create definitions for ourselves; we become "this kind of person." At some level we are content with this definition and reinforce it regularly. As we grow more and more comfortable with it, we can become very rigid in our beliefs about who we are and find it increasingly difficult to change.

However, as we mature, our bodies and attitudes change. For example, we may find that certain vegetables become very appealing and wonder how many opportunities we missed to enjoy vegetables because we believed we did not like them. Similarly, we may find that as we grow older we develop an affinity for warmer weather. This causes confusion. We say to ourselves, "Wait… I'm not this kind of person… what's wrong with me?"

What we fail to do is ask ourselves why we really feel the way we do, really look at the core of the issue. Our judgment is not anyone else's problem, it's ours. The important thing is to recognize what you think and understand why you think it.

HOME SWEET HOME

Consider: If we were raised in a culture very different than our own, would we have a completely different set of judgments? This could be a different country or even just a different part of the country we were raised in. What if we were raised in a different time period, with different religious influences, or by different parents? For example, in some cultures, such as Native American, a tattoo is a symbol of strength and accomplishment, something to be admired, not a symbol of rebellion.

In the endlessly relevant book *How to Win Friends and Influence People* [xxvii] Dale Carnegie talks about Abraham Lincoln's diplomacy in working with others. He relates that when others spoke badly of Southerners, Lincoln admonished them, reminding them that if they lived under similar conditions, they would likely have the same feelings and attitudes.

Cultural judgments have a tremendous power over our personal states of mind. Societies can be extremely judgmental, with cultural values ranging from extremely liberal and open, to harshly regulated and controlled. Some commonly held values can be innocent—such as a preference for warmer weather—while others can prove highly detrimental, e.g., beliefs about ethnic groups, subcultures, or "alternative" lifestyle preferences; in short, things that are different from the norm.

Historically, we can see the impact of cultural judgments in almost every society, as well as see their prevalence in the world today. These societal judgments can have devastating effects on individuals. They destroy self-esteem and can even drive people to suicide or violent revolts. All of this due to judgments, which again, have no basis in reality; they're just collective agreements.

INVESTIGATIVE REPORTING

In addition to parents and peers, one of the most powerful influencers in a culture is the media. As has been seen many times throughout history, media can be utilized to influence large groups of people, both positively and negatively. Politically, the media is among the most powerful tools for reporting and distorting the truth of a matter.

In order to validate what's being said, savvy citizens must now check multiple sources of information in order to glean a sense of what is truly happening with an event. One right-wing media organization will present a story with a specific angle and the left wing will present the same story with an opposing angle, each oftentimes assigning blame for the issue to someone associated with the opposing side.

Unfortunately many people are unaware of this issue and do not do any further investigation on what they are being told. They take what they see and hear from one source, typically the one that most closely matches their point of view and beliefs, as the unequivocal truth—the judge.

With the rise of social media and the Internet in the mid-2000s, the possibilities grew exponentially for the sharing of information and the opportunities to actively influence others. Now almost anyone in the world can find and connect with others who share similar attitudes and values, further reinforcing opinions and thereby validating judgmental beliefs and spreading prejudices.

Anyone with a computer and Internet connection can become a news reporter and influencer. Further, mobile communications and the rise of smartphones and devices have made it possible to access and send information from almost anywhere, thereby furthering the reaches of influence.

EXERCISE: OUTSIDE INFLUENCES

When examining a deep-rooted judgment, look at how it originated.

» From where did this judgment arise? What is its source? Were you taught or told this belief by someone whose opinion you valued? Was it something you picked up from the media?

» Has this judgment locked you into certain beliefs about the world that might now be challenged?

» What judgments do you notice that changed over time, either due to age or experience?

» Do you find yourself buying into media influence, specifically political values? Do you check what you hear against a variety of sources before rendering your verdict?

CIRCUS

As we said at the beginning of this chapter, judgments are illusions. They are based on people's ideas, and ideas are not facts. Judgments are a way of imposing our will on the world in order to feel in control. If we peel away the layers around a judgment (like the proverbial onion), we will see that nothing remains. *(Except for a mess of onion peels littering the table and floor, not to mention the tiny pieces that get stuck under your nails, those are the worst. Why does no one acknowledge this fact when using this concept? Personally, it sounds like an aversion to cleaning up after oneself. Really, I'm convinced that untidy people are going to be the downfall of society.)*

Deep-seated judgments are the hardest to work through. Often they are based on fear, and we are not apt to approach things we find fearful. If we have the willpower to look into the depths of these issues, we can see that they challenge something within ourselves, perhaps our self-worth, or our fear of being judged by the world.

By letting go of judgments we open up the door to compassion, not just toward others, but toward ourselves as well. We realize that we are all works in progress and we see that, like ourselves, everyone is doing the best they can with what they have—"what they have" being the key factor. To paraphrase Lincoln, "Might we not be the same as they are if we were raised or influenced to believe as they were?"

You may come to see that you have certain habits or thought patterns that have evolved into judgmental states of mind. For example, you may find that you make assumptions without knowing the full story and you are often proven to be incorrect. Perhaps you notice that you filter information so that you hear only what you want to hear, or expect to hear, and you base your decisions on that limited information. Again, these are just habitual modes of thinking.

The power of recognizing these habits, and others like them, is that once you become aware of them, you can begin to ask why you engage in them, and, in time, learn to stop them altogether.

ORIGINS

The key to examining judgments is to notice them immediately as they arise.

As mentioned previously, when you catch yourself making a judgment, immediately begin to probe inwardly and ask yourself: What is the basis of this judgment? From where did this judgment originate? Was this something that was told to me as a child that, because I knew no better and trusted the person who told me, I accepted as a fact? Was it something I heard on the news from someone who seemed to know what they were talking about, an authority, that I believed to be true? Was it something that has been reinforced by society over and over again, like definitions of attractiveness or success? Do my peers constantly reinforce this concept or idea? And finally, in my heart, do I really believe this judgment is a fact that cannot be altered? Is it black-and-white, one-or-the-other, with no middle ground? If so, why is that the case?

Start with noticing just one or two judgments—something simple that you evaluate as good or bad. You wake up in the morning to heavy rain coming down and immediately decide the day is going to be "bad." You see someone in an expensive car and instantly feel resentful, believing their life must be easy. People who don't shop at organic grocery stores are going to die a slow death because they're ignorant of the impact of processed foods. If someone has a liberal political sticker on their car, then their parents must have been long-haired hippie freaks. That hair color cannot be natural. Why would anyone in their right mind get a piercing there?

This does not include preferences, like favoring strawberry over chocolate chip (unless of course you've created a story in your mind, in which one is "good" and the other is "bad"). One is

CHAPTER SIX: UNDER THE INFLUENCE

not better than the other, they're just different. *(But strawberry is better... it's not a judgment, really it's not; it's a fact).*

Once you open up to the concept, you may be overwhelmed by the number of judgments that pollute your consciousness throughout the day—they're that insidious.

It is also tremendously important not to judge yourself for having judgmental thoughts. It's the way we all have been trained to operate. Instead, focus on the fact that you are trying to change a mental habit in order to foster more peace in your life; in time, your efforts may also serve as a positive influence on those around you.

A NEUTRAL STANCE

Be curious, not judgmental.

- Walt Whitman [xxviii]

Remember that the point of this examination is not to change something you judge as a negative into a positive. Rather, try to see that everything just is. It just exists. It is. No judgment is required. No change is required on the part of the object being judged.

Strive for neutrality, the way you approach things that do not stir a reaction in you.

Tattoos are just tattoos, piercings are just piercings. For his or her own reasons, a person decided to make changes to his or her body. It's their story and whether it's a celebration or a handicap in their life is up to them. You can be compassionate and know that you don't need to render a verdict. More than likely, if you were to get to know him or her personally, you would find that he or she is a wonderful and amazing person who could enrich your life in many ways.

Mindfulness is about discovering that life is as it is. Life does not require your input or opinions. Eternity has done, and continues to do, a pretty good job of taking care of herself.

And lastly, we may also see that we make many judgments about the judgments that other people are making. Recognizing this pattern within ourselves and curbing or stopping this behavior can alleviate a tremendous amount of stress. We can have the compassion to recognize the states of mind that other people are inflicting upon themselves, and hope that in time they too will come to an understanding of the choices they have.

EXERCISE: STOPPING THE MADNESS

Once you realize how your mind operates, you can more easily stop yourself when a situation arises where you are prone to engage in judgmental habitual thinking.

» Tell yourself that it's not necessary to make any judgments in the situation.

» Tell yourself that whatever the object is, it just is. It is as it is, just as you are as you are. No judgment is required; it never was.

» If your judgment involves another person, remind yourself that they too are doing the best they can with what they have—their education, upbringing, clarity of mind, mental or physical conditions. (Just as **YOU** are doing the best you can with what **YOU** have).

» Allow yourself the opportunity to see the recipient of your judgment objectively.

> » How do you feel, not making the judgment, as opposed to when you engaged in making judgments in the past?
>
> » Catch yourself if you begin to engage in assumption-making behaviors.
>
>> • Ask yourself what prompted you to make the assumption.
>>
>> • How did you feel when your assumption was incorrect? When it was correct?
>
> » Catch yourself if you begin to beat yourself up for making judgments against others. That only makes things worse. Simply acknowledge it as a habit you are working to break. Have compassion for yourself in knowing that at least you are working on it.

KEY POINTS ABOUT INFLUENCE

• Judgments are merely mental comparisons whose goal is to make us feel better or worse about ourselves (our self-image, beliefs, and values). They are illusions, not facts.

• Judgmental thinking results either in making us feel more secure and, therefore, less flexible in our view of the world (which leads us to feel angry or conflicted when challenged), or leads us to engage in argumentative or self-deprecating, self-hating states of mind.

• Judgments are often taught to us by parents, peers, the media, religion, and society. Too often they are simply accepted and never challenged or evaluated when we get older.

- It is critical to catch yourself immediately when a judgment arises in your mind and question it objectively.

- Mindfully, try to remain neutral when the urge to make a judgment arises.

CHAPTER SEVEN: EXPECTATIONS

People don't realize that the future is just now, but later.

- Russell Brand [xxix]

THE MOMENT EXPECTANT

When it comes to distracting thought patterns, one of the most common mental processes we engage in is setting expectations. This activity entails projecting experiences and their associated states of mind into an unknown realm we generally call "the future." *(Perhaps you've heard of it? It's commonly believed to be the place where all of our dreams come true and where things will be increasingly better than they are today.)*

The mind states associated with expectations utilize escapism as a means of diverting our attention from being present. They can also be among the most detrimental emotionally. Despite what we may like to believe, the future is a time over which we have no control.

When setting expectations, we are planning for, anticipating, and creating a future state of mind based on a fictional experience—fictional in that the experience has not yet happened. While, at the time we are envisioning it, we are embedded in an entirely different state of mind. *(Get all that?)*

In setting expectations, we are subtly putting wheels into motion with an intention of manifesting certain experiences that will eventually lead to or bring about a hoped for or justified state of mind, a planned outcome. In doing so, we believe we are in control of destiny.

Be it a positive or negative outcome, we are looking to be fulfilled in some way. We may be looking to be loved, admired, respected, satisfied, justified, or just feel a sense of belonging. Or perhaps we are looking for the opposite: to be feared, disrespected, loathed, or rejected. We set up expectations because these anticipated states of mind will bring us some level of satisfaction. In both scenarios, we are exerting force to try to control a future event.

Setting an expectation is another means by which we try to control the world and the environment around us. We believe if we can predict the outcome of certain events, and if those events do in fact resolve themselves in the general vicinity of what we had planned, then it affirms, and even strengthens, our hold on our environment and our relationships with the people around us.

Distracting ourselves by imagining future experiences creates a conflict with what is actually taking place in the present moment, typically something we are unhappy or bored with. Mindfully, our goal is to recognize what we are dissatisfied with, then step back and allow the current experience to unfold as it will. Experience the situation fully without judgment and without trying to make anything happen.

Additionally, we may expend a tremendous amount of time and energy trying to manipulate our circumstances, with the aim of bringing about our expected result. Here too we are so focused on the future that we ignore our present situation.

To clarify, expectations are different than goals. When we have a goal, we are focused on the completion of a task—for example, an academic degree, a creative project, or losing weight—over which, through our actions and motivations, we have a level of control in that goal being achieved. The expectation comes believing that certain things will happen as a result of achieving that goal—that we'll land the perfect job, get a promotion, find the perfect mate, live happily ever after, etc.

COLLISIONS AND DANGEROUS WAGERS

The primary impact and most obvious drawback of setting expectations is that it forces our attention into the future and away from what we are experiencing right now in this very moment.

When we focus on future events, we are telling ourselves that the moment that is unfolding right now is nowhere near as important as the future moments we are anticipating, which may or may not play out as we hope or expect.

While you're sitting in a meeting or class in the current moment, your mind is disengaged from what is happening around you and dwelling in a future moment that doesn't exist—and, more than likely, will never exist exactly as you play it out in your mind.

When you are not present, and are completely engaged in fantasy, you are not at peace. You are focusing on another place and time that you believe will bring you a certain emotional response— an anticipated sense of peace or sense of control greater than what you are experiencing now—and you believe it to be more important than what is occurring presently.

When we do this, in a way we're setting up a bet with Eternity, gambling on destiny. We are hedging our bets, pretending that we know how the dice will land and what cards will be uncovered, based on our investment in the expectation.

The expectation could be focused on a large event or experience, like a promotion at work or meeting the perfect mate, or it could reflect a subtle change that we would like to see, like an acknowledgement from, or change in attitude by, someone. In placing this bet, we're betting against the house (and the house always wins).

EXERCISE: DROPPING IN UNEXPECTEDLY

Start to become aware of how your mind engages in setting expectations.

» When observing your thought patterns, if you find that you focus on the future often, review the scenarios you're creating in your mind to see if they are based on circumstances in your life presently.

  • If so, what is the nature of the scenario? Is it to gain or lose something, such as a job or a relationship? Perhaps just acknowledgement from others?

  • What emotions do you experience in the current moment while you are playing out these future scenarios?

> - What is your intent in creating this situation, what need or void is it filling for you? What is lacking in your current situation that this fantasy addresses?
>
> - What emotional investments do you have in these expectations—hope, fear, dread?

RULES OF THE GAME

The act of setting an expectation is a manifestation of our natural desire to control the world and our lives in it. Whether we are expecting something good or detrimental, these extremes fit into a definition of what we believe we deserve or are capable of experiencing.

If we know the rules, then we can play the game. We find a sense of comfort in knowing. Where we experience fear is in the unknown. When we don't know what to expect, we become anxious and potentially fearful. The truth is, of course, that there are no rules. *(But if it makes you feel better to believe there are, please indulge yourself to your heart's content. It can provide hours of entertainment for everyone involved.)*

We set up expectations around a future event and plan for certain states of mind to be achieved from that event coming to fruition. When the event finally plays out, if these states of mind are not achieved, we will become preoccupied with comparing our planned states of mind to our actual states of mind. In struggling to bridge that gap we again miss out on the authenticity of what is actually occurring in the current moment.

We struggle to figure out what's wrong with us or with the other party, if another party is involved, or what is going wrong with the situation we so diligently planned in advance. We're now busy re-planning and re-strategizing in the hope of salvaging one of our planned outcomes and getting back on track.

Not to mention the states of mind we will engage in after the expected event transpires. If the situation fails to meet our expectations and we were attached to that certain outcome, we will now be spending a good amount of time nursing our wounds or making excuses and finding justifications for why our planned outcome was not realized.

We may beat ourselves up for believing that certain things would be possible for us, and start to doubt our worthiness. We may spend days or weeks in dark and depressed states of mind shaking our fist at the heavens and brooding over the experience.

We may blame others and form lasting opinions of certain people, believing that they are the reason we did not achieve what we wanted, the irony being that we alone created that expectation in our minds in the first place.

Others might have fanned the flames of desire for us in achieving said expectation, but ultimately we brought it on and bought into it, and we alone are responsible. *(I'm guessing you're shaking your fists at me now, aren't you? Just please don't harm the book in the process. It always spoke well of you and never meant to hurt your feelings.)*

Conversely, if the experience turns out better than we expected, we may put ourselves on a pedestal and believe we are worthy of, even entitled to, more glory in the future, thus raising our expectation bar for future experiences.

We may also come to believe that we are an authority on what the future holds, thereby elevating ourselves in our minds and creating a fixed and rigid vision of the world, while limiting our ability to allow situations to evolve organically.

LET IT RIDE

Oftentimes, we plan for a fifty/fifty, yes-or-no, succeed-or-fail, black-or-white result when we project the outcome of a future experience. Even if we have multiple outcomes mapped out, we plan all-or-nothing for each of those outcomes. But how can we conceivably anticipate all of the possible outcomes?

In our world of unending possibility (yes, this world, for those of you that are unclear), outcomes, or what we perceive to be results, are infinite. But because of our need for control, we have our blinders on to only see the possibilities that we can imagine and the outcomes we desire.

We block out possibilities, push away opportunities, and attempt to drive others toward believing in or affirming our expected outcomes. We miss the opportunity for spontaneous or organic alternatives to arise and be explored, experienced, and investigated as they unfold.

Anything is possible. Anything! Yet we believe, and thus predict, that x, y, and z are the only things possible. Setting expectations in this manner becomes an exercise in futility, as we can never know what the future brings. As a wise spiritual teacher once stated, "Like all women, it's Eternity's prerogative to change her mind as she sees fit."

THE CATCH (WHY IS THERE ALWAYS A CATCH?)

Neither state of mind, negative and demeaning, or celebratory and victorious, can ultimately be satisfying because they are transient states of mind which are dependent on worldly experiences over which you have little or no control.

States of mind will come and go, as will worldly experiences; in setting expectations, you build a dependency on worldly situations to bring about a desired state of mind.

Here is where we begin to mistakenly believe in the paradigm "if only $x, y,$ and z situations would occur, then, and only then, would I be happy and at peace. Until those situations transpire, I will not be capable of experiencing happiness or peaceful states of mind."

AN EXPOSITION OF REPETITION

Another real danger begins to emerge when similar experiences play out in much the same manner a number of times.

We may now come to believe that comparable situations will always play out the same way, setting up an always/never paradigm, where exceptions are perceived to be flukes of nature or dismissed altogether for extraneous reasons we devise.

This repetition tightens our grip on controlling situations and trying to force certain outcomes. We may even wind up blocking situations from developing because we've created an expectation that a certain experience is just not possible for us, so why bother trying?

It may also be the case that the mental anguish we suffered from a failed expectation (or multiple ones) is too much for us to face again. We may then do whatever we can to try to prevent the situation from ever arising again.

To draw a distinction, I'm not saying that you should not plan for events and potential situations occurring in the world. If you're travelling to a cold destination from a warm one, it's best to pack your winter coat to shield you from the elements.

What you want to avoid is creating the expectation that you're going to be miserable in the cold when you arrive and how horrible it's going to be trying to navigate through the packed-up dirty snow on the roads, because you just never know what this experience will actually be like.

Maybe, just maybe, this time Mother Nature will surprise you by showing you just how exquisitely beautiful and peaceful a fresh snowfall can be, something you've never had the opportunity to witness before. And just maybe, that lasting image will change your entire attitude about snow and the cold.

KNOWING THE UNKNOWN

It's not uncommon to use an expectation to justify questionable actions in the present moment. "Well, he's going to be mad at me anyway, so I'm just going to go ahead and do this." "They're never going to find out about this mistake, they're not that smart." "I've never been caught before." "Go on and do it, they're not going to care."

If we project into the future what an outcome will be, it opens up a new playing field for our actions in the current moment. More dangerously, it provides us with a sense of justification for those actions. We are, in fact, justifying something now (stating it as fact), based on something that's completely unknown and unknowable.

If you act in this manner repeatedly, then you can easily start to lose accountability for your actions. It fosters a false sense of security, authority, and control because we become confident that we "know" what's going to happen.

FALSE SENSE

Many people have been taught to believe since they were children that their wedding day (or wedding days, as the case may be) will be the "best day of their lives." However, when the blessed day arrives, often they are anxious and tired from excitement and anticipation.

They may very well find themselves not experiencing the "best day of their lives." Instead they experience some moments of joy, some moments of anxiety and fear, some moments of exhaustion, and an overwhelming desire for rest. As a result, they may begin to doubt themselves because they are not having the experience they had come to believe in, or they believe they've done something wrong.

Whether it's the "best day of your life" or any future day, how can you conceivably know what state of mind you'll be in at that future moment? More than likely, it will be different from the current moment in which you're planning for that future moment. You have absolutely no way of knowing what your state of mind will be at that future moment in time; there are just too many variables.

For example, you plan at the beginning of the week for a night out on Friday with a group of good friends. Then circumstances throughout the week prove to be challenging or upsetting—personally, professionally, or both.

When Friday arrives, you may still be looking forward to the evening out because you remember what your state of mind was when you set up the plans initially and what you anticipated your state of mind was going to be. However, your actual state of mind is such that a wiser choice might be to stay home, enjoy a quiet environment, and watch a comedy.

Regardless, you go out, and wind up being miserable. You are miserable because you want a fun experience and the associated states of mind that go along with it, and you're not experiencing them because the circumstances of the week are weighing greatly on you.

You then feel disappointed because you're so miserable. You, and even your companions, may come to believe that there's something "wrong" with you because you're not having as good a time as they, and you, are accustomed to and were expecting.

EXERCISE: FORWARD THINKING

Many times, when we live in the future, we model situations to fit desired outcomes. Take some time to reflect how you might set up these mental paradigms:

» Do you find that you set an expectation around being in a specific state of mind at a certain point in the future?

» When that future time comes, and you are not in that fictional state, how do you react? Disappointed? Frustrated? Do you even realize that you had set up this paradigm?

SELF DEFEATING

We're disappointed when we don't enjoy an experience as we thought we would or, perhaps more truthfully, the way we wanted to. If we don't reflect on why we're in the state of mind we're in, we may start to believe there is something wrong with us for not having the experience we expected.

When this happens, it can become increasingly difficult to make future plans. When we make a plan, we're in one state of mind with certain expectations. Then, when the future time arrives, we're in yet a different state of mind, perhaps even with new expectations, or we're in a state of confusion because we are not in the state of mind we expected we would be in originally.

This is not to say that you cannot change your state of mind by dropping or temporarily setting aside all the stress and frustration you're holding on to so that you can be in a more agreeable mood. The power to make this choice about what your state of mind is at any time is something to strive for. While you may not currently believe you possess that strength, willpower is something that can be cultivated and increased over time. Recognizing the thought patterns and habits your mind is engaging in is crucial to this effort.

WAITING ROOMS

Setting expectations not only keeps you from being present because you are busy planning out all the future scenarios, it further wastes time and keeps you from being present by having you wait in a state of anticipation, marked either by excitement or dread.

Typically, it's not a one-time effort: you don't set an expectation and then, *voila*, you're done. Between the time that you start building the expectation and the time the experience comes to fruition, you are on hold or in limbo, frequently fueling your desired outcome with added pressure and emphasis, tweaking it for optimal impact and living in excited anticipation or dread (as opposed to living in the present, which usually has more comfortable furniture and better sandwiches).

174

Granted our active little minds will bop around all over the place and land on various expectations throughout the day, as well as land on a multitude of other ideas and attitudes (which we're generally better off not sharing). That time in between expectation and actual experience, where you are anticipating, dreading, reinforcing desired outcomes and exploring new brilliant options toward your expected experience, is all time wasted not acknowledging and appreciating what's going on around you right now in the present.

EXERCISE: STRONG-ARMING

Check in with yourself:

» Do you find yourself manipulating or steering situations toward an outcome that you fantasized about previously, instead of letting situations play out naturally?

  • If a situation is not playing out as you planned, do you find yourself becoming increasingly disappointed or frustrated?

  • If a situation exceeds your expectations, do you find yourself being overly proud of yourself and your capabilities?

  • How often do situations play out exactly as you expected—not in a general sense, but exactly?

A STEADY SUPPLY

Expectations can manifest around as many different experiences as can exist in the world. Thus there are innumerable possibilities that people can think of for how an experience will play out; it's exponential.

Let's say there's a party with a hundred people attending. Each one will arrive with expectations for how the party will play out for them. Consequently, the attitudes and behavior of each person at the party will model the expectations they brought with them.

Some are looking forward to having "the time of their lives," while others are dreading the event and will only stay as long as required to qualify as "making an appearance." Still others will come with the expectation of finding the man or woman of their dreams (or both, no judgment). Some will come wishing to "run into a certain someone again" in the hope of furthering their relationship; others are dreading running into "that certain someone." Very few will come as they are, open to any and all possibilities that may unfold.

When a child is born, a parent may create a million expectations for what that child's life will hold, as well as how it will reflect back on the parent, although they may not see that aspect of it at the time.

They mull over how the child's life and personality will evolve and what kind of person the child will become. More than likely, they create expectations regarding the kind of experiences the child will be involved with.

Based on the parent's life experiences and stature, he or she may have an expectation that the child will go to medical school and become a doctor, the fourth generation in the family to do so. *(No pressure there, little one.)*

In subtle ways, the parents may try to influence the child to embrace certain studies, hobbies and interests, and shield them from things they believe to be wastes of time, or which the parent has little understanding of or control over.

While believing they have the child's interest at heart and that they are acting out of love and concern, they may overlook the innate talents and natural proclivities of the child. In other words, the child may never stand a chance. *(That's a lot of pressure to put on a being that's just entering the world, don't you think?)*

When the child does not conform to the parent's wishes, the parent may get upset and feel disappointed, while failing to see that it was the parent who created the entire situation in the first place. The child is just acting on his or her own natural interests.

DATING (AKA SELF-INFLICTED TORTURE)

For most people, the lure of relationships and societal pressure to be married is overwhelming. We see advertisements daily telling us how a relationship will make us happy and fulfilled.

Movies, commercials, news, television shows, and even video games push this idea of relationship fulfillment. It's almost impossible to hide from it. Additionally, one of the main topics of conversation among teenagers and adults is the status of their search for a relationship or the maintenance of one they're currently in.

When one is not in a relationship and is bombarded by all this pressure, the impact can be overwhelming to our states of mind. If we are not in a relationship, we begin to believe there is something wrong with us or that we are inadequate in some way. We begin to believe (expect) that if we were in a relationship we would be happier and more fulfilled.

Ironically, many people also feel that if they were not in the relationship they are currently in, they would be happier and more fulfilled. However, the idea of not being in a relationship is even more daunting than being in an unhappy one, so they choose to stay. *(Oddly enough, I've always wondered why they have not created more celebratory "Congratulations on the end of your relationship" greeting cards. I'm getting quite tired of making them from scratch personally.)*

And, finally, there are those who are content without a relationship and have successfully blocked out or become numb to the social and media pressure. *(I personally believe this superpower to be as impressive as those of the Gods.)*

FAIRY TALES

Most people believe that a relationship will provide the happiness that we idealize and the fulfillment we long for from the world. When an opportunity arises to go on a date, one that we are excitedly looking forward to, we will play out in our heads a hundred different scenarios for how the date will flow.

Based on our proclivities and past experiences, we may believe that it will be fantastic and that lifelong companionship is on the horizon. Otherwise, we may dwell on how horrible it will be and how the other person will be disappointed in us and in the experience in general.

In either case, we will invest great amounts of time, energy, and thought in these mental nightmares. We'll fantasize about what we'll say, what we'll talk about, where we'll go, how they'll react to what we say and how we'll respond to their reactions. We may even get to the point where we've got fifty scenarios scripted out precisely, complete with soundtrack, lighting, and costumes.

When the time for the date arrives, something may happen that does not fit our scripts and we'll find ourselves searching for a response to this new situation, or judging what's unfolding against our playbook of success and failure scenarios.

However, since we've scripted everything precisely—"I'm going to say *x* and they're going to respond with *y*"—we now must struggle with how to recover. If this pattern occurs repeatedly, we may find ourselves so frustrated that we beat ourselves up, make false judgments about the other person, or feel unsure about our own self-worth.

This is a tremendous amount of work and pressure to put ourselves through for an unknown outcome. It is impossible to know for certain what the other person is thinking or feeling or what their state of mind will be at the time of the date.

The other option (one I highly advocate) is to step back, let go, and let the experience unfold as it will. Experience the other person and that situation fully without judgment and without trying to make anything happen, rather than playing a role you scripted in your head. *(Allow it to play out organically, without any harmful chemicals and pesticides, such as doubt, fear, and hope.)*

We may respond to this idea with fear or feelings of inadequacy, and that's what's important to look at. So many people suffer from low self-esteem based on previous experiences, societal expectations, media interpretations, as well as a whole host of other issues. We may even believe that if we don't rehearse our interactions, we'll definitely screw it up and disappoint the other party.

The point is, being present and in the moment does not involve inwardly stepping back and criticizing, judging, or devaluing oneself as the situation plays out. It just means being there, accepting and experiencing everything as it unfolds.

Contrast the idea of planning for an initial date with the experience of meeting someone spontaneously and spending time with them. Which situation feels more authentic, more enjoyable?

When it is spontaneous, there is no time to build up expectations and fear of possible outcomes. You simply go with the flow during the time you are together and allow the experience to play out naturally.

YOU SANK MY BATTLESHIP

When we decide what the future will be, that's all we allow ourselves to see. We become blind to anything else that may present itself to us.

For example, we may be convinced that another person is going to behave or respond to something in a specific manner. Thus when we approach that person, we are now looking only for $x, y,$ and z behavior so that we can feel validated and more in control; we were right. *(Congratulations on that, we're all very happy for you. No, really, we are.)*

In these situations, we may overlook every other behavior exhibited by the person to prove our point. Even if during the time we were with them they only exhibited that expected behavior 10 percent of the time, this is what we remember and hold on to.

"I knew such and such would happen… I knew this is the way it would play out… I knew they'd react in such and such a way… See, I told you that such and such would happen…" The fact is, experiences don't and can't play out exactly as we expect. We're just not that powerful (so get over it).

Many situations in the past only played out the way we predicted they would because we were focused solely on what we wanted to see. In focusing only on outcomes, we miss out on all the potentialities, opportunities, and possibilities unfolding in each and every moment during an experience.

Be completely honest: Even when a situation turns out better than you expected, do you still put the emphasis on the negative aspects and downplay the positive when reviewing the situation afterward? And do you do this to reinforce your perceived sense of control, your expectation?

Try now to reflect on a situation where you had expected a traumatic outcome, yet that in the end went better than you expected, even better than you had imagined possible. In these situations, you were probably exceptionally relieved by what transpired because the scenarios you had painted in your mind were painful to imagine and caused you a great deal of stress.

Here again, by creating expectations, you brought unnecessary stress into the present moment by focusing on a future uncertainty marked by fear of the unknown.

OF GREAT AND DISMAL EXPECTATIONS

Our attempts to control the outcome of a situation in advance can apply to what we may consider negative as well as positive situations. And, as we saw, both scenarios go against the intent of being mindful. However, what's also interesting is how we can actually influence our perception of the entirety of a situation through our expectations.

Based on our proclivities, we can willfully invoke certain states of mind and thereby affect the outcome. Some people may naturally focus on the negative to achieve a desired result, while others may naturally focus on the positive. What's interesting to observe is that the same amount of effort is used in both situations.

For example, you tell yourself that a certain experience is going to be horrible, an absolute nightmare. And it does turn out to be an absolute nightmare because that's what you've set it up to be. You block out any possibility of it changing because, when an opportunity arises for something positive to occur, you're so focused on it being horrible and sustaining a negative state of mind, that nothing else was possible, regardless of what transpired.

You frame everything to fall into the perception of a horrible time to give yourself a sense of validation and control. It's as if you're wearing glasses that only reflect back what you expect, and feel empowered and validated because you "knew that it was going to be horrible." This scenario is easy to play out because it's always easy to blame and find fault.

Yet, while it can be challenging for many people, it's also possible to approach the same situation with a positive attitude. There is a tremendous amount of power in doing this, in learning to willingly shift your perspective to a peaceful and positive state to approach a situation.

Feel the difference when we change to a positive point of view. We'll take the sentences from above and exchange the negative words for positive words: You tell yourself that a certain experience is going to be wonderful, an absolutely fantastic time. And it does turn out to be wonderful because that's what you've set it up to be. You block out any possibility of it changing because, when an opportunity arises for something negative to occur, you're so focused on it being wonderful and on sustaining a positive state of mind, that nothing else was possible, regardless of what transpired.

Ultimately, through mindfulness, we are working to have a more neutral stance, to not influence in either direction, but to allow a situation to unfold organically and react accordingly. However, as an exercise to observe how easily your emotional state can be influenced by your state of mind, it's beneficial to look at it both ways.

Perhaps you have an event coming up that you're not looking forward to, and you feel a sense of fear or dread. The night before, you go to bed anticipating that the next day will be "bad" or "rough," or you wake up telling yourself this.

As we saw earlier, if you set that expectation, it's likely that you're going to look for anything over the course of that day to validate that declaration.

You'll do what you can to locate it, feel justified about it, and you even may feel more in control because of it. The traffic is worse than usual, you're out of coffee, etc. You eliminate the possibility of acknowledging anything positive occurring throughout the day, or changing your outlook to it being a "good" day or even a neutral day. You are, in fact, quite content with "knowing" you're having a "bad" day. The battle is over before it's even begun.

EXERCISE: KNOWING

Review these concepts about expectations and compare them with your own modes of thinking:

» Do you regularly validate your feelings by stating that you "knew" that certain things would happen or that certain people would act in a certain manner in specific situations?

» Do you tell yourself that something is going to be a horrible experience, and as that event unfolds, do you look for every available opportunity to validate that expectation?

> » As miserable as you perceive things are working out, do you feel a greater sense of control in your life, or a sense of pride, when things play out as you had expected?

OVERRULED!

Insanity is doing the same thing, over and over again, but expecting different results.

- Narcotics Anonymous (attrib.) [xxx]

The setting of expectations can be very subtle and often reflects habits we've developed over time. We may find we are setting expectations for large events in our lives, or small day-to-day ones. The traffic is going to be impossible, so let's not even try to go. The presenter has always been boring or the topic is not exciting, so we don't even allow the possibility that it might be interesting. This meeting is going to be horrible.

"Always," "never," "it's going to be," "know it will," "I expect that," "I don't expect that." These words and phrases are unconditional and absolute. What we fail to recognize is that we create truths relative to our own little world that are limited to just that. We'd like to believe that our truths apply to others and the world at large, and we will seek validation from others to prove our point. But that proof and validation is false and limited.

Nothing is unconditional and absolute except the way in which we choose to see the world, regardless of how many people we get to agree with us or how many "facts" we collect to support our view.

Positive and negative states of mind are based on our perceptions and vary in their duration. We, individually and as a society, form judgments that one thing is better than another and even assign value or worth to individuals who embody those qualities.

Individually, we have all developed our own sense of "neutral" that falls somewhere along the spectrum between two extremes. Some people are more comfortable residing closer to the negative end, while others favor the positive end.

Periodically, based on the situation we find ourselves in, we visit one or the other extreme for a short time, although it may feel as if we are stuck in them endlessly. Within the bounds of our spectrum, we adapt our state of mind to the situations we encounter in order to maintain a feeling of comfort and control.

A MENU OF OPTIONS

We must understand that a state of mind is a choice, a choice that can be made at any moment: a choice to act, react, or remain unaffected and unattached.

What's required to make that choice is willpower, the strength to move from what's comfortable and familiar to something different or unknown. We also must use our willpower to look honestly at why we act and react in the ways we do in certain situations. Through willpower we can foster the strength to expand or change our spectrums completely.

We all possess a certain amount of willpower, and that amount can be increased. Like all levels of strength, it is variable and can increase with practice. We must look at our fear of venturing into the unknown, uncomfortable or unfamiliar, and do it anyway. Unfortunately, many of us back away from change because of the perceived effort required or a disbelief in our own abilities to make a change happen.

ALTERNATIVES

Setting expectations is different than planning. You may wonder, when you're so busy being present all day, how you can get anything done or figure out what you're going to do later in the day, or next week.

This question has come up a number of times in my workshops. As one participant stated, slumped down in his chair with his arms crossed, "So... if I'm working so hard on experiencing everything as it occurs all day long, how can I possibly get anything done? I feel like I'm just going to be standing still all day just experiencing. I won't be able to move, to eat, to get dressed..."

When you're ready to plan out your day or plan out future activities, stop and plan them out. Simply plan. Don't create stories about what you're going to do for the day and how that's going to play out *(expectations)*, or who you're going to run into and what that interaction is going to be like *(expectations again)*, or how you're going to feel later *(expectations—starting to see a trend?)*. Just stop and plan, then execute the plan.

As situations change throughout the day, as they are apt to do, simply stop and re-plan. You may re-plan your day every half hour if required, and that's fine. You might even figure out what your big "to-dos" or milestones are for the day and let everything flow freely around those items.

(Now, if your milestone is to just stand still all day and experience the day unfolding, which personally sounds like a fantastic plan to me, especially if it's at a lush tropical beach, by all means, execute that plan. I hope there will be few reasons to re-plan in that situation, unless it's just to change the direction you're facing.)

On the morning news, the weatherman tells you to pack your umbrella and you end up carrying it around with you all day, but it never rains. Are you disappointed or upset throughout the day because you have to carry your umbrella with you, or are you just experiencing carrying the umbrella and returning it to its proper place when you return home?

Do you find yourself frustrated at the end of the day because you had planned on rain and you really enjoy rain or think we needed the rain? Do you feel betrayed in some way by Mother Nature because she didn't deliver like the weatherman said she would? Do you feel better about your situation when you blame the weatherman for your inconvenience? Does that blame provide you with a justification for your frustration?

(Do you find this line of questioning as exhausting as I do?)

There is much to consider when looking at expectations and mindfulness. As with all of these concepts, in time you want to become aware of when you are demonstrating these behaviors and witness for yourself how they impact your state of mind on a moment-to-moment basis.

RENDEZVOUS

I've had innumerable magical experiences where, by getting out of the way and not trying to force things to happen, they've turned out better than I could have imagined or anticipated. And I've come to the conclusion that, when something magical does occur, it's easier to just accept it than to try and figure it out.

In order to do some advance advertising for a workshop that was being held in a large city out of state, three friends and I, all dutiful practitioners of mindfulness, decided to fly out and hang posters. We arrived early in the morning and split up into two groups, each with its own car. As one of my friends and I would be staying an extra day, we decided to work together.

The city was new to all of us, so we simply headed out in opposite directions and drove until we found areas that we thought looked appropriate for posting the information. Towards the middle of the afternoon, I received a call from the other team asking for our exact location. They needed to head back to the airport, but they had extra posters they wanted to leave with us. As my partner and I had stopped using maps and had been following our instincts, we had no real idea where we were. Finally growing weary of listening to us trying to figure out our location while driving, the other team told me not to worry about it, they would find us. Amused, we went back to looking for places to post the flyers.

We pulled into an outdoor shopping center that looked promising and started visiting stores. As we were walking up the stairs to the second level, our companions drove up, honking and laughing hysterically. I was in shock. It had been less than ten minutes since we spoke. When I asked them if they had been following us or knew where we were when they called, they swore that they hadn't. They had set their intent to find us and just happened to drive by and see us as we were walking up the stairs.

Coincidence, in a city that large? Maybe. Magic? Absolutely!

BEING MINDFUL OF EXPECTATIONS

Here are some tips for starting to see how you may be engaging in expectation-focused thinking:

- Become aware of when you use words such as "always" or "never" or speak in absolutes. Our thoughts and words carry power, and strong words make for strong ties. If we repeat these words to ourselves often enough, then the concepts involved will become fixed in our minds, with little or no room for change to occur.

- Look for patterns of when you might engage in future-based thoughts and the constraints these impose. Are there certain situations where this is prominent, such as dating?

- Catch yourself when, in the midst of a mundane activity, you are planning for some future event as an escape. See if you can refocus your attention on what is unfolding presently, regardless of feeling bored or uninterested.

- Look for trends of thought that dictate your beliefs about how similar situations are going to play out. Typically these are the always/never situations.

- Catch yourself when you're focusing on the outcome of a situation you're in, instead of experiencing the moments that make it up. Recognize what's happening and the influence the future-based thought is having over the current moment.

- Learn to train your will by forcing yourself to think positively about a situation where you currently hold a negative expectation or belief. When you see your mind trending toward the negative, focus on something, anything, to bring it back to the positive.

KEY POINTS ABOUT EXPECTATIONS

(You expected key points, didn't you?)

- Setting up expectations is a learned habit based on our previous experiences in the world. Like all habits, they can be changed, and we have the power to change them.

We just need to be willing to recognize the patterns when we are engaging in them.

- Mental habits are more difficult to catch because they have no physical manifestations, and they don't trigger obvious alarms. Mindfully and objectively watching what our minds are engaging in throughout the day is the key to spotting these habits

- In letting go of expectations, being open to endless possibilities, and paying attention even when you don't want to, there is always something new you can experience and learn. If there are no expectations, there can be no disappointments, only possibilities. Ideally, you can strive to experience life as it is, not as you want it to be.

CHAPTER EIGHT: STORIES

A man is but the product of his thoughts. What he thinks, he becomes.

- Mohandas K. Gandhi [xxxi]

ONCE UPON A TIME

When reading about the adventures and feats of famous historical figures throughout the ages, it can easily feel as if we're reading a book of fiction, even though those experiences occurred on a day in time no different than today. To the people who lived those experiences, they weren't fiction at all, they were their lives, their experiences. It was all real, it all happened.

Similarly, when we watch documentaries about inspirational figures or significant events in cultures other than our own, these too can feel as if we are seeing something other-worldly, since it is outside of our own realm of experience. In fact, the entire world outside of our own experiences can seem like a work of fiction. We can really only comprehend the world that we are familiar with, and within it we are locked into who we believe we are, our role, and what we believe we are capable or incapable of accomplishing.

An important exercise in mindfulness is to step back and consider ourselves, our lives, objectively and without judgment—much as we watch or read about the stories of other people. In so doing, we can begin to see how we each have created a story about who we believe ourselves to be, our definitions of ourselves.

Upon examination, we may find that we have unwittingly imposed countless limitations and constraints on ourselves and our beliefs about what we are and are not capable of achieving. Too often we base who we are on our history and who the world tells us we are, without questioning it. However, if we can see through the illusions and see how these walls have been constructed, we can begin to take them down and redefine who we believe ourselves to be—in effect, changing our story. *(And I'm sure there's lyrics for a killer rock song somewhere in all that.)*

AUTOBIOGRAPHY: THE STORY OF ME

In our minds, we are the main characters in our stories, and rightly so, because in our lives everything is happening to and around us. We perceive everything through our own point of view and we believe we are doing the right things through our actions. *(Feel free to go ahead and give your story a title now, because that's one of the most fun parts of creating your story. Personally I waver between "Uber-Fabulous Adventures in Plaid Pants and Silk Ties" and "Smutty Stories of the Smurfs and Their Unspoken Impact on Modern Poetry." It all depends on your perspective.)* For simplicity, here we'll just call it "The Story of Me," until you've had time to come up with something more fitting for your personal story.

In "The Story of Me," we've each created very solid definitions of our character: who we are, our place in the world, what we are and are not capable of doing or becoming, and what we believe to be "right" and "wrong."

We have also created our own story about the world in general and how it functions, based on our history, judgments, and perceptions. We have, in effect, created a script to follow that defines how the world operates and how we operate in the world, "our place in the world."

Within our stories, we've created many beliefs that help us navigate our day-to-day experiences in the world, which we'll call our operating system. This operating system tells us that we only possess certain limited capabilities, based on what we have or have not done in the past.

We also use our past experiences to determine which specific events will or will not happen to us in the future. For instance, you may believe you will never run a marathon because you don't like to run, are not in good shape, or have a debilitating injury. You will never travel to a certain place because you will never have the money or time. You will never get married because your dating life has been disastrous, which makes you feel unworthy or unattractive. You will never become a manager because upper management does not believe in your capabilities or you're not part of the Boys' Club. You will never be happy because horrible things continually happen to you and manure rains down on you from the gods above. *(Cheer up already, would you? You're really starting to bum me out and we just started this chapter.)*

WE ARE WHAT WE THINK

In T*he Dhammapada: The Sayings of the Buddha* [xlii], translated by Thomas Byrom, there is a beautiful poem that explores the idea that everything we are is a product of our thoughts, to the extent that we essentially create the world through what we think.

Reflecting on this, we can introduce the idea that we, in fact, do create the world, our vision of the world, with our thoughts and beliefs. Further, we have a choice in how we perceive and experience the world by mindfully being aware of what we choose to hold in our minds and what thoughts we choose to think. We may also confine ourselves to a limited number of experiences and possibilities due to our restricted view of ourselves and our place in the world, our story and definitions.

We set up stories about our limits, conditions, and ability to function in the world. For example, you may believe that because you only got five hours of sleep the night before, and your "minimum" amount to function adequately is seven-and-a-quarter hours, that you're going to be exhausted all day long. And, in fact, if you keep reinforcing this belief by repeating it to yourself throughout the day (as well as repeating it to everyone around you who's lucky enough to hear it), it will come true; you will believe all day that you're exhausted.

Even if you find that you are alert and energized for periods of time—even lengthy periods when you are very productive because you are more relaxed and have not yielded to your normal levels of stress—you'll overlook those periods in favor of the periods of fatigue because your lack of sleep is at the forefront of your consciousness. Perhaps you'll make tremendous progress on certain tasks you needed to complete because, due to your exhaustion, you will see things in a different light and be able to overcome certain mental roadblocks. This will be overlooked because you will hold on to the generalization that you're tired all day until the time comes when you're able to get your "full night's rest."

And if you have advertised your lack of sleep and how exhausted you are to everyone you've come across, then it will be further reinforced by those people repeating it back to you all day, validating and reminding you that you are exhausted and will continue to be so until you can get more rest.

In this example, we have created a world that is fraught with difficulty and strife because we are burdened by exhaustion. On this day, the world is difficult and challenging. We reinforce the belief all day that we are tired and barely able to get by because physically we feel the tiredness of our body and it's what we repeat in our minds over and over. What we fail to recognize is that we may have had periods when we were mentally and physically alert and able to function well. We may even have had some huge successes in the day that were overshadowed or lost altogether.

ACCORDING TO WEBSTER'S

As we grow, certain experiences add to our definitions. I like going to the gym, thus I'm a sporty person. I have a doctorate, thus I'm smarter and more educated than most other people. I gave money to a charity, thus I'm a compassionate and caring person. I've had a divorce, thus I'm damaged and bad with relationships.

Unless we are prompted to make drastic changes in our lives or undergo a significant experience, such as a challenging health issue, most moments and experiences in our lives simply serve to further reinforce and validate our story. At this moment, we are the sum total of all of the moments and associated experiences in our lives to date.

PERSONAL HISTORICAL FICTION

Our history can also become confused as time passes. When we look back at what we consider to be the large or significant events of our lives, those events might appear to be somewhat detached from what we perceive as reality today. It's as if they happened to someone else in another time and place.

We also may find that we have lost a feeling or emotion connected to past events and, when we try to re-experience it, the exhilaration of that past experience escapes us, although it changed our lives at the time. Or we may look back at a daring event from days gone by and ask ourselves in disbelief, "Did I do that?"

Our lives in this moment may seem very far from who we were at moments in the past. Perhaps when we were in high school, the world was an adventure and authority was to be challenged. We may have been more "footloose and fancy free" with our clothing and attitudes. Now, it may seem that we are the ones who exude authority and maintaining the status quo is our top concern.

CASTING CALL

In our story, the main character (in case you forgot, that would be you) lives and works in specific settings. There are supporting characters, friends and family, who influence and support or demean and degrade our main character (or otherwise just bug the heck out of us).

Our main character has strengths and limitations that come out in different situations: x, y, and z capabilities; x, y, and z strengths; and x, y, and z limitations. Thus, more often than not, our characters are completely defined, with little room to change. Our associates are also aware of these capabilities, strengths, and limitations, and will helpfully remind us of them periodically, should we forget them or try to alter them in some way.

YOU'RE THERE NONETHELESS

It's beneficial to look at how much we strive to control our story and our associated definitions of how the world works. You can ask yourself: Because of these definitions, do I create filters to see only what I want to see, in order to reinforce my beliefs about the world? Do I tune out or avoid what I find unfavorable to me so that I can make believe it doesn't exist? Do I enjoy focusing on the unfavorable to reinforce and validate my negative state of mind?

We all do this with our own story. As we saw in Chapter Seven, often we have expectations of certain experiences happening in our lives, both "good" and "bad," and we seek out opportunities to have those expectations become reality. You say, "I'm not going to have a good time at the party, I really, really don't want to go." Then, when you're at the party, you seek out experiences that validate the belief you've created. You focus on people whom you didn't particularly want to see. You focus on how uncomfortable your clothes are, or how hot the room is, or that you don't like the food being served. You overlook anything that does not reflect what you want to see—mainly, that you're not having a good time, just like you knew you wouldn't.

Because you're so set on seeing what you want to see, you overlook the fact that you have the opportunity to spend time with people you generally like, that the architecture of the building is spectacular, that the band is playing wonderful covers of some of your favorite songs, that the decorations are some of the most creative you have ever seen.

If you were to attend the party in a more ambivalent frame of mind—e.g., "I'm not really in the mood to go to a party, but I will anyway and I'll be open to whatever comes up"—you might be genuinely surprised by the experience. You would notice the things you find favorable, and perhaps put less emphasis on the things you don't. Since you're there anyway, you might as well experience it.

Bonus Tip: The next time you're someplace you don't particularly want to be, say to yourself (without any bitter and sarcastic inflections, please), "I'm here now, let's just see what happens." **Extra Bonus:** Let's practice, so when the time comes, you'll have the confidence to say it. Say it aloud right now, or if you're bashful, at least repeat it to yourself silently: "I'm here now, let's just see what happens."

THAT'S MY STORY AND I'M STICKING TO IT

Never be bullied into silence. Never allow yourself to be made a victim. Accept no one's definition of your life; define yourself.

- Harvey Fierstein (attrib.) ^{xxxiii}

The real challenge is that all of these definitions, scripts, and stories can come together and create a very solid and inflexible outlook on the world, locking us into specific beliefs and patterns, many of which have no basis in reality. This is similar to how judgments operate.

Naturally, creating and reinforcing our story gives us a sense of control. If we have a solid story, then we have a semblance of control over our lives and the world we inhabit. We are in the driver's seat, and who likes a backseat driver constantly correcting or making "helpful suggestions"? *(Poor backseat drivers, always getting a bad rap. They really might want to think about organizing, since they could become a powerful political force, or have a union, at least.)*

Thinking or believing that we are not in control is disturbing. It means that our perceptions may not be correct, that there's something "wrong" with them, and we need to make a change. And again, change—for the majority of us—is frightening, if not outright terrifying. Not to mention how it's been drilled into our minds that "wrong" is "bad," and so we feel as if we're being judged negatively. However, if we can open up to the possibility of changing our stories and let go of the judgment, then we can change the way we see and experience the world, thus changing our currently inflexible states of mind.

EXERCISE: SELF-DEFINING

Here are a few questions that may help you begin to look at some of the structures you've put into place around yourself and your life:

» What are the definitions you have used to describe yourself?

- From where did these definitions arise? Were they beliefs that you came up with on your own or were they definitions told to you by others?

- What validates them as being the ultimate truth, unwavering and unchangeable?

- What happens when they are challenged?

- Are these definitions absolutes? Do you employ words such as "always" or "never" when looking at your capabilities?

- Do you cling to these definitions and beliefs even when the possibility of changing them arises?

- Do you say, "I could never do that, I'm not adventurous, brave, ambitious, smart, sexy, clever, or coordinated enough?"

» After reflecting on the definitions you've created for yourself, start to examine some of the definitions you've created about the world.

- From where did these definitions arise? Were they beliefs that you came up with on your own or were they definitions told to you by others?

STORY INTERRUPTED

Often we will hear or read about people involved in natural disasters or accidents who say that the experience seemed surreal, "like a dream." Many times they say that their lives have not been the same since it occurred. In these instances, they were moved, or forced, out of the comfortable context of their story. They were overloaded with new information and may not have had any control whatsoever over what was happening. They probably fought as hard as they could, but eventually they had to let go of control and just go along for the ride; they had to just experience the scene unfolding around them.

During the financial crisis that began in 2008, people were shocked to hear that large investment firms were in danger of collapsing. The perceived pillars of stability were crumbling and the emerging reality threw people's beliefs about financial stability into chaos.

The majority of the public believed that the people running these companies would be responsible and honest, and play by the rules that protect society's best interests. When people learned of the corruption that had taken place, there was mass disbelief followed by outrage. Where were the authorities who should have been watching over these institutions and keeping the average worker safe?

Similar scenarios are seen anytime corruption is uncovered. Sex scandals within the Catholic church, which began to come to light in the early 2000s, threw many devout churchgoers into states of disbelief and denial, causing them to clamor for reasons and excuses to justify such behavior. Political corruption and sex scandals (which are, sadly, common at this point in history, and are no longer scandals, but pretty much the norm), also challenge the structures people believe and have faith in.

Individually, we can get nervous or fearful when we go into new situations where we don't know what to expect and our sense of control feels limited. Going on a job interview or starting a new job, for example, can seem very stressful, since we don't know what kind of environment we are walking into or whether we will measure up to the new employer's expectations of us.

Other examples are the first day at a new school, a first date with someone we've had a crush on for a time, having to make an appearance in court, or entering a new social situation where we believe we are not in the same social class. In all of these situations, we are facing the unknown and our emotions react accordingly, mainly with differing levels of fear, stress, and anxiety.

When you encounter an unfamiliar situation, you may become nervous or anxious if the situation doesn't fit into one of your preexisting definitions of the world and how things are known to operate according to your story. Instead of surrendering to what's unfolding, you may spend the entire time trying to fit the situation into a definition or category you're comfortable with. In doing so, you miss the opportunity to expand your story, your capabilities, and your world.

When struggling with change, we are challenged to reconcile new and often unforeseen and unexpected events with our existing strong definitions. We thereby experience internal conflicts for which the world seldom has any answers or consolation.

Ideally, if we are able to adapt to changes, even those forced on us, we discover parts of ourselves we didn't know existed; moreover, the changes are rarely as detrimental as we feared. We may find that we are far more adaptable or passionate than we ever imagined and we may be able to utilize those newfound strengths in other areas of our lives.

EXERCISE: WORLDLY DEFINITIONS

Some questions to ask yourself about how well you handle and adapt to changing situations:

» Do you engage in the "always/never" paradigm when the possibility of change arises? (For example, "Things will always be this way, I'll never do x, y, or z.")

» When you encounter change in your life, how do you react?

» If you find that you resist change, is there a trend or pattern to that behavior?

» How do you typically react in new situations? If you often feel fearful or have a sense of trepidation, can you investigate why you feel this way? Ask yourself what

> there is to be fearful of. What is the worst thing that
> could happen? Would the sun still rise tomorrow?

BECOMING CULTURED

Communities as a whole create collective stories and agreements in an attempt to create standards for conducting their lives; we'll define this as culture. Each culture has an identity, its own story, complete with general rules and regulations, boundaries and limitations defined by its history. As children, we are taught the constructs of our culture: its rules and limits, constraints, social norms, customs and protocols.

Over time a cultural identity can change, but seldom do those changes occur quickly or radically. Even after upheavals in government or revolutions, a culture's customs, traditions, and values tend to stay intact. Often cultural identity is built around a religious belief system that dictates the roles of power, levels of modesty, and moral and ethical guidelines for the conduct of its members.

We also see how cultural identity can define and reinforce personal attributes, such as general strengths and faults. These cultural influences significantly shape and add context to our personal story. For example, if one culture promotes extremely long ears as a sign of exquisite beauty, and another defines it as a gross disfigurement that should be covered up, imagine how different the life of a person who possesses this specific trait would be living in each of the two cultures. Similarly, imagine how your perception of a person with this characteristic might be different if you lived in these cultures.

EXERCISE: DEFINING CULTURE

Take some time and review how your culture has shaped your view of yourself and of the world:

» What are the stories and beliefs your culture has impressed upon you?

- How might they have limited or empowered you?

- Are there attitudes or beliefs you currently subscribe to that would be strongly challenged or criticized in other cultures?

LIVING UNDER THE INFLUENCE

Almost everywhere we turn, we are inundated with images and advertisements from companies and organizations that we unquestioningly accept as authorities for setting standards of beauty and normality. It is most often only because they have defined themselves this way. *(Pretty nifty trick, huh?)*

Billboards, magazines, television advertisements, the Internet, and the fashions and attitudes of others all influence us in both subtle and not-so-subtle ways. By simply glancing at a large magazine rack, one may observe the large number of publications claiming to be authorities on what is hip and trendy; this feeds, shapes, and reinforce our own definitions.

Television shows perpetually reflect back to us definitions of masculinity and femininity. Infomercials tell us why our lives are incomplete without the latest exercise equipment or set of razor-sharp knives. *(But wait, there's more...)* Movies tell us what relationships, love, danger, and adventures should look like. You can't have an awards show without an accompanying fashion review, which, sadly, also often involves a subtle, or not-so-subtle, critique of the person wearing the outfit.

Media outlets also present ideas of what "happiness" looks like. Advertisements featuring people laughing and appearing joyful while engaged in a certain activity convey the idea that if you also engage in this activity, you will be as happy as the people in the advertisement. If you use a certain floor-cleaning product, everything in your life will work out favorably: You can finally sit back, serene and at peace, knowing that your floor is germ-free. Ads tell us that eating a particular food or using a particular product will cause the pounds to drop from our bodies overnight.

Ads also create the belief that there might be something wrong with us if we are not experiencing the joy, peace, and satisfaction that the people in the advertisements are experiencing. If we are not aware that this manipulation is going on, we may find ourselves believing that we should be feeling something other than what we are feeling in the current moment and that we're missing something. This prompts us to go out and purchase the product to rectify the issue.

It's also easy for us to buy into group beliefs and attitudes in the real world; if everyone else is engaged in an activity, then the behavior must be acceptable. This is the psychology of crowds. Illegal activities become easily and conveniently justified when everyone else is engaging in them. *(Such is the case with flash mobs; however, sometimes there's just no excuse for badly rehearsed dancing and lip-synching.)*

In the early 2000s, television shows began mimicking (or mocking) what we consider "reality," and the line between fact and fiction became even more blurry. Competition and relationships devolved into contests of who could physically or mentally outwit their rivals or who could appear the most "trashed," pretentious or self-righteous and condescending. *(And, sadly, it's often too close to call.)* When watching these programs, we may compare our own actions with those of the participants, and make adjustments where we think we might derive benefit.

EXERCISE: INFLUENCED

Reflect on how the media and advertisements have influenced your views of yourself and the world:

» Do you find that you compare yourself to models in advertisements, and actors in films or television?

  • How does this typically manifest? What thoughts arise with these comparisons? Do you feel that your life situation would be better or more fulfilling if you appeared as they do? Does this lead to states of depression or sadness?

» If you do compare yourself, do you find that you devalue or demean your self-worth when making these comparisons?

  • Do you also demean or devalue the worth of other people you know or observe around you?

  • Do you justify certain behaviors you engage in because they are reinforced by what you observe in others or what you see in the media?

WHAT VERSION ARE THEY ON?

As discussed in detail in Chapter Six: "Under the Influence," we spend a tremendous amount of time putting our lives and situations into context by comparing ourselves to the people around us. Those comparisons result either in feeling empowered and righteous if we judge the other party negatively, or feeling bad about ourselves if we judge the other to be superior to us. Unfortunately, we don't spend much time looking at other people and their circumstances objectively, free of judgment.

We are all capable of experiencing a multitude of states of mind, some clear and free of outside influences, and some less clear. Knowing this about ourselves allows us to recognize that others also experience diverse states of mind. We may ask ourselves about other people's decisions or actions, "What in the world were they thinking?" To them, however, their actions were justified and correct, and made perfect sense at the time.

As we discussed in Chapter Five: "Perceptions," judging others' actions is inherently a futile activity. Unless you are that person, you cannot understand their rationale. You are not them. You do not see the world as they do. Nor do they see the world the way you do. How can they? Their story and many of their definitions are different than yours. There may be some similarities and common norms, but their story and their view of the world is not yours, nor can it ever be.

We may strain to understand the actions that we find disagreeable in others. We try to fit their actions into our story, our view of the world, and hold them up against our own standard. When their actions are drastically different than ours, we may categorize them as "sinners," derelicts, mentally damaged or deranged. This can make us feel better about ourselves and give greater justification to our own actions and beliefs because we are not like that.

According to their own story and definition of the world, everyone thinks they're correct and justified in their actions, even the cruelest dictator. No one sees themselves as the bad guy in a

situation, or what they are doing as detrimental. They feel justified; otherwise, they wouldn't do it.

As stated earlier, when we adopt a more compassionate
standpoint, we can see all people everywhere as doing the best
they can with what they have (just as we are). Again, as Lincoln
instructed, don't criticize other people, for we may act in the same
manner and have the same beliefs if we were in similar circumstances. People grow up in different situations and cultures. They
are taught different beliefs and ideas of right and wrong, and live
in different physical environments, even within the same country.
There may be commonalities, but they are inherently different.

Imagine what your life would be like and what your outlook
on the world would be if you were born and raised in the Congo,
the outback of Australia, or in the Middle East. They would be
much, much different. Material things that are vitally important
to you in your life now might seem frivolous or ridiculous if you
were raised in one of these regions. The way you present yourself
and interact with others might be 180 degrees different than how
you present yourself today in the world. Your idea of what is attractive or valuable could be drastically different as well.

PASSIONATELY PASSIONATE

Understanding that everyone has their own point of view
about themselves and the world around them can help in teaching us compassion for others. Through compassion, we can relieve
ourselves of the many negative states of mind we suffer from,
because they often originate in judgmental thinking that we
habitually indulge in.

We can also look compassionately at some of our own experiences for which we have regretful feelings and try to put them
in perspective. When we look back at a poor judgment we made

in the past, it may continually reinforce our feelings of remorse and regret over that experience. However, if we go back to that moment in time, to that exact experience, we may see that at the time of the event, for some reason, we, in that particular state of mind, felt justified in our actions.

At that point in time, in that moment, what we were doing made sense, as crazy as that may have seemed in the moments that followed and seems in this moment. We thought we understood, or didn't care about, the consequences of our actions and we were willing to accept them. Our story and definition of the world at that time reinforced that view. We later came to see that past situation in a way that, at the time, was outside of our realm of possibility, outside of our story. That became the source for our feelings of regret.

EXERCISE: DEFINING OTHERS

Explore the ways in which you consider the stories of other people, as well as some of your own actions from the past.

» When you find yourself becoming judgmental or aggravated with regard to the actions of others, try to see the world from their point of view. Like us, their situations and circumstances formed their life view.

  • Can you adopt a compassionate stance and see that the way they are acting is based on how the world has been defined for them, that they too are doing the best they can with what they have?

» Reflect upon an experience in the past where you exercised poor judgment and about which you may currently feel regret. Think about the circumstances at that time and in those moments.

- Try and take yourself back to your exact state of mind in those moments. What was your level of clarity then? Could you have anticipated the future outcome at that moment, in the state of mind you possessed at the time?

- Once your understanding of the possible outcomes and the impact of your actions grew, did you continue to take that same approach, or did you alter your behavior based on the new information? What you did or didn't do is something worth acknowledging and examining.

» Reflect on a time when someone you know similarly exercised poor judgment. In trying to compassionately understand their story, explore the differences between the states of mind you experienced in your situation and the states of mind they experienced in their situation. Aim not to judge either. Strive to see how both situations gave rise to actions motivated by desired outcomes.

REVISIONS AND SECOND EDITIONS

Changing, revising, and adding new chapters to our stories is not as difficult as you may believe. This is in fact the central idea of this book (and if you haven't realized that by now, then I should be fired).

Hollywood has made a tremendous amount of money presenting stories of seeming nobodies who turn into heroes and champions. These movies are inspiring to watch and can provide motivation. Recently, with the advent of affordable video cameras and sharing on the Internet, we have been able to witness great feats and transformations by ordinary people (as opposed to actors trying to be ordinary).

One well-known video highlights the struggle of a Gulf War veteran who lost the ability to walk unassisted, and his descent into disparaging states of mind. Then, through the grace of an unlikely ex-wrestler turned yoga coach, he completely turns his life around and is running on his own within a year of starting his practice. I'm sure he questioned the possibility of such an achievement on a daily basis; yet he persevered. [xxxiv]

If people can make such drastic physical transformations through will and commitment, may we not also be able to make similar changes in our ways of thinking? Both take practice, patience and perseverance.

As with judgments, it's beneficial to look at where and how the definitions in our stories—about our capabilities, strengths, and weaknesses—originated. All of these definitions can lock us into belief structures which limit possibilities for transformation.

Look at how friends and family influence you. Do they confine you to certain definitions that they wish to believe about you? How does the media influence you? Do you buy into the ideas and concepts they present?

One of the greatest joys that mindfulness brings is the ability to see things in the world, and attitudes within yourself, in entirely new ways that you never dreamed possible. And it's not as difficult as you may believe. It just requires a shift in perspective—sometimes bigger shifts that take more effort, and sometimes smaller ones that require less.

Do you believe that your story is immutable and fixed? Remember, if everything we are is a product of our thoughts, then if we can change the way we think, we can change who we believe ourselves to be.

KEY POINTS FOR STORIES

- Over the course of our lives, we each create a story about who we believe ourselves to be, based on our circumstances and experiences. This story can lock us into certain beliefs about what we are and are not capable of achieving or experiencing in our lives.

- We reinforce our stories in innumerable ways, often just to avoid change, which we can find overwhelming.

- Our culture and the media also strongly influence our story and our definitions of the world. They can create beliefs that are not real or true.

- Mindfully becoming aware of the limitations and mental structures we put in place and reinforce on an ongoing basis will allow you to see how you restrict yourself and your view of the world. These restrictions limit what you believe yourself capable of, or worthy of experiencing or being.

- It is important to understand that everyone has their own story, with absolute definitions and differing views of the world. Compassionately, we can understand that we are not so different from one another in the way we operate in the world.

CHAPTER NINE: PROJECTIONS & REFLECTIONS

The life which is unexamined is not worth living.

- Socrates ^{xxxv}

MIRROR, MIRROR...

As discussed previously, in early childhood we begin to learn how the world operates with regard to our relationships with other people, both in our family and in society. Additionally, we begin to grasp how the world and our specific culture function. From these observations, we begin to form an operating system that tells us how best to navigate this maze, based on our story: who we believe ourselves to be, our capabilities and limitations, and our understanding of our place in the world.

We must also acknowledge that our story is shaped significantly by outside influences telling us who we are, both culturally and personally. The specific form these take will depend on our gender, our family's income level, our nationality, and our culture's relationships with other cultures, among others.

In order to maintain our comfort level with our story, or validate our attempts to make changes to it, we may seek agreement from the world and the people around us that the story we have created, or the changes we are trying to implement, are legitimate. They confirm through our interactions with them that we are a good person, a funny person, an attractive person, a strong person, a threatening person, or a meek or weak person—whatever we believe our story to be at the time.

Like looking in a mirror, we seek reflections in the world in order to show us that we are indeed the type of person we are comfortable portraying, or that we are being perceived in the way we wish to be seen.

Imagine standing in front of a mirror and examining yourself. When we do this, we are often imagining what other people will see when they look at us. You may notice what you think are flaws and try to cover them up in order to achieve the look you want reflected back to you. You may feel pride about how good you look and find yourself preening in front of the mirror, trying to see your body, and perhaps the outfit you're wearing, from every conceivable angle. Otherwise, you just want confirmation that you are "presentable."

Conversely, perhaps you don't care how you look. You don't care what other people think. You have confidence in yourself regardless of what you're wearing. Perhaps you even practice flipping yourself off in the mirror in order to confirm you can convey the appropriate level of disdain for your audience. *(Personally, my third-period Angst 101 class was the source of my most cherished high school memories. It's heartwarming to see that budget cuts have not eliminated this most important component of a well-rounded high school curriculum.)* Or to be more extreme, you believe yourself to be the most hideously unattractive of beings and, no matter what you do, you cannot escape that belief. *(Standing in front of the mirror, you sigh in resignation, then turn and unlock the cage of winged monkeys and send them out to do your bidding.)*

Now imagine that the mirror has transformed into the world you interact with on a daily basis. Everyone you encounter becomes a source of reflection. Your coworkers at your job, passers-by on the street, people in the grocery store, at the gym, on the bus, in the car next to you, your partner or spouse, your neighbors and family—all of these are sources of reflection, like little walking mirrors.

When we interact with people, we pay attention to how they react and respond to us. If we act nicely and they react favorably to us, then we are a good, kind, and likeable person. They are validating how we wish to be perceived—as a nice person. If we act cruelly or are dismissive, then they may react negatively, validating that we are a powerful and threatening person or that we just don't care what other people think. If we flirt and the recipient flirts back, then we feel desirable. If the flirting is not returned, then we feel foolish and humiliated. As you can see, each action and subsequent reaction has an immediate impact on our state of mind in that moment.

Throughout the journey of our lives, we make modifications to our behavior when necessary, in order to maintain the level of reinforcement we receive from others. From a mindfulness perspective, challenges arise when we are unaware of our dependency on these reflections. It is helpful to examine why they are important to us. We must also look at the beliefs we've constructed regarding what they provide for us that we feel we are lacking.

COMMODITIES EXCHANGE

One of the most prevalent examples of projections and reflections in the West, and throughout much of the world, is our perceived attractiveness. For it is through our attractiveness that we seek to locate a suitable mate, or obtain acceptance or admiration from the world.

Some may believe that their attractiveness entitles them to certain commodities, for example, someone equally, or perhaps even more, attractive as a mate. Again, this stereotype is continually reinforced in the media and even in our fairy tales. As children, we learn about the rejected ugly duckling that in time grows to be a beautiful swan and is then, and only then, accepted by his flock. Cinderella can't catch the eye of the prince as a maid, only when she attends the ball dressed as a beautiful princess.

Men and women will flirt and throw sexual "vibes" at one another in an effort to procure a mate, even if just for a night. When going to a bar or nightclub, people fret over what to wear, their "window dressing" for putting themselves on display. We wear what we think will make us appealing to whatever mate we hope to attract.

Interactions in bars and clubs (or gyms because, sometimes, what's the difference?) provide immediate feedback and validation, projection and reflection, for many people. However, we can also find reflections in our daily actions, where the feedback is completely self-created.

If you feel a sense of pride in being able to shop in a higher-end retail store, it may be because it makes you feel connected to the people in that store. You are part of that club or tribe, and the mere fact that you are in that store validates that you belong with that group. If you feel uncomfortable in that kind of environment, it's often because you feel like you don't belong, that you're an outsider, or unworthy.

When you go to an organic grocery store, you're happy when you're there because you feel you are a health-conscious type of person. If you prefer to eat at higher-end restaurants, perhaps it's because it gives you the sense that you are the kind of person worthy of frequenting such establishments.

These reflections can be innocent, but it is important to look at them and recognize the power they have in continually reinforcing our story.

ON THE PLAYGROUND

Having a strongly defined cultural and social structure also helps validate our actions and reassure us of our place in society. Most people constantly compare and contrast themselves, their actions, attitudes, behavior and appearance with the people around them to provide a sense of comfort.

We compare what we're wearing to the clothes worn by those we associate with, or with others who project what we wish we could also project to the world—be it a Wall Street executive, a Hollywood starlet, a rap artist, a favorite relative, the popular kids at school, a cultural icon, or the lead singer of a popular Goth-grunge band.

We pay attention to the fashion, food, technology, and lifestyle trends in the media and strive to be up-to-date with the things we want others to notice and reflect back to us. We want them to see and acknowledge that we are indeed the "type" of person that we are presenting to the world.

WHY THIS MATTERS

(I know, I know. Seriously, it took this long to get to the point of all of this?)

In pointing out the various ways we look outside of ourselves to add to or reinforce the definitions in our story, I do not mean for you to create any judgments against yourself. I want you to be aware of the various subtle ways we all seek validation from the world and be able to step back and ask yourself: "Why is this kind of reflection important to me? How is it tied to my story, my definitions and operating system, and how flexible am I about them? And why is a particular definition so important to me?"

We all seek reflections of who we are through a multitude of methods. For example, both men and women often wear provocative, tight-fitting clothing in order to have other people reflect back to them that they are sexy, healthy, and attractive. They enjoy the subtle looks and blatant stares from passers-by because it is reinforcement from the world that they are desirable, that they are in good shape, that they are maintaining their youth, that they are stronger than others, and perhaps even that they are superior to others.

With plastic surgery increasingly common, we can see the often drastic measures that people are willing to take in order to receive validation that they are youthful, and therefore, they believe, more attractive.

On the flip side, some people are more comfortable being perceived as nonconformist and going against the norm. In order for them to get the validation from the world they desire, they may dress in a dramatic fashion, cover themselves in offensive or shocking tattoos, or get multiple piercings in multiple places. They'll do whatever is considered antiestablishment in order to receive confirmation that they fit the definition of antiestablishment. (And how pissed are they when their look becomes the new norm?) Here too they may feel superior because they abhor the status quo.

The need for reflection and validation can become like an addiction over time. We may find that we are constantly in need of feedback from people around us. This manifests as constantly looking for people to notice us, or by constantly evaluating ourselves against our perceptions of those around us. "Am I better-looking than they are? Am I better-dressed than they are? Am I more successful? Are they accepting of me?"

We may look for acceptance from others in what we wear, what products we use, even in our choices of furniture and life-style. We want to be like the Joneses and, when we're not, we may fall into negative states of mind, thinking that we must change because we are inadequate as we are now. All of these reflections serve to reinforce our story.

A CASE IN POINT

The following example illustrates how a shift in perspective can allow one to see a surface issue on a more subtle level. Interestingly, in this case, reflections were a main component of the experienced challenges.

A woman who attended a number of my classes was working diligently on understanding her feelings of frustration toward her children, who were in their late teens and early twenties. When she asked herself why she was getting upset over some of the choices they were making that she did not agree with, her answer was that she loved them and she wanted the best for them. She would always come back to this conclusion, regardless of the situation. So while this insight was a lovely display of her affection, it wasn't examining the situation at a level where the source of the conflict could be observed.

When she did eventually probe deeper, she realized that her frustration was actually based on her desire to control aspects of her children's lives that she didn't approve of. She hoped to spare them the negative consequences of what she perceived as choices similar to those that she had made in her own life. She was convinced that they too would suffer by making the same mistakes, and she was not willing to let them experience those choices on their own, possibly with different, more positive outcomes. Additionally, she was afraid that others would cast judgments on her for their behavior.

While reaching this realization was somewhat painful and upsetting, she came to understand the source of so much of her aggravated and frustrated states of mind. She also understood that she had a choice: She could continue to engage in these states of mind, or she could start to gradually let go of her fears and desires, and accept that her children were not like her. Perhaps they could engage in those same activities and not have the same results that she had. Perhaps what was best for them was for her to accept their choices and support them as best she could.

THIS HAS BEEN A TEST OF THE EMERGENCY BROADCAST SYSTEM

The danger in this habit of comparing is that it sets up a paradigm based on desiring acceptance and fearing rejection. We falsely believe that acceptance will provide happiness and a sense of control in our lives. The problem is that, if we depend on others for this sense of comfort and control, we'll then do whatever we feel is necessary to sustain this.

It becomes an addiction, and we may not even recognize the misery we put ourselves through in order to sustain those feelings and feed the cravings for those reflections. For if acceptance provides happiness and control, then rejection must lead to the opposite.

What we must ask ourselves is why we care what others think. Why do we allow our sense of worth or happiness to hinge on the opinions of, and reflections from, others? By doing so, we are giving away all of our power by relying on them to confirm our story and definitions.

If we are completely at peace with ourselves in this moment, then we will no longer look to others, or to the world, to provide us with the fulfillment we desire, the reflections. They simply won't matter.

THE SLAVES OF SOCIAL MEDIA

While I was in the process of writing this book, I had an eye-opening experience that exemplified one of the many ways in which reflections are sought from the world.

I often do my writing in college libraries. As will be discussed in Chapter Ten: "Clarity," I find that being in an academic atmosphere, surrounded by others who are focused on academic tasks or expanding their learning, to be conducive to writing. For me, it can be easier to concentrate and focus in these locations than in my home, which provides many tempting distractions.

In these environments, it's very easy to observe what people are working on, as they dutifully tap away on their laptops. What I quickly noticed was that the top distraction for students was whatever social media application was popular at the time.

Like a zoologist observing beasts in the wild (it was a college library after all), I was constantly amazed. I would often observe people uploading photos and arranging them strategically, perhaps with the hope of being perceived in a particular way, or as a means of reinforcing or growing their reputation. *(Jocks being jock-ish, sorority girls being sorority-ish, nerds being nerd-ish.)* Others would peruse the comments on acquaintances' photos, sometimes adding to them. Still others would spend time investigating people's profiles, perhaps with the intent of finding out what they had in common, or to know how to approach them to ask them out. Many spent time updating items in their own profiles, analyzing how world events related to them, or stating what they thought about those events.

It became clear to me that social media is yet another source of reflection. How do we wish to present ourselves to the online masses? How many people are connected to us? Who enjoys the same things we enjoy? Who approves of the things that we post?

I want to emphasize that there's nothing "wrong" with these actions. What's important is to look at why we feel we must be perceived in a certain manner in order to feel validated or happy. Why do we care so much what other people think of us? How does that bring us a sense of peace? Our online manipulations may make us look good in others' eyes, but how do we look in our own eyes?

This kind of examination can show us the ways in which we have a dependency on the world to validate who we are or our behavior. The amount of time, effort and energy we can spend seeking that validation is exhausting. Why not spend that time becoming comfortable with the reflection in your own mirror?

REPROGRAMMING THE OPERATING SYSTEM

The truth will set you free, but first it will piss you off.

- Gloria Steinem [xxxxvi]

Again, the concepts being presented are not meant as judgments; it's just interesting to note the ways in which we seek reflections in order to make ourselves comfortable.

The goal is to begin to see how you seek validation from the world and why you see that as being important to you. This internal investigation requires a tremendous amount of honesty and can be somewhat frightening to engage in. *(So please do not begin this activity while holding sharp objects and always remember never to run with scissors, you'll put your eye out.)* However, once the behavior is recognized, then change becomes possible.

Perhaps instead of seeking so much feedback from the world, we can find the feedback and the reflections we want inwardly. Are we feeling greater peace in our lives by learning about and working through our internal struggles? Only we ourselves can validate that. When we are truly at peace inwardly, everything is OK as it is. We don't have to change the world or ourselves to match some perceived definition.

We can find peace within ourselves if we try to exist in the world as if we were watching a movie—detached and objective. We can experience what is happening in the moment without trying to change it, evaluate it, or change ourselves to appear more favorable in it. *(Unless it's a horror slasher film you're watching, in which case I recommend changing the channel to a hysterical cartoon.)*

GETTING OUTSIDE MORE

In your interactions with the world, it's not necessary to ignore people or disengage from them in order to shield yourself from reflections. All that's required is to be aware of them and our dependency on them. To break yourself out of this pattern, though, it can be helpful to shift your mode of engagement. When interacting with people, instead of looking for feedback, focus on what you can do for them.

One of the best ways to stop focusing on ourselves is to learn to be of service to others. This does not necessarily mean spending hours engaging in volunteer work, although that can be a great spiritual exercise. You can also be of service through brief interactions in which you make someone's day a little bit better. Following are a few exercises I encourage you to try. In all of these, it's important to make certain that you are not looking for a reflection, you are giving of yourself with no expectation of receiving anything in return.

- When interacting with someone in the service industry, take some time to acknowledge them. If you have ever had, or currently work in, one of these jobs, then you are aware of how monotonous and physically taxing they can be. This could be an order taker in a restaurant, or the cashier in a store. Make eye contact with them and ask how their day is going. Try telling them a joke or see if you can make them laugh or amuse them in some way. One interaction like this can help ease hours of mental monotony.

- Have patience when calling a customer service line to register a complaint or request help. Whatever your issue may be, keep in mind that, more than likely, the person on the other end of the line is not the cause of the situation. They are just trying to earn a living like all of us. It's likely that they have been listening to people complain for hours. Imagine how you would like to be spoken to if you were in their place. If you use a friendly and patient tone, seeking assistance instead of going on the offensive, then it will likely help them feel better about the work they do.

- Take time to acknowledge the people who often go unnoticed. Smile and chat with the person at the toll or ticket booth, the janitor in the building, or the reception-ist in the office.

Just to reiterate (because it's important): It's not about you be-ing perceived as a nice person or being nice to get more out of the interaction. In fact, you shouldn't care how they respond. What matters is that you acted, that you made a selfless gesture. You are getting outside of yourself and making an offering of yourself.

EXERCISES IN REFLECTIONS

To see how you may seek your own reflections from the world, explore the following:

» Step back and objectively look at your interactions. Do you find that you seek reflections from people in the world much as you would seek a reflection from a mir-ror? As in the examples discussed previously, can you pinpoint certain situations where this happens?

» For example, do you flirt with people in order to feel attractive or desired? How do you feel when that is suc-cessful? Unsuccessful?

» Do you avoid people because you feel unworthy or uncomfortable being around them? If so, can you determine the basis for this belief?

» Are there activities you engage in or places you frequent that give you a sense of pride that you use to judge others?

  • Why do you think these reflections are important to you?

» Do you seek acceptance from others in what you wear, or what you own, or where you hang out?

As mentioned throughout the chapter, the intent of this line of questioning is not to judge yourself or others. The point is to begin to understand your dependency on knowing how the world perceives you.

KEY POINTS ABOUT PROJECTIONS AND REFLECTIONS

• Like looking in a mirror, we seek reflections back from the world that show us that we are indeed the type of person we are comfortable portraying, or that we are being perceived in the way in which we wish to be perceived.

• Throughout the journey of our lives, we will make modifications to our story when necessary in order to maintain the level of reinforcement from those who provide us with reflections.

• In a mindfulness practice it is essential to look at the reflections you seek from the world, how they manifest, and why they matter to you.

- If your inner peace is dependent on what others tell you about yourself, then you will be unable to find peace without that feedback.

- Once you begin to understand what's happening beneath the surface, you can change aspects of your operating system. The first step is recognizing what's really going on.

CHAPTER TEN: CLARITY

You cannot fail in any laudable object, unless you allow your mind to be improperly directed.

- Abraham Lincoln [xxxvii]

I CAN SEE CLEARLY NOW

Up to this point we've focused primarily on general observations about how we operate and perceive ourselves in the world, including the specific strategies we employ to navigate through it. These include perceptions, judgments, future-based thinking, dwelling in the past, and self-evaluation. We've looked at how we each manifest these characteristics in our interactions.

One of the most important aspects in cultivating mindfulness is understanding how our states of mind are constantly shaped and molded by the world and the people around us. To do this, we must find ways to separate ourselves from the influences of the world in order to identify them, much as we work to detach ourselves from our thoughts to observe the patterns.

Through this effort we strive to gain clarity about what we are currently experiencing—our thoughts, our states of mind, our emotions, our physical sensations—and determine how much of this is an organic part of us and how much is due to an influence from the world.

In other words, we want to understand how much of what we are feeling at any given moment is genuinely our own—our own thoughts, moods, emotions, feelings—and what part is due to something impacting us from the world—from our environment, location, another person or group of people, or a combination of these.

By default, we automatically assume everything we experience is part of our own psyche; we take ownership of it all. Often though, that's not the case. But how do we know? If we can discern that something we're experiencing is due to an outside influence, then recognizing this will give us greater clarity and awareness. And if we find that it's not organically ours, then we can discard it.

This is extremely important because in recognizing when and how we are being affected by something outside of ourselves, we dissipate its impact and learn how to avoid it going forward. It's like discovering the source of an annoying sound that's been bothering us for hours, shutting it off, and eliminating it from our lives.

DISCLAIMERS

This chapter will explore some of the more esoteric ideas and concepts associated with mindfulness. Accordingly, you may be inclined to dismiss it as New-Agey, metaphysical, or just too far out for your liking. If that's the case, then I ask you to put mindfulness into action by putting those judgments aside, and seeing if the information presented provides a new perspective or resonates with you at some level.

In this section, I'll start referring to our state of being, as opposed to just our state of mind. What we are looking at here is the effect that something apart from us can have on us, not just mentally, but physically as well. Additionally, we can start to see how the physical affects the mental, and vice versa.

EXERCISE: SETTING A BASELINE

The goal of this exercise is to objectively observe the world unfolding around you. At the same time, try to get a sense for how you feel, both mentally and physically, in different environments.

» Find a place where you can observe the world as though you are watching a movie. As best you can, relax and clear your mind of all activity. Tell yourself that for the next five or ten minutes there's nothing else you need to be doing, there's nothing you need to figure out, and there is no one you need to think about.

» Take yourself out of the equation. Imagine what this place would be like if you were not there, if there were no one to add commentary, evaluate, or judge. Just try to see it in its pure form.

• If possible, the first time you try this exercise, do it in nature, somewhere peaceful, with few people and distractions around.

• Look around and take in the view. What do you see? What are the sounds you hear? The smells you smell? What is the temperature and how is it affecting your body?

- Also notice how easily your mind is pulled away and distracted. When you find your mind wandering—judging, evaluating, critiquing, or creating a story—just catch yourself, come back and refocus on observing. Catch and come back. Catch and come back.

- See that everything just is as it is and try to accept that. There is no need to judge, evaluate, or change anything. There is no need to create a story around or categorize anything. Just simply observe.

- Notice how different this may feel, compared to how you normally react to this situation.

GOOD VIBRATIONS

At its essence, the world and everything within it has energy, a vibration that can be experienced and quantified in different ways. We can imagine this spectrum of energy ranging from a sluggish churning or "low vibe," to vibrating so fast that it appears to be completely still, a "high vibe." This is often expressed as a "feeling." For example, a dilapidated old car with smoke billowing from its exhaust pipe has a radically different feel from a new luxury car in a showroom window. Not better or worse, just different.

We are all aware of the energies and vibrations (feelings) in the world to some degree, although most of us are completely unaware of how and when they are affecting us. Becoming aware of their impact is something that can be cultivated through the practice of being mindful. Once we understand how we are directly and indirectly affected by the things we feel from the world, we can begin to change how we react to those experiences and eliminate them as obstacles that prevent us from being peaceful.

To demonstrate this concept, let's look at how our body reacts to a physical experience in nature. Imagine how you would feel mentally and how your body would react if you were to jump into a pool of ice-cold water. For most of us, upon hitting the water, our bodies would tense up in shock and our movements would become abrupt and exaggerated, anything to bring up our body temperature and fend off the assaulting cold. Our thoughts would be focused on getting away from this situation immediately, with an almost primal urge to flee.

Now contrast that experience with jumping into a lake during the summer, when the water temperature is close to your body temperature, or a little bit warmer. In this situation, upon hitting the water, your body would relax and expand into the water as if you had been engulfed in a loving embrace. Your active mind and thoughts would be quelled and you would allow the warmth of the water to envelop you.

Your mental reactions changed as a result of your physical circumstances. Here we have two similar situations with very different impacts on our body and, subsequently, our state of mind.

Taking this a step further, the following analogy illustrates how we react, physically and mentally, to changing circumstances in the world: Picture yourself moving through the world as you would kayak around an island in the tropics. Imagine your mind is like the kayak.

You launch from a beach where the water is still and easy to move through. Here the boat (mind) meets little resistance and moves easily through the calm water. As you travel around the island, you begin to encounter and observe the different relation-ships between the ocean and the land. Your boat (mind) reacts to those changing conditions much as your mind reacts to changing worldly conditions.

In one area, you see the ocean slamming into the rock cliffs with tremendous force, causing large, violent crashes of water. You know that if you venture into that area, your fragile kayak (mind) will be decimated. You try to avoid that area and those currents in your vulnerable kayak. You compensate by paddling harder to break free of the currents to keep yourself from harm.

At another point in your journey, you get caught in a riptide and, while the water around you appears to be calm, you find you are being pulled off course and out to sea, farther and farther from the island. Understanding what is happening, you paddle parallel to the island, break free of the riptide, and aim your boat back toward land. This is similar to zoning out. When you're not paying attention, you slowly get lost.

At still another point, you sight a beautiful and serene lagoon, separated from the ocean by a beautiful reef. Here your boat is quiet, at ease, and undisturbed.

Water, being fluid, will change its behavior based on its sur-roundings and circumstances. We're the same way. While every-thing is not as obvious as boats reacting to currents, our minds and bodies react to different situations we encounter. By cultivat-ing a clear understanding of our environment and circumstances at all times, and seeing how they affect our state of mind, we can make adjustments when needed to get us back to a more peaceful and stable state.

NOTHING SAYS FUN LIKE...

On a more esoteric level (keep working with me here), we can illustrate the concept of awareness in the world by completely shifting our attention away from our thoughts and focusing solely on our physical sensations. To accomplish this, you imagine that all of the open space through which you move has solidified, filling your environment like water in a sunken ship. Thus you move through the world acutely aware of every sensation, much as we washed the dishes in Chapter 1.

As in the different manifestations of water, and the relationship of the ocean to the island that your boat/mind experienced in the previous example, the following exercise can help you see how the world is made up of different energies or feelings and how they can affect you.

Again, it is extremely important to stress that these observations should not be perceived as judgments. Strive to see situations as neither good nor bad, but just as they are. We are simply looking at how situations affect our state of being (thoughts and physical reactions), and feeling the differences between them.

EXERCISE: JUMPING IN

The only way to have these concepts work for you is to try them yourself. If you think this exercise is ridiculous (because you're a pro at this mindful stuff now), then that's just a judgment you can investigate, can't you?

» Walking in Gelatin:

  • Imagine that all of the open space of the world through which you move has solidified, like clear gelatin.

- All of the air has become a tangible substance that blends into all of the physical objects in the world: trees, cars, people, animals, etc. However, you can continue to move through this substance as if it were air, no differently than you move through the world today.

- Become aware of the feeling of this substance all around you and pay attention to it continually, as if you're feeling your whole body at once, not just focusing on a part of your body in particular.

- Give your full attention to what you feel or sense around you and pay less attention to your thoughts.

- Like swimming through water, your body may perceive changes in temperature and changes in flow.

- Try out this feeling in a variety of places. Does the area you are in feel like a still pond (nature), a slow-moving stream (suburbia), a raging white-water rapid (a busy mall), or a tumultuous ocean (a dance club)? Can you sense a difference in how your body feels?

- Become aware of how your bodily reactions can affect your thoughts. In these different situations, is your mind more active and agitated, or is it naturally quiet and still?

THE PHYSICAL WORLD

Like water adapting to its environment, everything in the world has a feeling or vibration to it. Differences in energy manifest in countless combinations in the physical world, just as each person has his or her own unique personality with varying levels of energy. For example, compare a dilapidated, abandoned part of town to a thriving, upscale avenue full of shops and boutiques, or a contaminated waste site to a pristine nature preserve.

Reflecting on these examples may elicit a physical or emotional response, and shift your attention in small ways, as if you were in that place. This can happen even when looking at pictures of different places and situations.

Now imagine how you would feel physically and mentally if you were to spend a few days in each of these areas. For most people, if you were in the dilapidated or polluted areas, you would likely feel sad, depressed, and even physically tired or exhausted. Whereas in the flourishing and thriving areas, you would likely feel energized, invigorated, optimistic, and peaceful.

PHYSICAL IN-ACTION

Periodically people will have epiphanies while discussing this topic in my workshops. In one case, a gentleman began to realize how his living situation had been affecting his mental and physical health. He lived in San Francisco, which contains vastly different neighborhoods backing up to one another.

He stated that he had lived in the city for many years and had always enjoyed living in a busy urban setting. To save money, he had moved to one of the "seedier" neighborhoods about a year previously.

Upon reflection, it dawned on him that since moving to that location, his health and mental outlook had declined significantly. He recalled that, prior to living in that location, he was happier and more energetic. Friends had even expressed concern about the changes they had noticed in his behavior, but no one considered his living situation as a possible cause of these changes.

For the first time in his life, he had been having difficulty sleeping, was often depressed, and felt a lack of energy. Putting two and two together, he realized that whenever he returned home from his job, which he greatly enjoyed, his mood and outlook would decline.

Soon after this epiphany, he began to closely monitor his states of mind and validated his theory that his mood and physical condition felt worse after he returned home. To test his theory further, he house-sat for a friend for a few weeks in an area of town where he always felt comfortable and at ease.

Soon his previous energy levels returned and remained constant throughout the day. He became more optimistic and happy in general. When he completed his house-sitting and returned home, because he was monitoring his physical and mental state closely, the reappearance of the low states and lack of energy was very apparent.

He quickly made plans to relocate to another area of town, where he was more comfortable living. Soon after relocating, he began feeling a greater sense of equilibrium.

Here the participant was fortunate to be able to get away from his home and neighborhood long enough to regain his former positive attitude. With that as a baseline, he felt the impact of his return in a more pronounced way.

If we live in a location for a long period of time, we become accustomed to how the area feels. This can make it difficult to be aware of how the energy affects us, since we don't know what it is like to feel otherwise.

If we are unable to live in another location in order to see how it feels to be away from our normal environment, then spending time in nature, or by a body of water, can serve to cleanse and calm our body and mind. These excursions can provide a level of clarity to help set a baseline if needed.

Not only where we live, but also our work location and places we like to hang out have an impact on us. Interestingly, some people prefer pristine areas, while others enjoy more rundown locations, regardless of how they feel physically. This is something that can provide insight and is worth examining. Again, neither is good or bad, right or wrong (no judgments required).

ON A LARGER SCALE

Taking it a step further, the feeling of an area will also contribute to the culture. In the same way we can compare the personalities of individual people, we can contrast the attitudes of cities such as Manhattan, Los Angeles, and Chicago. Each of these has its own vibrancy that allows certain things to thrive, and people are attracted to them for this reason.

If you've had an opportunity to visit these locations, you've experienced for yourself the different energy of these vastly different cultures. Perhaps, while you were there, you even started adopting local characteristics. You picked up your pace in New York or slowed it down in the Midwest.

You may have been extremely uncomfortable in a particular location because you felt like there was no way you could fit in long-term; conversely, you might have felt as if you could stay in another indefinitely because it resonated with you so profoundly.

If you've visited or lived in a large city such as Manhattan or San Francisco, you might have noticed that the environment can shift even within a single block. One block may be a bustling area with many stores and businesses; then, you turn the corner, and you're in a rundown area where you feel vastly different. If you're paying attention, you may even find that you become anxious or experience bodily discomfort, such as your muscles tightening or some fatigue in your body.

The point is, all of these locations have subtle and not-so-subtle impacts on our being and state of mind. If we're not mindful of how our environment affects us, we may incorrectly believe there's something wrong with us emotionally, or blame our feeling on an unrelated situation we're currently struggling with in our lives.

IMPACTS OF THE WORLD

Countries, states, cities, and neighborhoods all have different feelings and can affect our states of being. With practice we can begin to notice the impact they have on us to some degree. Like circling an island in a kayak and experiencing the relationships between the ocean, the land, and our boat, we can start to understand how an environment affects our attitudes, moods, and feelings.

Think again of walking through a world of gelatin, where our mind is quiet and we are paying attention exclusively to our physical body. Imagine you are walking through Times Square in New York and are acutely aware of your senses. At almost any time of the year, you would be surrounded by hundreds of people. Your movement would blend with, or be in conflict with, the currents of people moving down the street. Meanwhile your senses would be assaulted by advertisements for Broadway shows you're being told you should see, by clothing in storefronts you're being told you should purchase, or by the makeup store that will make you look as beautiful as the model or celebrity displayed in the front window.

Unless you are focused, you will probably feel overwhelmed by this environment, exhausted yet simultaneously energetic, your body tense and nervous, in complete sensory overload.

Now compare that feeling with the feeling produced by taking a hike on a gorgeous spring day in a beautiful and serene nature preserve, devoid of people. In this situation, more than likely, your body is relaxed, your mood is calm and contemplative, and you feel profoundly peaceful.

Nature has a magical way of rejuvenating our bodies and minds. For most of us, just looking at pictures of beautiful islands, trees, flowers, lakes, oceans, and rivers can elicit feelings of peace and tranquility. It's as if when we look at them, our bodies give a subtle sigh of relief.

As mentioned previously, driving or walking through a run-down area may decrease your energy levels and cause you to feel sad or depressed, while in a more cultivated part of town, you're energized and alert. You also may feel more or less comfortable in one or the other area, which will also affect your state of being.

If you walk through a college campus, you might feel youthful and hopeful, with a sense of vigor and excitement. *(Although, if you were to walk through it during finals week, you might find you are nervous or stressed.)*

HOME WORK

Many people find it difficult to be comfortable or at ease in their homes if their house is a mess. With increasingly busy lives, we find we have less time to keep the house clean, and may resign ourselves to simply keeping it as manageable as possible.

If there are several people living together, especially with young children, we may give up altogether.

We may get used to it looking so cluttered, to the point where it becomes the norm. However, often when we decide to clean up and put things in order, we feel more at peace and optimistic, and regain a sense of organization and accomplishment in our lives. We may even wonder how we lived with our house in such a mess for so long, and vow never to have it get away from us again, at least until we get busy again.

Might our living situation be a reflection of our state of mind? While it may be a stereotype, a teenager's bedroom can be a picture of chaos. During this stage of life, the world is a very dramatic place as we search for meaning and understanding. We struggle to find our identities and sort out just where we fit in the world. Our minds are chaotic and our environment reflects that.

As adults we tend to decorate and furnish our environment in ways that reflect our preferences, and perhaps even our character. Some prefer modern furniture, others are drawn to antiques. Some desire a very full home, while others are minimalists. If you are passionate about your home environment, pay attention to your level of comfort when you are in a home that is drastically different than yours. Are you physically or mentally uncomfortable in these environments?

Similarly, we try to live in areas where we feel comfortable or where we feel we belong. Some people choose midtown Manhattan, while others choose a small town in Iowa. Neither is better, they're just different.

EXERCISE: CLEANING UP OUR ACT

(No, this exercise was not included at the request of your mother. Although she did ask if you've increased the number of peas you eat at dinner from fifteen to twenty.)

» Pay attention to how you feel in your home before and after it's cleaned.

- Take time to clean your home when it becomes significantly disheveled.

- Before starting, take a mental snapshot of how the place looks and how you feel in the space, mentally and physically.

- Set aside all of your judgments about cleaning and focus intently on each activity while you're executing it: vacuuming, sweeping, straightening, or dusting.

- When you're done, take in how the space feels when it's organized and clean. How do you feel in the space now?

- Compare that feeling to the mental snapshots you took at the beginning of the exercise.

- Notice how you perceive your home in the days following this exercise.

SIMILARITIES

Like our feelings about our home, we have different comfort levels with the things we interact with in the world. If you look at your favorite places to hang out or frequent, you may notice similar characteristics among them.

For example, do you find you are more comfortable in newly opened venues or established places? Perhaps you have a fondness for antique-themed settings. Do you favor neighborhoods in your town that are similar, such as historic or newly renovated ones? Do you prefer chain stores and restaurants over independents? Do you prefer places that are frequented by hip crowds or by more conservative ones? Younger crowds or older ones?

On the flip side, by noticing what you're attracted to, you'll also start to notice what you have aversions to, and the places you tend to avoid. You may feel anxious in expensive restaurants or annoyed in family-themed ones. Again, these should not be taken as judgments. The point is simply to start becoming aware of your preferences.

As you work on this, you also may start to notice how your state of mind is impacted by these preferences. This insight provides a tremendous advantage to you in your quest for a deepening sense of awareness through mindfulness. If you can understand how a certain environment affects you, you can proactively plan how to handle it if you are required to spend time there. You can anticipate your probable states of mind and how your energy levels will be affected, and think about what you can do to avoid being adversely affected.

It is also tremendously insightful to look at why you have strong aversions to certain places. Again, it's not judging, it's self-awareness. If something that you experience limits you in some way, you can examine it and explore how you can change that behavior.

EXERCISE: HANGING OUT

Reflect on the places you like to frequent and see if you can identify any trends or similarities in their energy.

» For example, when you go to a restaurant, are you more comfortable in a diner, a chain restaurant, or a finer establishment? Antique-themed restaurants or those with modern art and atmosphere? Are you uncomfortable in restaurants of other cultures?

» Look for trends in your preferences in restaurants, clothing stores, coffee houses, grocery stores, and malls. Do you go out of your way to shop at specific stores because you just like them better?

» How do you feel when you are in different neighborhoods in your city?

  • How does your body feel when you are in a new or revitalized area? How do you feel when you're in a dilapidated or rundown area of town? Again, neither is "good" or "bad," they're just different.

INFLUENCES IN THE MEDIA

In interacting with the world, one of the greatest challenges we face on a daily basis is dealing with fears produced and fostered by the media. Fear is a means of controlling people, getting them to act or react in a certain way. Of all the emotions, fear has the greatest power to motivate people to action.

When we sense fear, we do all we can to escape the feeling. And fear has the power to completely overpower us. It can break us down and make us feel helpless, or it can elicit reactions such as outrage.

People who feel powerless in the face of a looming threat can be easily incited and manipulated. Governments, extreme religious organizations, political parties, and the media know this all too well and use it to their advantage.

Political advertisements and speeches have become the worst offenders in using fear to elicit a response. Every few years we are inundated with political advertisements that lambast opponents and warn of the apocalypse that will ensue should the other guy win the election.

Many religious organizations are quick to point out the faults of other religions and the price that non-believers will pay.

Media and news outlets purposely present sensationalized stories to lure viewers in and keep them coming back for more. The media will often present information in a gossipy format, making you feel that to be part of the "in crowd" and "own" the information that only exclusive people can own, you must tune into their broadcasts.

Information has become like currency, and if we own a coveted piece of information, our value goes up. We perceive that we are more informed than others, and are thus in a better position to make correct decisions.

When reading or watching the news, it can be helpful to pay attention to your reactions, both immediate and lasting impressions. How does one outlet's portrayal of the news make you feel vs. another's? Do you question what you are told, or do you take it as fact? How does this affect your state of mind? If you read or hear the news in the morning and you find the content upsetting, how long does that feeling stay with you, and how does it impact your view of the world that day?

TRUTH IN ADVERTISING

Advertising also operates by employing its best friend, insecurity, or the feeling of not being in control. Advertisers know they can spur you to buy their products by establishing them as the norm, the standard. If you do not purchase the product, then you do not belong.

Often their messages imply that there is something wrong with you, eliciting a sense of fear. To remedy that fear, all you have to do is purchase their product. *(So convenient! Who knew?)* Cleverly, they also target those who want to be different by suggesting that, if you don't want to be mistaken as belonging to the norm, you'll want to use their product. *(You can run, but you can't hide.)*

Advertising tells us how we "should" look, what we "should" be eating and drinking, what products "should" make us happy and give us a sense of belonging or improve our stature. *("Clueless consumer, what are you thinking? You're nothing without me.")* It provides definitions that we can then add to our stories. "If you're this kind of person, then you must use this product because all the other folks who are this same kind of person are using it. Don't you want to be like them?" *(Beware your fall from grace should you not.)*

It's advertisers' job to understand your insecurities and play directly to them. If they can make you feel insecure enough, then you will go out and purchase their products to alleviate that feeling of insecurity, of fear.

At some level, everyone is seeking their tribe, the place they belong, where they feel secure. Associations with like-minded individuals validate our own feelings and mind states. Advertising and the media work by telling you where you should belong and what it takes to belong.

For example, if you purchase a certain brand of clothing, then you'll belong to a specific group of people. Your style will be a reflection of your economic class and allow you to display to the world the characteristics you value.

Insecurities provoked by advertisers can become very deeply seated within us. We may start to question our decisions or feel as if there is something wrong with us, which leads to sad and depressed states of mind. We may then come to believe that only through obtaining that particular product will we find salvation.

TUNED IN? BETTER TO TUNE OUT

The key to mindfulness with regard to the media is to be aware of when you are reacting to advertisements or other presentations and how that reaction is manifesting.

Notice if you have an emotional reaction to what you see. Do you react with fear, longing, shame, outrage, disappointment, or relief? What is the core of your emotional response?

For example, if you see an advertisement for a new tech product that you don't have, do you feel upset because you're behind the times compared to other people in your social circle? Is it a feeling of missing out on something, or of not having enough? Is it anger? Is it sadness? Why is this feeling present? Does it feel authentic or have you been told you "should" feel that way?

When watching news on television, do you feel despondent, outraged, exhausted, helpless? When reading the latest fashion magazines, do you feel unworthy, unattractive, or sorry for yourself?

If you do have any of these reactions, the first step is to be aware of them and try to identify precisely when you started to feel them. What prompted them? In time you can learn to identify their sources and then ask yourself if the reactions are authentically yours, or just something you've been led to believe by the media. As mentioned earlier, many news organizations are pushing political agendas; they want you to feel outraged so that you'll buy into and support their goals.

If the reactions do feel authentic, you can begin to work through why this is the case. For example, if you regularly become despondent and depressed when looking through fashion magazines, it may be a result of low self-esteem. If that's the case, you can ask where and how that feeling originated and look for the different ways it manifests. Was it because you were taunted as an adolescent by your peers? Perhaps it was due to comments from an overbearing parent? In your teens, did you constantly compare yourself to others (as most teens do) out of a desire for acceptance?

In time, you may be able to understand why others acted as they did and recognize that their actions reflected their own issues and really had nothing to do with you. You just happened to be there. You can investigate why you put so much importance on what other people think of you. These are often not easy questions to ask ourselves, but if you're willing to inquire, you may be able to let go of that influence and release yourself from that burden.

Or you may discover that these feelings are in fact completely due to media influence—that you continually compare yourself to the (airbrushed and digitally altered) models in the magazines and developed the idea that the only way you will gain acceptance, admiration, or respect in society is to look the way they do. You may then notice that this is exactly the message pushed by the media: that it is only through your appearance that you will earn acceptance and approval. But whose acceptance and approval do you need and why exactly do you need it?

I CAN RELATE

Other people also affect our state of being, either en masse or through one-on-one relationships.

Everyone has their unique personality, which comes through in how we present ourselves to the world, what we choose to wear, our physical stamina, the food we eat, and even what we think, the thoughts we hold in our minds. Our closest friends often possess personality traits similar to our own; we say that we "have a lot in common." Frequently these are people we were comfortable with on our first meeting. When dating, for the most part, we are attracted to certain types of people, "our type."

REACH OUT AND TOUCH

People affect us in a variety of ways—some less apparent than others—through the connections we have with them.

Many of us have had the experience where we begin thinking of someone, then suddenly the phone rings, and it's that person on the other end. We nonchalantly say, "I was just thinking about you." *(Insert* Twilight Zone *theme music here.)*

To visualize this concept, imagine that there are lines of energy that connect us to the people we know. Some of those lines can be thick and strong like steel cable, while others are thinner and weaker, like wisps of smoke. Typically, with our closest friends and family members, the lines are stronger, and with our casual acquaintances, weaker.

When you focus on someone, you pull on that line to the other person. If someone you have a strong connection to is going through a difficult time and looking to you for support, he may pull on that line with a good amount of strength, which may leave you feeling depleted and weak. In a way, whenever you focus on that person, you are holding his energy inside your mind, in the same way that thinking of images of nature produces feelings associated with them.

From a mindfulness perspective, it's interesting and helpful to observe how people affect us, and how we affect them.

Perhaps you have a friend who is an incarnation of Eeyore from *Winnie the Pooh*, someone who sees the glass as perpetually half-empty (if not completely empty); that is, a person who sees the world through a negative lens. If you know someone like this, try an experiment where you monitor your energy level before you meet and talk with this person, and then check in with yourself afterward and see how you feel. Try this with all of your relationships, and see if you notice any trends.

On the flip side, perhaps there are people you absolutely love to be around because they are so energetic that they actually lift you up. They shift you higher when you are feeling low. You seek them out to help you with difficult questions and situations. This is what many noted preachers or spiritual teachers do, and is one of the reasons we seek them out. Their presence is so calming or soothing to our being.

With our closest friends, the give-and-take of energy is typically quite balanced. We comfort and soothe each other in difficult times, and celebrate together in good times. We thrill to see the other grow and thrive. They make us feel that we are not alone in the world. We have a place where we fit in and are accepted as we are.

EXERCISE: I CAN'T GET YOU OUT OF MY HEAD

Try the following exercises the next time these situations arise:

» If you're thinking about someone excessively, see if there is a reason why they may be on your mind.

- Is there something you're expecting from them or want from them, or does their mental presence seem totally random?

- If you're confident that you're not stalking them, call them and see whether the feeling subsides after you hang up.

- If it's because you're upset with them, realize there is more power in not focusing on them than giving them control of your consciousness, which is essentially what you're doing by focusing on them.

» When you find yourself thinking about people throughout the day, notice whom you're thinking about and when you're thinking about them, and pay attention to how you feel emotionally when you focus on them.

» If your mind is relatively calm and someone pops in from out of the blue, make a note of when it occurred and how you felt. If they continue to stay in your attention, try reaching out and making contact with them. Afterward, see if they continue to come into your mind.

HYPOTHESIS

Monitoring your relationships with other people can be hugely insightful with regard to the beliefs you've created or been taught.

For example: You notice that whenever you spend time around a particular individual, you become exhausted, mentally and physically, as a result of their pervasive negative attitude. After noticing this, you may not want to make yourself as available to them as you have in the past. It's not that you need to isolate yourself from them completely; you may just want to become a little more strategic in your interactions with them.

Of course, helping the person change his attitude is always a compassionate course of action; but if you find that he doesn't want to change, that he is completely happy in his negative state and you are continually drained after interacting with him, then something needs to shift.

If you notice that you think about a certain individual often, this is a good opportunity to look at why you are focusing on them. Are you hoping that this person will provide you with something that you feel you are lacking?

Again, these exercises should not lead to judgments against other people, or yourself. This is all simply part of self-awareness and discovery.

DISRUPTING THE STATUS QUO

People change slowly over time, based on their life experiences, or sometimes they can change very quickly in response to a specific event. As we mature, our interests may change, our tastes may change, and the way we think may change.

This can pose difficulties in romantic relationships or close friendships because, if one person starts to change, the other may not like the changes that are taking place. One partner may feel they are losing the person they fell in love with or are close to, as well as the comfort and control they've had in the relationship.

If someone sees their partner or friend changing, they may feel threatened and think that they should change too; however, they may also fear what that change may entail. Many times, in these situations, the one fearing the change will try to hold the other back.

Through mindfulness, as you let go of fears and negative actions and reactions, you will inevitably change. Acquaintances might find this uncomfortable, since you are no longer the person they knew; more, this may cause them to question their own perceived inadequacies.

Change can make human relationships extremely complicated.

PEOPLE EN MASSE

Needless to say, if one-on-one relationships affect our energy levels, then you can imagine the kind of impact a large group of people can have on us.

For example, imagine that you are at the most popular mall in your city on the Friday after Thanksgiving. *(Feel free to take a moment to prepare yourself mentally for this, if you need to.)* You are surrounded by hundreds of people all starting their frantic search for holiday merchandise. There is a frenetic energy in the air, as shoppers comb through aisles and racks of merchandise, worrying whether what they are choosing will please the recipient. *(Or honestly not caring if it would please the recipient, it's on sale for God's sake! They damn well better like it.)*

While you are in this environment, you may feel stressed, exhausted, frustrated, and even depressed. You may even begin acting frantically yourself, even if you walked into the mall in a peaceful state, not stressed in the least about your shopping plans.

Let's look at another example: If you're stuck in a lengthy traffic jam, more than likely you'll be frustrated and anxious, like everyone around you. Your body will be tense, your shoulders will rise up to your ears, and you may even start honking your horn in aggravation or slump down in your seat in resignation. Your body will become tired from impatience. But if you stop to reflect on it, unless you're running late for an appointment, are you in a hurry to be anywhere or are you just unhappy about being slowed down?

The influence of group behavior is most evident when large-scale conflicts arise, creating a mob or herd mentality. In 1992, the verdict in the closely watched Rodney King trial in Los Angeles created a frenzy of rioting and crime. It was as if there was an open invitation for anyone who had ever wanted to create a disturbance to go out and do so.

The riots in London in mid-2011 had a similar outcome. Starting as a protest against the authorities, this event quickly escalated out of control and led to widespread general lawlessness and looting. It's as if there's an infectious state of mind: If some people are breaking the law and getting away with it, why shouldn't I do it too?

MINDFULLY PREPARED

Understanding what you are walking into in any situation can be incredibly helpful. As a mindfulness exercise, when you know you are about to enter a place where you will be surrounded by many people, monitor your state of mind before entering the area. If you are going with the express intent of accomplishing something specific, notice whether that changes once you are in the crowded environment.

Pay attention to how your body feels and your energy level throughout the experience. How do you feel as you leave that environment? Over time you can create your own strategies for either avoiding these kinds of situations in general, or navigating through them with minimal loss of life.

FROM OUT OF NOWHERE

Another participant in one of my workshops was diligently monitoring her thoughts in order to understand why she suffered from so much internal anger.

Over time she had become extremely mindful of when the anger would arise and the triggers that would prompt it. She related the following story about a situation in which she became acutely aware of feeling the energy of another person and how it affected her state of mind.

> One afternoon I was running some errands and was waiting on the corner for the light to turn so I could cross the street. A few other people were also on the corner near me. Suddenly I started indulging in my common habit of getting into fights with people in my mind over things they had done that I had found to be unjust. I was a good minute or two into this fight when I realized what I was doing.
>
> Immediately I stopped and asked myself why I was indulging in these angry thoughts. I tried to retrace my steps and see if I could figure out what trigger had been pulled and when they had started. This had surprised me, as I had actually been in a really happy mood most

of the day. I came up blank. I couldn't identify a trigger. So, by coincidence, I began to look around me.

Immediately I noticed that a man standing right next to me was silently fuming. His face was red and his eyes were squinched and set like he was ready for war. Glad that I wasn't on the receiving side of that face, I nonchalantly stepped away from him. It dawned on me in that moment that it's possible I was feeling HIS anger, that it wasn't mine and it didn't belong to me. What else could it have been?

Running through my arsenal of therapies, I quickly diffused my own anger. Later I would begin to see how often this occurred and it was more frequent than I would ever have believed possible. It got to the point that I was able to pinpoint this occurring consistently with specific acquaintances and situations.

The power of this insight was that it allowed me to quickly identify and disengage my habits of getting angry when I knew that the source was an outside influence.

EXERCISE: MONITORING

Being aware of sudden changes in your state of mind can help you recognize when you may be picking up on the feelings of people around you.

» While being mindful, pay particular attention to any dramatic changes in your state of mind or if you start thinking something that seems out of place.

> » If you notice an inexplicable change, pay attention to your location and who might be in close proximity to you.

THINGS IN THE WORLD (STUFF)

Over time we tend to collect objects: home decorations, knickknacks, gifts, etc. Some people prefer to possess very few items—minimalists—while others, hoarders, collect as much as they can. Most of us fall somewhere in between.

Each object we possess connects us with a certain time or place, and a feeling or emotion. If we received the object from someone, whom did we receive it from and what were the circumstances around receiving or acquiring it? A story is created around that object. *(Was it a holiday gift that we have no idea why anyone would give it to us? I'm sorry, that's right. Those are complete anomalies. We've worked through this. My apologies.)*

If it's an object we purchased, did we think the object might do or provide something for us? An object can be connected with one or many states of mind. So when we focus on that object, we will often ruminate on its story, and all of the emotions attached to it come flooding in.

More often than not, we're not even aware that we are spending time reflecting on these stories. They are simply interwoven into the hundreds of other stories churning in our consciousness of which we're unaware.

Perhaps you inherited an item, a vase for example, from a departed family member toward whom you had very negative feelings. *(Don't worry, your secret is safe with us, this is a circle of trust.)* You received this vase after their passing and, as a good family member, you felt obligated to hold on to it and display it.

Every time you glance at it, you experience a momentary feeling of dislike, disgust, or guilt, however subtle. If you step back, you can observe that this is just one of hundreds of items that can pull your attention in the world every day.

You could ask yourself why you should hold on to this vase. Is it out of a sense of obligation? What is that obligation based on? Can you throw it out? If not, can you store it in the garage or in a closet somewhere and only bring it out when family members visit?

If it's valuable, I would recommend selling this theoretical vase and giving the proceeds to a local charity. If it's not valuable, then donate or destroy it. In other words, free yourself of the object. Alternatively, with effort, you can try to change your outlook and make peace with the relationship it calls to mind, turning the vase into something that triggers good feelings. It can be a significant act of personal accomplishment to change that energy around, but may not always be warranted.

As most of us know, it can be exhausting to move from one residence to another. One reason is that everything we own has a feeling and a story tied to it. When we pack up our belongings to move, physically touching these objects can bring up the memories and emotions associated with them. This can be exhausting.

Again, our minds really don't know the difference between what is happening now and what we're focusing our thoughts on. We are, in fact, reliving all of the moments tied to those objects.

In the same way, music can take us back to times in our lives that we may have unpleasant feelings about. Hearing a specific song can create a visceral reaction. If we are not paying attention, we may find that when we are listening to the music, we begin to tap into the sad memories associated with it, and before we know it, we're wallowing in a state of sadness and not even sure how we got there (*cigarette in one hand, martini in the other, soft jazz in the background, and spilling our guts to the bored, underpaid bartender*).

WINDOW DRESSING

Our clothing can also tie us to a time or certain events in the past. Perhaps we wore a specific suit or outfit for a job that caused us to feel depleted and depressed for months or years, until we were able to change jobs. How do you feel when you put on that suit now? When you look at it, does it remind you of that job and those challenging years?

Do you have the desire and energy to turn that into a positive experience in your mind? Can that outfit now serve to remind you of your strength in being able to change jobs, or does it pull you back to the difficult time? If you're not able to change it or you don't see a need to, then either destroying it or donating it might be a good option.

Like our other objects, our clothes also have stories connected to them, especially if particular items were worn for specific occasions or events. Our clothing can also be a reflection of, or even influence, our states of mind. When we go for a job interview or on a date with someone we want to impress, we dress up. We take extra care to make ourselves more appealing and consciously attend to the details.

Conversely, in our day-to-day activities, we may throw on whatever's handy or comfortable when we interact with the world. Unless we are concerned with "keeping up appearances" (something you might want to mindfully examine) when we make our weekend trip to the grocery store, we often grab the closest pair of sweats to wear because we are not concerned about interacting with others there. *(Until, of course, you inevitably run into someone in the bakery section, chocolate cake in hand, look of guilt on face. Hate that!)*

If you are going somewhere with a group of people and everyone is much better dressed than you, then you will likely feel uncomfortable or out of place for the duration of the event. Similarly, you may feel uncomfortable if you are overdressed.

People react to how you are dressed and you react to how others around you are dressed. At some level you know that the judgments you make about others are the same judgments they make about you, and being on the receiving end is much more traumatizing than being the sender.

All of these situations can have an impact on our state of mind at any time. We need to become aware of when it's occurring and how and why we are reacting as we are. Once we understand what's happening, we can make changes in our responses if we choose to.

PLAYING DRESS UP

You may find that when you wear formal wear, or even a suit, you hold yourself differently and may even walk and talk in a sharper, more distinguished way. If you're in beat-up jeans, a T-shirt and flip flops, then you probably behave in a more relaxed manner.

Notice how clothing shifts your state of attention, and use this to your advantage. Perhaps you are rewriting your resumé and sending it out to recruiters, or calling businesses about job opportunities. How do you think you will present yourself in a phone interview if you're wearing a suit versus wearing pajamas? Do you think you'll hold yourself differently, that you'll speak differently? Absolutely!

EXERCISE: CLOTHES MAKE THE MAN

One of the easiest things to notice about your attitude is
how you feel when wearing different kinds of clothing.

» When you wear formal clothing, such as a business suit
or outfit, how do you feel?

  • Do you have automatic judgments about differ-
    ent types of clothing and the people who typically
    wear them?

  • Take some time to try putting on different clothes
    and see how you feel when you wear them.

  • Do you find that you carry yourself differently
    when you wear a suit compared to when you're
    wearing jeans and a T-shirt?

  • Do your mannerisms and your behavior change as
    well?

DISCERNMENT

Know thyself.

- Thales (attrib.) [xxxviii]

The cultivation of discernment, that is, understanding how
and why you are affected by the world and the people around
you, is one of the most powerful aspects of a mindfulness practice. Through it, you can begin to recognize what you are feeling
at any moment; what comes from your own thoughts, ideas, and
proclivities and what should be attributed to your environment,

friends, and relations; what is inside you versus outside of you; organic versus imposed—you get the idea.

In time you can begin to see where and how your ideas and assumptions have been influenced or manipulated by the media, or reflect the ideas and ideals of other people.

EXERCISE: DEVELOPING CLARITY

Use the following exercises to assist you in learning about the various ways you are impacted by the world.

» As with all mindfulness exercises, start by reminding yourself to check in on your state of mind and what's holding your attention, what you are focused on.

- Perhaps hourly to start with, set an alarm or use some other mechanism to remind you to check in with yourself.

» When checking in, ask yourself:

- "What is my current state of mind?"

- "Where has my mind traveled to since the last time I checked in with myself?"

- "What experiences have I been through since that time?"

» Things you can reflect upon as the situations arise:

- "Whom do I think about throughout the day and how do I feel when I think about that person?"

- "How do I feel in different clothes? Do I carry myself differently and act differently?"

- "How do I feel in different neighborhoods or around different people?"

» Try to spot how energy changes in different neighborhoods. Go to different extreme (but safe) areas and purposefully examine how you feel mentally and physically in them. Take a snapshot of your state of mind before (so you're aware of your general state), then take a snapshot during and after.

» Think about the places you like to frequent and see if you identify any trends or similarities in the energy of those places.

» Notice over-the-top changes in your thoughts or emotions. Notice emotions that seem out of place or out of the blue.

» If you've been able to identify what some of your biggest issues are—anger or anxiety, for example—try to determine how and under what circumstances these states of mind arise. Can you identify any specific triggers?

- Do they begin to arise around certain individuals or in certain situations?

- If they arise in specific situations, when and how are those triggers pulled? Once you understand how they operate, you can proactively avoid the situations or people that evoke these states of mind until you gain greater control over them and you're no longer affected to such a degree.

> • Ask yourself why. Why are you reacting in this manner? Try not to blame it on another person. You can change yourself much more easily than you can change others. Really look beneath the surface to see what's underlying this emotion. Why does this matter so much to you?
>
> *(Lastly, be sure to say "hello" from me when you're having these internal conversations. Sometimes they can feel so one-sided.)*

HIKING THOUGH WORLDS

As I have suggested throughout this chapter, it can be extremely beneficial to seek respite in nature when working through difficult states of mind. *(Because of issues I was working through, there were times in my past when excursions into nature would happen almost daily. Drama, drama, drama…)* Gratefully, upon leaving these areas, I would always feel better than I had when I arrived: uplifted, with a new sense of clarity and possibility.

Fortunately, I lived in an area where many pristine and beautiful places were within driving distance. One place in particular was so soothing that it was easy for me to quiet my mind down and give my focus to the beauty that surrounded me at every step. I would walk for hours, focusing on my footsteps, chanting peaceful affirmations, and stopping periodically to sit and appreciate the music that only nature can provide (always an original world-premiere tune, never again to be replicated).

To reach this beautiful wooded area, you needed to walk through a small open field before entering a canopy of trees and taking a trail that followed a stream for several miles. When I first began these hikes, it would take at least a half hour for me to quiet down once I was on the trail. As my practice evolved, I would focus on calming my mind as soon as I left home, so that

I could appreciate this special place the entire time I was there. Eventually, by the time I arrived my mind was already pretty quiet, and soon the walk through the field became part of the hike as well.

I also noticed that something interesting would happen when I entered the tree canopy. A noticeable shift would occur, both mentally and physically. It was as if I had passed through an invisible wall. On the far side of that wall, the world went away, or it was a different world. There the story of my life didn't matter, didn't even exist. My body felt lighter and the things that weighed me down seemed to drop off instantaneously. When I returned to my car, I could feel the same shift in the other direction. But of course now I was returning to a different world. It wasn't because the world had changed; it was because I was no longer the same person I had been when I started the hike.

Over time, I would notice this phenomenon occurring in different places on the hike—these shifts of energy where I would begin to feel lighter and things appeared brighter. Conversely, there were also a few times when, not heeding how I was feeling (aka not being mindful), I would enter areas where, seemingly out of the blue, my thoughts would begin to focus on anger that would amplify quickly. Soon I would start to get a headache or feel nauseous. Once I smartened up, I was able to turn around and leave quickly and, as fast as they had come on, the headache and angry thoughts would begin to subside.

I highly recommend seeking out magical places as part of your practice. It doesn't need to be someplace magnificent; it can be a small park in the middle of a busy city, the shore of a river or lake, or even an art gallery or museum. If you have the opportunity to travel, take time to explore the wonders of nature at your destination, instead of spending all of your time surrounded by buildings and concrete.

KEY POINTS ABOUT CLARITY

- One of the most important parts of cultivating mindfulness is learning to understand and foster clarity. Ultimately you are seeking to discover what you're feeling at any given moment, which part of that is organically your own (your own thoughts, moods, and feelings), and which part is coming from the world—from a location, another person or group of people, or both. This is important because, once you understand when and how you are being affected by things outside of yourself, you can learn how to avoid them or, more importantly, learn to not let them influence you.

- It's like discovering the source of an annoying sound that's been bothering you for hours and shutting it off, eliminating that distraction from your life. You might also find that things that once were sources of great irritation or distress become mild nuisances, or stop bothering you altogether.

- Locations can have subtle and not-so-subtle impacts on our being and state of mind. If we're not being mindful of how our environment affects us, we may believe that there's something wrong with us emotionally, or incorrectly blame what we're feeling on an unrelated situation in our lives.

- Start to notice how your attention is impacted by your preferences. What are you attracted to and what do you have aversions toward? These insights can be of great help in your quest for a deepening sense of awareness through mindfulness.

CHAPTER ELEVEN: HAPPINESS AND GRATITUDE

A thankful heart is not only the greatest virtue, but the parent of all the other virtues.

- Cicero [xxxix]

C'MON GET HAPPY

The idea of happiness is one of the most challenging concepts we encounter in our practice of mindfulness because we have been sold a bill of goods by the world regarding what happiness is and what it takes to obtain it.

As we grow up, we learn that it's not as cut and dried as we've been led to believe and this can lead to feelings of frustration and confusion on many levels.

There have been many books written about happiness in the psychology and self-help genres, and endless classes taught on what it is and how to realize it. While my examination may be similar to things you have heard before, it's important to take happiness into consideration when discussing and practicing mindfulness.

For our purposes, I'm separating the concept of happiness from the concept of being at peace. We may believe that ultimately happiness will bring us peace or that these two concepts may be one and the same, but for now, let's keep them separate.

WAVING AS IT GOES BY

Happiness, or being happy, is an idea, a concept based on an emotional state typically dependent on something occurring, or not occurring, in the world. Like all states of mind, it is transitory in nature; it will come and it will go. However, the idea that happiness is transitory can seem counterintuitive because of what we've come to believe about it.

As children we were told that people lived "happily ever after," suggesting that happiness can and should be a permanent state or destination. As we get older, we continually hear that people "just want to be happy" in their lives and so we strive to obtain the elusive badge of happiness.

We may start to believe that we should be happier than we are, and thus begin to think that there is something wrong with us. If we develop the perception that other people in the world have achieved the badge, we look for reasons to validate that belief. "Of course they're happy, they have x, y and z things which I don't have. Until I too have those things, I will continue to suffer."

We say, "If only I had a faster and sexier car I would be happy," or "If only I could find the right guy or gal, then I'd be happy." "That great house, job, or computer will make me so happy." "If only..." These ideas reflect the belief that something outside of us is required to move us out of our current state of mind, which is lacking in contentment. *X, y* and *z* are the missing ingredients and, without them, we will be, and remain, unhappy and unfulfilled.

But even the Founding Fathers of the United States understood that happiness wasn't something that could be bequeathed. The Declaration of Independence refers to the rights to life, liberty, and the pursuit of happiness. Notice that they say we have a God-given right to life and liberty; however, with that happiness thing, while they acknowledge its importance, there's not much they can do about that... with that one, you're on your own. *(Best of luck, send postcards.)*

IF ONLY...

We also believe that a happy state of mind is better than other states of mind and that we should be dwelling there at all times. We believe that we must get away from, or avoid, other states of mind to live in the land of happiness.

Even the phrase "if only," inherent in so many of our beliefs, reinforces the idea that things are not okay as they are right now in this very moment. It means we believe that we cannot be content as we are. We find ourselves living in a state of want, and imagine that a material object, achievement, or experience will bridge the gap.

Although it may bring with it an enhanced level of comfort or a new appreciation of life, that object can't sustain our happiness, because our state of mind will continue to fluctuate over time as we grow accustomed to having it around. Eventually we come back to the state of wanting where we focus on the next elusive object, which we believe will return us to that temporary place of happiness. If only…

EXERCISE: CONTEMPLATING HAPPINESS

Looking at your idea of happiness can provide tremendous insight. Take some time to examine what you associate with happiness.

For example, do you believe that in this state everything will "go your way"? That you will have no worries and that people and the world will be kind to you? That all of your physical, mental, and social needs will be met without any effort on your part and that you will never be burdened with tumultuous states of mind? That you will acquire everything you've ever wanted? That you will be in continual physical comfort?

» How specifically do you define happiness for yourself?

» Do you create rules and constraints around this state of mind?

» Does your happiness depend on other people or certain situations?

SELLING THE DREAM

Advertising and marketing firms sell to us constantly, telling us that if we possess a particular item we'll be happy. Ads generally use images of people with big smiles on their faces, or people looking dreamily peaceful, as the result of buying some product.

Automobile ads show us people driving contentedly in their new sexy vehicles, cosmetics ads show us women blissfully, ecstatically happy, all because of twelve-hour non-smearing mascara. *(No doubting the value of this miraculous invention, but, honestly, I've walked past plenty of makeup counters in department stores and I have yet to see someone experiencing this level of happiness. However, a man looking at new barbeque grills—now that's a special kind of ecstasy.)*

Whether it's the right electronic device, the newest toy, a yoga or exercise practice, the latest snack food or drink, or the most popular cocktail, we're led to believe that only when we have acquired the advertised product will we be complete. Taking this further, we begin to think that if we don't feel complete generally, there must be something wrong with us. *(Amazingly enough, we've got a product right here to fix all that. If only…)*

These subtle and not-so-subtle messages create a longing for an elusive state. In a barely perceptible way, we look at these advertisements and start to question our own happiness, or compare our lives unfavorably to what's being presented.

"I don't possess that item; will I be happy once I have it? Perhaps I'm lying to myself—I thought I was happy, but I don't look nearly as happy as the folks in that advertisement. Maybe there's something wrong with me. If only (if only) I had that product, I'd experience a deeper, more true and lasting, level of happiness. One, perhaps, that I didn't think possible." *(The Shangri-La of happiness.)*

IT'S A CHOICE

Most folks are about as happy as they make up their minds to be.

- Abraham Lincoln (attrib.) *xl*

While you may have a strong emotional response to the following statement, please take a moment to reflect before making a judgment: ***Happiness is a choice.***

Every state of mind is a choice, really. *(That comment, I hope, will take some of the pressure off... or make the whole thing even more baffling... Eh, to each his own.)*

If we have a hard time controlling our minds and thoughts, then it may be difficult to see how happiness could be a choice, but work with me here.

WORK WITH ME HERE

As mentioned in previous chapters, if our minds are adrift in thoughts of sorrow or sadness—reminiscing about the loss of a loved one or a disagreement with a partner—then our state of mind will temporarily be depressed and sad. Conversely, if our minds are focused on joyful or humorous thoughts, then our state of mind will temporarily be one of happiness.

The key concept in both situations is temporary.

When we are in a state of unawareness or are struggling with our emotions, we feel we have no control over ourselves, that we're trapped in our current state of mind. However, this state of mind will change at some point.

As the earth dances with the sun and moon, every day brings light and every night brings dark. (*Unless you live in the Arctic, where this comparison would totally lose its point; however, you're working with me here, remember?*)

States of mind come and go, it's the nature of thoughts and the mind. And some states of mind last longer than others. In the space of five minutes, you may encounter any or all of these states of mind: hungry, happy, tired, sad, depressed, excited, angry, joyful, cranky. *(On the other hand, you may just be cranky for five months… it happens.)*

Additionally, like the United States, which consists of fifty individual territories, we can easily have fifty unique states of mind, some similar to each other, others drastically different. But they're all states, each with its own overriding characteristics.

Many people are comfortable living in one place, while others wish to relocate to another place, where they believe they'll be more comfortable. Sometimes when they do relocate, they find that they are indeed much happier than where they were before.

Others find that they are uncomfortable with the new place and that it did not live up to their expectations, so they desire to return to their original place. Some places will agree with us, some will leave us feeling unfulfilled. So too will our states of mind.

Some people are actually comfortable in a sad or depressed state of mind. And while they may complain about it, in actuality, they're not willing to change it. This could have to do with their self-esteem, fear of change, or a belief that they're not worthy of another state, among other reasons.

KEEP WORKING WITH ME HERE

Once we understand how our minds behave and how thoughts move through various states, we can begin to change our thought patterns. We can examine why our mind dwells where it does, and train ourselves to avoid the states where we do not wish to spend time.

(As we've discussed before, this is the whole point of this book, in case you weren't paying attention up to now. And if you made it this far without paying attention, that's a pretty impressive feat.)

How long the learning process takes is also a choice; unfortunately, it's difficult to see this while we're in the midst of it. When we come out the other side, though, we can often see that we made things unnecessarily difficult for ourselves.

For example, we might see that we could have implemented a change earlier, and that we were just being resistant—typically because it involved facing fear, guilt, or shame, or giving up a sense of control. On the positive side, recognizing this may allow us to move more quickly through other similar challenges that may arise.

Like exercising our muscles at the gym, we build up strength over time until we are able to lift weights we previously believed to be beyond our capabilities. Similarly our mental strength, or our willpower and ability to focus and concentrate, allows us to look at the truth of why we dwell in certain states of mind and why we might even be uncomfortable with other states, perhaps even uncomfortable with happy states.

Through the practice of meditation and mindfulness, we can condition ourselves to more efficiently redirect our unproductive states of mind toward a more agreeable, peaceful place. Instead of travelling down a dirt road in a car with no shocks, we can locate a freeway that takes us there infinitely faster.

Gradually, we can grow strong enough to choose to no longer visit, even briefly, old unproductive states of mind. Or if we do decide to visit them, perhaps in response to an emotion, we can choose how long we wish to remain there.

In the beginning, you may feel as if you are a slave to your emotions and your varying states of mind, as well as to the circumstances that cause them. You may feel you have no control over what you wish to overcome mentally or that some things are just too big to tackle. But with practice, perseverance, patience, and a large helping of compassion for yourself, you will be amazed at what you can accomplish!

(See, I told you I'd get us there! Thanks for working with me.)

EXERCISE: EXPLORING HAPPINESS

It's important to reflect on your own labels for happiness and your relationship to the concept.

» Do you find that you often engage in thoughts based on the belief that you are lacking something in your life that will bring you happiness or make you complete in some way?

  • Do you find yourself saying things like, "If only x, y, or z would happen, then I'll be happy"?

  • If so, what is the source of this belief and what makes you think this assumption is valid? If it is because you perceive that x, y, and z have produced happiness for other people, how do you know you will experience it the same way?

» Do you believe that specific events in life are meant to bring you happiness?

» Do you believe that happiness can be a constant state of mind?

  • What are the influences that have shaped your definition of happiness (e.g., the media, family, or peers)?

> » Strive to pay attention to the various states of mind you traverse over the course of a day.
>
>   • Do you find that you tend to generalize your overall feeling of how your day went based on a few moments to which you had a strong emotional reaction?

LIFELINES

There should be no shame in working through issues that arise from mindful work. But, if you want to get through states of mind that you don't like, you must be open and willing to look at what is happening beneath the surface.

Some days it may feel like your car is broken down on the side of the road in a particular place, but in due course, if you stand by the road and wave your hands (or call AAA)—instead of waiting for the car to fix itself—you'll get the help you need to move further down the road.

The important thing is, you must actively keep an eye out for potential remedies and continue to try new things, anything that seems feasible. They're not all going to work, but some will. You're stronger than you think, and you should always remember that just being willing to confront and work on your challenges is a great accomplishment in itself.

Consider the alternative. When we give up and just sit back and wait for the solution to come to us, it's as though we're taking up residence in a town and forgetting that we were just passing through, that we're on our way somewhere else.

There are times when you may need to call in professional help to work through certain issues and there should be no shame in doing so. Read books (*Oh wait, you're already doing that, aren't you? I really sincerely hope it's helping, by the way*); take classes; do whatever it takes.

There are some places, like Rhode Island, that you might zip through in a matter of hours; others, like Texas, might take days or weeks (or even years). But eventually you can make it through them, or at least make them less difficult to endure.

DEFINING HAP-PI-NESS

It is said an Eastern monarch once charged his wise men to invent him a sentence, to be ever in view, and which should be true and appropriate in all times and situations. They presented him the words: "And this, too, shall pass away." How much it expresses! How chastening in the hour of pride! How consoling in the depth of affliction!

- Abraham Lincoln [xli]

In your examination of happiness, ask yourself if you believe a state of happiness can exist only when things go your way or when you obtain the things you desire. Are you happy when you satisfy the people around you whose opinions you value? Does achieving something that's important to you, or being recognized for some accomplishment, lead to a state of happiness?

It's important to look at what happiness is to you so that you can be aware of the associations you make. You can then examine the beliefs associated with those dependencies and determine whether they are valid.

Perhaps you feel a sense of happiness when others around you notice your accomplishments (reflections). While there's nothing wrong with this, it's interesting to look at what it means. Ask yourself why this matters to you. Does it fulfill a need to be accepted? If so, then why do you need that acceptance? Is it something you came to believe when you were growing up?

It's quite possible that you won't be able to put your finger on it exactly, which is fine. It's helpful if you can, but if not, you can still try to understand the feelings and emotions around it. What does this approval give you that you don't already have? Do you feel unworthy of happiness unless someone validates you in some way?

At some point you can ask yourself, "Is happiness really what I'm looking for, or am I looking for something else? Perhaps it's a feeling of contentment, a state where I desire nothing—strive to change nothing—where I just dwell peacefully and have a sense that everything is okay just as it is."

EXERCISE: DEFINING HAPPINESS

Our definitions are critical in forming our beliefs. Reflect on the following questions about how you perceive happiness:

» First, look at your definition of happiness and any dependencies associated with it.

- Then ask yourself: "Is this what I am really seeking from my life?"

- Then, probing more deeply: "Why is it that I want that?"

- Then, even deeper: "What keeps me from experiencing that?"

> » If there are things in the physical world that you feel are in your way, do you believe it is possible to change your perceptions about those things? If you perceive that it's another person holding you back, ask yourself whether you've given over control of your state of mind, and have become dependent on them.
>
> » Next, create a list of things that you believe will bring you your defined happiness.
>
> > • Here again, you can ask yourself: "How will each of these things bring me happiness?"
> >
> > • "Will they have a temporary effect or a permanent one?"
> >
> > • Reminder: If the things on your list are tied to the material world, then they will be subject to the rules of this world; they are transitory, they will come and they will go.

WEATHERING YOUR THOUGHTS

As we'll discuss in greater detail later, the counterpart to mindfulness is meditation. During meditation, you can experience profound levels of mental quietude and inner peace.

What you may come to see is that those states of inner peace are always there. They become accessible when your mind is still and you are no longer wrestling with your thoughts. When you can't find them, it's because they're clouded over by the storm of thought currently ruling your mind.

Through building up the muscles used for meditation and mindfulness—focus, concentration and will power—you can abide in these peaceful states for longer periods of time, instead of residing in the turbulent states where you may currently be spending time indefinitely.

GAINING LATITUDE WITH GRATITUDE

One of the most effective tools in our quest for greater peace is gratitude. Typically what keeps us from happiness are thoughts about not having, of being without, those "if only" thoughts. When we're in these states of mind, we're focusing on what we believe is missing from our lives; if we possessed this thing, we would then be happy. *(If only...)*

We dwell on what we do not have, as if there were a void in our life, which, when filled, would bring a sense of completeness or wholeness. This is a manifestation of future- and expectation-based thinking. We are not focusing on what we possess already, and often, what we take for granted. We fail to recognize and appreciate what we already have, what is present in our lives now. By focusing on gratitude for what you have already, what is present now, you can fill the void created by wanting.

Desire sends us running to the world to grab what we believe will bring us satisfaction. Gratitude is stepping back, acknowledging and resting in a sense of completeness with what is, as it is. Once we understand and begin to practice this concept, we find that there is less that we want, or believe we need, from the world, and we are able to see that our lives are very full just as they are.

We can see that our feeling unfulfilled was only a belief that we created. We believed that we lacked something and that, by possessing it, we would be complete. But that feeling of completeness only remains until we again come to believe that we need something else—which happens sooner than we care to admit. This back-and-forth is a vicious cycle, and we become slaves to the world; we are dependent on it for things to "make us" happy.

In time, we will see that the idea that we need something to make us complete contributes to our low states of mind. When we begin to see how complete we are already, we will experience greater peace and happiness in our lives and let go of the belief that we are lacking something or are deficient in some manner.

AS SIMPLE AS A BREATH

We can find opportunities for gratitude in the most basic situations, starting with something we take for granted every day. For many of us, it's our good health.

It requires a shift in perspective. If you are in good health, take some time to reflect on what you are able to do because of it, even something as seemingly mundane as climbing stairs. Perhaps climbing stairs is a daily activity barely worth acknowledging; however, imagine what life is like for someone who does not possess this ability, someone confined to a wheelchair, for example. The ability to climb just a few stairs would make their lives so much easier.

If you do have health challenges, you can still change your perspective from focusing on what ails you to being grateful for the abilities you still have. Doing this shifts the emphasis from what challenges your well-being to that which contributes to your well-being.

And, sadly, it's often not until something is taken from us that we realize its importance and how it contributed to our lives. In so many instances, we do not fully appreciate something because we're so used to it that we take it for granted. Learning to appreciate what you have now will enrich your experience of life and everything it consists of.

Focusing on gratitude will open your heart. It allows you to let go and surrender the things you believe constrain your life. We can even surrender those feelings of needing or wanting.

EXERCISE: CONTEMPLATING GRATITUDE

To make the concept of gratitude really resonate for us, we can choose something we feel deeply grateful for and ask ourselves, "Why am I grateful for this thing?"

» Specifically, look at what it provides. There may be more than one thing. Once you find one reason, many more reasons will likely start to emerge. For example, a beloved pet dog provides companionship, as well as gives you an added sense of security.

» Next, take it a step deeper and explore why the things it provides are important to you.

- This is not something you can do haphazardly; continue to drill down into the "why" until you feel it resonate within your being and fully realize what your life would be like without this gift. Then you will truly know the value of it.

  For example, while your pet provides you with companionship, it also gives you a sense of responsibility for another being. While friends and relations my come and go, your pet remains a constant in your life. Your pet displays unconditional love for and trust in you. When your world is in upheaval, a pet can be a consistent source of joy.

- In exploring your reasons, you may discover much more than you ever took into consideration, which reveals the richness and fullness of your circumstances. You may even come to see the world in a different way.

- Additionally, the desire to change what you possess will lessen. You may even find that the perceived void doesn't exist at all, and is only an idea that you created.

FILL IT TO THE RIM

When we take time to reflect on things for which we are grateful, it can bring a feeling of fullness and contentment in that moment—the opposite of wanting and desiring. Focusing on gratitude fills the false void of not having. Dwelling on our desire for the things we don't possess brings sadness and other low states of mind because it makes us feel incomplete.

When contemplating gratitude, our natural inclination is to look at the larger things that comprise our lives: our health, relationships, dwellings, material belongings. Almost always, we will find that they are sufficient, often more than sufficient, in spite of the fact that they may have perceived flaws.

GRATEFUL MOMENTS

To see a world in a grain of sand
And a heaven in a wild flower,
Hold infinity in the palm of your hand
And eternity in an hour.

- William Blake, "Auguries of Innocence" [xlii]

In looking at the things in your life for which you're grateful, even if you see them as flawed, an interesting thing happens. By breaking the larger things down into smaller components, the "whys," you'll see your life in greater detail.

For example, in contemplating your health, consider your ability to breathe. Granted, your life would be much shorter without this ability, but it also gives you your sense of smell. You can come to appreciate this ability more deeply by reflecting on specific moments, such as encountering the sweet aroma of flowers blooming, the smell of your favorite food filling a room as you walk through the door, or the invigorating scent when you walk past a coffee stand.

All of these experiences bring with them moments of happiness and make you feel more alive and aware. When we are unaware, these moments blend into other moments and the general chaos of our lives. Yet, if you can stop in those moments and recognize how wondrous this ability is and how the scents affect you, however briefly, you can be grateful for the experience. And, even more importantly, you can also be grateful that you didn't miss acknowledging that moment.

As we've repeatedly seen, our experiences in the world are made up of moments. When you begin to see the preciousness of these moments where you are aware of a feeling of gratitude, you'll also see that there are opportunities to be aware of it **all the time**.

The possibilities are endless: a meal shared with loved ones, an unexpectedly beautiful sunset and the peace and calm it brought you, a kind gesture witnessed between two people, a cool breeze on a hot day, the sound of a bird singing against the cacophony of city traffic, running late and missing your bus so that you were able to help a woman with her baby stroller get on the next one—these are all moments to feel gratitude. When you recognize how much the experience means to you, in these moments where you feel a sense of gratitude, you'll want to savor every moment of that experience and appreciate its meaning even more.

A LONG-TERM LOVE AFFAIR

When you regularly recognize the beauty of being present and acknowledging gratitude, you will start to feel a greater sense of contentment and peace in your life. You will see that your circumstances are more optimistic than you had previously believed. You may find yourself wanting less, and see that there are fewer and fewer voids to fill.

You'll find that there is beauty all around you in the world, in places you never thought to look (perhaps even in a grain of sand), unfolding in every moment. Further, and even more important in my opinion, you will be grateful for the opportunity and awareness to see and appreciate these moments. You may come to find that the thing you're most grateful for is the ability to experience gratitude.

RESISTANCE

If you find that it's difficult for you to experience gratitude, what may be missing is perspective. If so, there are a few things you can try that can be extremely effective.

First and foremost, spend some time with people who are truly suffering. Visit—or better yet, volunteer at— a homeless shelter or hospice. However you may feel about why people are there (and remember, those feelings are just based on judgments, perceptions, and stories anyway), it's important to experience that situation directly. There is no lack of real suffering in the world. Don't be afraid to look at it.

If you're able to travel, you can witness firsthand extreme poverty in a third-world country. People here are deeply grateful for small things that many of us take for granted. Try to see the world through their eyes and bring that perspective into your own life, and the way you see the world. Regardless of your situation, you'll see that your life is infinitely more comfortable than theirs. Consider what your life would be like if you lived in a war zone or in a harsh environment with few natural resources.

In contrasting these conditions with your own, you may come to more fully appreciate what you have. Conversely, you may have a negative reaction, perhaps feeling a sense of entitlement about the things you possess. ("I've worked hard, so the world owes me.") Again, this kind of examination may be difficult, but it can be very enlightening. The point is not to beat yourself up for uncovering these feelings, but only to become aware of them and see where else and how they might manifest.

Witnessing this kind of suffering on television or online won't give you the full impact, but it's a start if it's all you can do. Be willing to look at the things that society tends to hide away and not discuss. This is not about instilling feelings of guilt. Our circumstances are as they are. However, if our circumstances allow it, we should do what we can to help others. And this doesn't necessarily mean financial help. Sometimes just giving a stranger a smile or acknowledging another's suffering is more helpful to them than money.

RESISTANCE AGAIN (SEE, IT'S FUTILE)

There are innumerable things in this world that can cause suffering, and we all suffer to some extent in our own way. However, the most powerful tool we have is choice, and we can choose how to deal with suffering.

Admittedly, some days it may seem impossible to believe that there is a choice. And some individuals have challenges that impair their ability to choose. However, just knowing that it is possible to make a choice can help, even if you're not at the point where you can see exactly how to do it. Just hold onto that belief until you've built up the strength to turn the possibility into reality.

EXERCISE: ENGAGING GRATITUDE

» On a daily basis, towards the end of the day, stop and take stock of the major and minor events that transpired. If it's helpful, write them down. Within each experience, see if there is something you can be grateful for, whether it's having gained knowledge or a new insight, or just having experienced something new.

  • Focus deeply on why you are grateful for it.

  • Each day, pick new things. Try not to repeat something unless you've gained new insight into why you can be grateful for it.

» Experience twenty-four hours of gratitude. One of the most effective means for bringing about a change in the way you see life is to keep the idea of gratitude in your attention as often as you can.

  • To remind yourself, set an alarm or use another alert to indicate when an hour has passed. Stop and reflect on something that you're grateful for, either in general, or that occurred in the previous hour. Again, focus on the "why," not just the "what." Make sure to pick something new every hour. You can even be grateful that something didn't happen.

- Put small sticky notes with reminders in your wallet, in your car, and on your fridge. Put them anyplace that will help remind you about the exercise.

- Chant. Keep the concept in your attention by chanting the word "gratitude."

» Finally, review the things you're grateful for. See if you can identify any trends or patterns. These reflections might also provide some insight into your view of the world that you weren't aware of previously. You may notice, for example, that you've been focusing on being grateful for your health and come to see that you've been carrying around many subtle health-related fears.

IN SESSION

During my struggles with the multiple manifestations of anger that would linger in my mind for seemingly endless amounts of time, I sought the advice of a counselor. As I've mentioned, I highly recommend seeking the input of a therapist or counselor on your big issues, since friends or loved ones may be hesitant to provide this kind of feedback. It also may not be fair to put them in a situation that could lead to feelings of resentment on your part.

I also want to emphasize that some of these larger challenges we face may take years to work through, as was the case for me with anger. But, while this process may be difficult, the alternative is considerably worse. At least you're working on your challenges.

If you're able, I would also recommend interviewing four or five counselors prior to committing to working with one in order to make sure you're comfortable and understand their specific approach. Therapists utilize many different techniques and, in my opinion, if you can't buy into a specific method, then it's not going to work for you. For example, one therapist with whom I met focused extensively on the "inner child" concept. While this approach works well for some people, it just didn't resonate with me.

During one of my conversations with my counselor, we were discussing surrender, love and peace and how I differentiated among them. Although I don't recall the exact details, or why this answer came to mind, I gave an example involving standing on the beach and watching a beautiful sunset. I said that when taking in and appreciating the view, you can surrender your need to control the world and find momentary peace in looking at the sky, but it's not necessarily feeling love for the sky.

Immediately after I said that, I experienced something that can only be described as mystical or metaphysical (and, of course, magical). Suddenly I was out of my body, and I was up in the sky looking down at a beach from the vantage point of the clouds. In fact, I was the clouds. I saw my body and a few other people standing on the shore looking up at me. Then I heard a voice that said, "But that's how it sees you." I was then overwhelmed by a feeling of unconditional love. A love for the beauty of all beings.

Just as quickly as the vision appeared, it went away. Suddenly back in my body, I was speechless. My face was wet with tears and my mind was completely still, while my being was somewhat in shock. My counselor was staring at me with one eyebrow raised. Once I collected myself, I asked him, "Did you feel that?" He nodded and asked, "What just happened there?" I tried my best to explain it, but the eyebrow still remained slightly raised.

Again, I understand this may sound mystical or metaphysical, and I can't explain what happened; neither do I feel a need to explain it away. To do so would seem disrespectful and dishonorable. Instead, I focus on being grateful for this moment of magic I was graced with. The experience left me in an elevated state for some time to come. It was as if I could see and comprehend things with greater clarity. In the time that followed, I reflected on this teaching often and developed a deepening compassion for the struggles that all beings endure.

And I've never looked at a sunset quite the same way again.

KEY POINTS FOR HAPPINESS AND GRATITUDE

- The concept of happiness has become so commercialized, conditioned, and collateralized that it is difficult to know what it means anymore. However, since it is the mind that creates and experiences happiness, we know that it is a state of mind, which means that, by its nature, it is transitory; it will come and it will go.

- The idea that happiness is transitory may seem counterintuitive, since we were told when we were children that people live "happily ever after." This suggests that it can and should be a permanent condition.

- We may believe that we are missing something, which, if we had it, would bring about happiness or a sense of peace. If we can shift our focus to what we already possess, we may find that we want less from the world, and come to realize that we are more fulfilled than we thought.

- Gratitude is one of the most powerful tools we possess. When you find yourself in a distressed state of mind, remember to focus on gratitude. That act alone has the power to change your state of mind in the current moment.

SECTION THREE: BE... SIMPLY BE

[He came to understand that] Eternity and the ever-beautifully-changing Now were identical.

- Robert Heinlein, *Stranger in a Strange Land* [xliii]

In the previous section, we focused on what we identified in Chapter One as the first component of mindfulness, i.e., paying attention (or the lack thereof). It explored the structure of a few common states of mind that keep us from being present—those habits that keep us so preoccupied throughout the day that we are unable to keep our minds quiet and appreciate where we are at the present moment, this moment.

This section will explore in greater depth the second component of mindfulness, the idea of being present—a concept that can seem almost foreign to us because we spend so much time reminiscing about and evaluating our pasts and fantasizing about our futures.

Chapter Twelve: "Now is the Time" will explore the following topics:

- The concept of a moment and how we regard the idea of time.

- The past and the future vs. the present.

- Actively invoking willpower to bring focus to the present moment.

- The concepts of "doing" and "being."

- Embracing stillness when we are conditioned to constantly move forward in our lives.

- The mental states involved in propelling us through life.

- Tips and techniques for intentionally shifting to a more being state.

Finally, in Chapter Thirteen, we'll briefly explore the practice of meditation and how it can be used in conjunction with your mindfulness practice. Since meditation involves setting aside time to focus on quieting the mind and intentionally inviting more peace into our lives, it is the natural complement to mindfulness.

Meditation can help make the concept of a quiet and still mind more understandable and easier to embrace. When we meditate, we are not interacting with the world; we are purposefully taking time to step away from our engagement with the myriad events playing out in our lives and the world and just focusing on being still.

So pour yourself a hot cup of green tea, make yourself comfortable in your oversized organic beanbag chair, and enjoy sim-

ply being. *(Flower garlands in your hair are completely optional...
Ladies, that includes you as well.)*

CHAPTER TWELVE: NOW IS THE TIME...

Therefore do not worry about tomorrow, for tomorrow will worry about its own things. Sufficient for the day is its own trouble.

- Matthew 6:34 [xliv]

A DEFINING MOMENT

What is a moment and how can we adequately define it? This philosophical question is a difficult one. We all have an idea or feeling about what constitutes a moment, yet putting it into words can prove to be quite challenging. It may be easier to compose a poem, haiku, or other creative work to capture the essence of a moment, rather than constricting it to a definition that might explain away some of its meaning.

It's common to conceptualize a moment as a brief period of time or a placeholder associated with the occurrence of a strong emotion or an experience to which we attribute special significance.

Perhaps it is a dramatic or romantic experience like a first kiss, being awarded a long-sought promotion, completing a difficult task, or achieving a personal goal. A moment could also mark a tragic accident or painful emotional experience, such as the passing of a loved one.

One key thing that makes a moment special is the feeling that, at that instant, we are fully aware of what is occurring as it unfolds, **to the exclusion of everything else**. We are, in fact, completely present when we experience these moments. As sometimes exemplified in the movies, it may feel as if time slows down and we experience everything with heightened awareness and in slow motion.

Either because it is something completely outside of our usual experience or because we wish to fully embrace it, we are captivated by what is happening and we bring our full, undivided attention to it in order to take it all in.

If it is something we enjoy, we savor it, soak it in, and ignore distractions; its significance is just too big. We want to bookmark this moment in time, inscribe it in a chapter of our lives, and hold onto it. We may be so overcome with emotion, positive or negative, that the moment is imprinted in our consciousness. Later, if we reflect back on it, we can almost relive what we saw, what was said, how our bodies felt, and the feelings and emotions we experienced.

The moments we remember stand out either because we willfully brought a particular focus to the experience, or because it was so outside the norm—possibly something that completely shattered our conception of the world—that we could not help but give it our full attention. Very much like the first time you drove a spaceship. *(Sorry, jumped ahead to the future there; I'm back now... now.)*

BOOKMARKS

Take a few minutes now to reflect on some of the significant moments in your life. What are the ones that immediately come to mind, that stick out the most? You can probably easily recall both positive and negative moments (although the positive ones are preferred for this exercise).

Reflect back to the moment itself, not the story about what happened afterward—e.g., a wonderful first kiss, rather than the tumultuous two-year relationship and painful breakup that followed. Just focus on the significant moment itself, the kiss. Perhaps it was winning an award; crossing a finish line; driving your new car off the lot; the first time you heard your favorite joke, or saw your favorite movie, or heard your favorite song.

EXERCISE: REFLECTING ON BOOKMARKED MOMENTS

As you recall the memorable moments in your life, ask yourself (and answer) the following questions:

» What made those moments special or different from other times in your life, from the day-to-day events?

  • At the time they occurred, did anything else matter?

  • When you reflect back on those moments, do the emotions you experienced at the time come back, as if you were reliving them again in this moment, if perhaps to a lesser degree? Do you find yourself smiling or frowning as you relive them and contemplate their significance?

» What do you think happened in those moments that was absent from other moments (like when you took the garbage out the other day)? What was different (besides the odor)?

The point is to recognize that something different was happening within you in those moments, compared to other seemingly more mundane moments. Experiences themselves just are. Moments simply exist. But something about you was different in those moments. *(And no, it's not what you were wearing at the time, although I'm sure it was something smart and sensible.)*

In those moments we remember so vividly, the difference is that we brought an undivided awareness, interest, and intensity to the experience. We were actively paying attention to what was happening—without distraction—because we were more interested in experiencing fully what was unfolding than in any random thoughts created by our minds. We willingly, willfully (Note: not-so-subtle reference to "willpower") brought a sense of awareness to those moments.

Now, consider bringing that same level of intensity to any and every moment, even to what you consider to be the most mundane of tasks, such as taking out the garbage, washing the dishes, or walking the dog. If you look closely, you'll see that your evaluation of a task as "mundane" is only a judgment, with no basis in reality.

You may wonder why you would want to bring your focus to a mundane moment. Why is it worth your attention? You have better things to think about when engaged in an everyday task. These moments are dull and not worth your time and attention. In looking at this feeling honestly, you might discover that you believe Eternity has an obligation to provide you only with entertaining moments; otherwise you're bored and resentful (a feeling we often express as though it were the fault of others). And boredom, like all states of mind, is a choice. *(Ooh, we just hate those "choice" statements, don't we?)*

A BLAST FROM THE PAST

There is only this moment, and we only have moments to live.

- Jon Kabat-Zinn, *Full Catastrophe Living* [xlv]

We can logically conclude that, since we are not physically living in the past or the future, we must be living in the present. *(Don't you just hate it when logic works out like that? So logical and everything. Believe me, I struggle with it too.)* Yet, despite this reality, we tend to spend a significant amount of our time visiting the past and the future via our wandering thoughts.

We are, in fact, always in the present. Unfortunately, we cannot live in the past or the future, no matter how hard we try or how much we long for times gone by. *(It's almost irritating. We just can't seem to get away from this present moment thing, can we?)*

Knowing this, we will still spend a tremendous amount of physical and mental effort trying to re-create moments—moments that contain special significance for us—that occurred in the past. Either we want simply to re-experience them or we want to change their outcome to something we find more appealing. But as we often find when we attempt to physically re-create them, they fall short of the original experience, leaving us disappointed and discouraged, perhaps to the point that we begin to doubt the splendor of the original experience.

For example, you remember fondly your parents taking you to an amusement park as a child and the connection it fostered between you and them. In the hope of strengthening your bond with your own children, you decide to do the same for them. Unfortunately, the experience doesn't go as you had hoped: the children fight and complain, the park is more crowded than you had anticipated, the weather is disagreeable; and so you leave the park disappointed and questioning your efforts. Or you reconstruct an incredible date from your past with a new partner, only they don't find the experience nearly as special as you and your date at the time did. You may wonder why it didn't go as well this time and worry that this new person is not as interested in you as you had hoped.

RECONSTRUCTION

The hard truth is that it's impossible to repeat an experience exactly, no matter how hard we try. If we consider the innumerable factors at play in a moment—our precise state of mind, the state of mind of others who may have been involved, the specific interplay of Mother Nature and the physical world; in short, the "ingredients" that created that moment—we see that each moment is truly unique. If we try to create the moment again, more than likely, we will spend the bulk of the time comparing what's playing out now to what happened in the original moment, which is something, of course, we did not do the first time.

While the original moment undoubtedly was memorable and had a strong impact on our lives, it's good to examine the reasons we wish to re-create it. If we ignore the physical circumstances and try to recognize the feeling we crave, it can provide tremendous insight.

Reflecting on past events can be beneficial, especially if we can learn something to help us with a current challenge. However, clinging to them and reliving them in order to bring an emotion into our present lives is counterproductive. Why do we believe that only that moment can bring about that feeling? Perhaps instead we should honor those moments in our hearts, and go out and seek new experiences, new moments. New experiences can open us to new possibilities beyond the limits of what we know today. If we stay as is, we will continue to experience as is.

A STITCH IN TIME

In *How to Know God: The Yoga Aphorisms of Patanjali* [xlvi], the translators, Swami Prabhavananda and Christopher Isherwood, discuss the great Hindu saint's description of a moment, explaining that while a moment is real—"like a dog, a diamond or a tree"—a sequence of moments (i.e., what we call "time") is "a structure created by our minds, an idea."

Yet because we buy into this idea of time, we also tend to generalize our experiences, seeing everything as continuous. So, for example, we say that we were unhappy all day, when in fact we were only unhappy at 9:03, 10:22, 1:45 and so on. In this way, we not only fool ourselves, but take on added (and unreal) suffering.

They go on to say that much of the suffering we experience is due to our habit of focusing on challenging times in the past or on fears of experiencing pain in the future. Therefore, by focusing on moments and not periods of time, we can eliminate much of our suffering.

Apart from causing us unnecessary pain, when this structure dominates our lives it also creates boundaries, limits, and conditions to our beliefs. For example, society may dictate, and we may come to believe, that we have designated amounts of time within which to pursue or complete an activity. If we are unable to experience it in that time frame, it will be lost to us altogether: If we don't get married and have children by the time we're thirty-five, we think we never will. If we're not at a certain point in our careers by the time we're forty, we fear we'll be stuck in an inferior position until we retire.

But, as we've seen, time is not real; it's a structure, a template we use to navigate this shared existence. This moment is real; time is not. This moment is all we have. There is only this moment, right here, right now. *(Please feel free to take a moment now, or two if you'd care to really indulge, and marvel at the glory of this moment, of every moment, really. We're happy to wait.)*

MOMENT(ARY) ABUSE

As we've said before, life is a journey, not a destination. The journey is the continuous flow of moments, the good, the bad, (the ugly), and the mundane. The journey is, in fact, the destination.

We can experience our journey more powerfully by becoming aware of the moments we choose to focus on and the states of mind we indulge in along the way. And why not learn to focus on each and every moment? If we're in the moment and the moment is all there is, why not be there for it? *(Seems kinda silly not to be, doesn't it? Not to mention disrespectful. I mean, the poor moment is doing all it can to be there for you. The least you can do is acknowledge it.)*

We say things like, "I have better things that require my attention than this mundane moment." Are there things that require our attention, or are we just creating an excuse for our minds to randomly ruminate about the past and future? *(And just how do you think it makes that poor moment feel to be discarded so haphazardly? Moments have feelings too, you know.)*

306

If we need time to plan or figure things out, then why not stop and give our focus completely to moments consisting of planning and analytic activities? Unfortunately, if we are not mindful during our planning and scheduling activities, they often turn into future fictional "what if" scenarios and ruminations on past experiences, culminating in emotional states of mind and judgments about the current state of our lives. We quickly end up a million miles away, cruising on autopilot, dwelling somewhere that doesn't even exist and that we have no control over. *(Now let's go back to that poor, discarded, unloved moment sitting there alone in the corner. How do you feel now, hot shot? Go ahead, pick it up, give it a hug and make up with it. Again, we'll wait.)*

We may not like where we are or what's happening in the current moment, but we're there nonetheless, so why not give ourselves to it? There is something to be learned and experienced in each and every moment.

Whether it's a challenging moment, a beautiful moment, a terrifying moment, or a mundane moment, if we can just be present in what is unfolding, in time we may become less attached to the good, less adverse to the bad, less bored by the mundane. Like snowflakes falling from the sky, there are no two identical moments.

ADDRESSING CHALLENGES

Many of us tend to dwell on things that pose challenges to us. If something agitates us, such as a disagreement with a friend or family member, we may hold on to that experience in our consciousness for hours, days, or even weeks, depending on the impact on our ego and emotions.

Over time, the emotion will subside as our consciousness is pulled elsewhere and we encounter new situations and experiences. However, if we repeatedly take ourselves back to the situation in our minds and re-live it, the experience will continue to cause us unhappiness.

When we indulge in revisiting these upsetting experiences with our thoughts, our minds don't realize that the experience played out in the past. To the mind, it's happening right now, because, in actuality, it is happening right now; we are creating the situation and feeling the emotions all over again in the present moment.

To ease this burden mindfully, we can remind ourselves that we are no longer in those upsetting moments—we are in this moment. In this moment, that past event is not happening. This moment is happening. *(Oh, and by the way, we're missing it because we're not here... poor lonely moment. They're going to have to form a support group for themselves if it keeps up like this.)*

This is not to say that we should ignore problems that cause us mental anguish. It's tremendously important to look at them to better understand our minds and their unique reactions, habits, and trends. As discussed in Section Two: "The Root Cause Analysis," once we are aware of these issues, we can create strategies for addressing them clearly and objectively.

TURN THE BEAT AROUND

There are a few situations where reflecting on past moments can be incredibly beneficial, especially during times where we feel stuck in a challenging state of mind and are having difficulty finding a way out. Here we feel trapped in dark suffering and it feels as if we will remain in this pain forever. At these times, reflecting on a beautiful, funny, or uplifting moment can be a strong tool to help you pull yourself out of the muck.

Holding that previous precious moment in your mind can provide that light at the end of the tunnel, a beacon to salvation. It's a reminder that your current state is transitory, it will come and it will go. By focusing on that past moment, you can pull all the light from the past into this current painful moment, shifting your state of mind to one of peace, or at least equilibrium. It may provide just a long-enough shift for you to be able to gain some clarity about what's causing you such pain.

Of course, the more present we were in these beautiful moments that we are bookmarking, the more solid they will be in our consciousness. If we were mindful in that past moment, it seals in the feelings to a deeper extent and allows us to reach back and grab hold with greater ease.

When using this technique, we must have the mental fortitude not to go off on any dangerous side roads. If you begin to feel remorse that you are no longer in that past moment and feel that you never will be again, or you reflect on how difficult your situation is now compared to then, or begin beating yourself up for getting so off-course that you begin feeling sorry for yourself, this will only make your current challenge more difficult. It defeats the entire purpose. So you must be vigilant and not allow your attention to waver and, if you spot it starting to go off-course, catch yourself and come back.

DOING VERSUS BEING

For most of us, our typical, and most comfortable, mode of operation in life is to actively keep ourselves busy doing things.

More often than not, though, the doing we are caught up in is thinking and analyzing, creating and changing, pondering and daydreaming, while mindlessly carrying out some physical activity. What we're not doing is focusing completely on what we are actually engaged in, or simply being in the moment, experiencing things as they unfold.

We tend to live much of our lives as if we're being pushed forward, carried down the stream as society dictates, churning and driving, with an incessant urge to do and achieve, to go forth and conquer. We are always moving forward to the next goal, the next place we think we need to reach, the next craving we wish to satisfy.

All of this doing activity is about getting us from where we are right now to where we believe we need to be at some point in the future. Whether that place is only a few minutes ahead or years away, we need to get there immediately! There's no time to spare! *(Um... literally and figuratively speaking, actually.)*

And since we're not there now physically, we think that the least we can do is put our minds there to bridge the gap and play out what we believe the experience will be like.

FUN WITH GERUNDS

Much as the definition of a "moment" can seem elusive, so the concept of being can be difficult to grasp as well. Being can be described as the absence of mental doing, that is, unnecessary mental activity. It is engaging in an activity and giving ourselves fully to it, to the exclusion of everything else.

It does not mean sitting on the floor, or standing in one place, devoid of action, drooling incessantly, although we can engage in that activity fully as well. *(Drooling is optional.)* What we mean by "being" is keeping the mind from wandering while actively focusing on experiencing, or engaging in, a situation as it unfolds.

In a state of being, we can be aware of thoughts that cross our minds without feeling the need to take action. Recognizing that they're just thoughts and urges, we can let them go and not follow the impulse to engage with them. They don't need to be resolved; they can simply be dropped.

Often we'll find that it's the thoughts to which we have emotional ties that are the most difficult to let go of. We may be so emotionally invested in them that we feel we're abandoning them by letting them go. It may even feel like an addiction. *("Hello, my name is Sam and I'm a worry addict." "Hi, Sam.")*

Paradoxically, when we stop all the doing and just be, it can be disquieting, even alarming. For what are we, if not the things that we engage with in our minds? Finding this stillness disturbing at first is not at all uncommon. However, the more you experience this feeling, the more comfortable you will become with it.

As always, it can be beneficial to look at why you're feeling uncomfortable. Is this a recurring theme in your life? Do you tend to feel anxious when you're by yourself? Are you experiencing feelings of guilt or shame because you're not actively "doing" something? Try to see the different ways this feeling manifests in your life and how it affects your state of mind.

EXERCISE: JUST BE

This is a repeat of an exercise presented in Chapter Ten. I'm including it again because it is fundamental to becoming mindful and developing a sense of stillness.

» Find a place where you can observe the world as though you are watching a movie. As best you can, relax and clear you mind of all activity. Tell yourself that for the next five or ten minutes there's nothing else you need to be doing, there's nothing you need to figure out, and there is no one you need to think about.

» Take yourself out of the equation. Imagine what this place would be like if you were not there, if there were no one to add commentary, evaluate, or judge. Just try to see it in its pure form.

  • If possible, the first time you try this exercise, do it in nature, somewhere peaceful, with few people and distractions around.

  • Look around and take in the view. What do you see? What are the sounds you hear? The smells you smell? What is the temperature and how is it affecting your body?

  • Also notice how easily your mind is pulled away and distracted. When you find your mind wandering, or starting to judge or evaluate something, catch yourself, come back and refocus on observing.

  • See that everything just is as it is. There is no need to judge, evaluate, or change anything. There is no need to create a story around or categorize anything. Just simply observe.

» Try this same exercise in a busy location, such as a heavily trafficked intersection. Ensure you are not at risk of being in anyone's way and just observe.

» Also try this exercise in a place you are very familiar with, such as a coffee shop or shopping mall. where you would normally be engaged in some activity.

> » In all of these active locations, reflect on what your normal state of engagement would be—such as evaluating and creating stories about the people and objects around you—and how different it feels to dis-engage and just observe.

NEVER BELIEVE IT'S NOT REAL

Often unnoticed in our constant doing, the world is overflowing with the brilliance of life. There is a vibrancy in the world and our experience of it that is frequently neglected because of our focus on doing.

As I mentioned previously, awareness can be a kind of magic. You may believe that magical experiences need to be spectacular in some way in order for us to acknowledge them. However, I suggest looking for the brilliance in more subtle phenomena, which can reveal a beauty and wonder of a profound kind. Here are a few more examples that I hope will make this concept clearer.

When I leave my technology industry job at the end of the day, I'm exhausted from hours of pressing deadlines and demands, as well as lengthy encounters with stressed-out coworkers. *(And yes, while you can remain peaceful in a chaotic environment, it can take a toll on your energy levels. You still feel the chaos, you just don't engage with or react to it.)* As I walk out to the parking lot, I'm struck by the beauty of what is being presented to me.

A group of trees blooming vibrantly in the spring warmth. Hundreds of flower petals falling and being carried by the breeze, decorating the lonely parking lot like pink and white confetti. The bright summer sun and soft wind working together to create ever-changing shadows on the ground as thousands of leaves dance on a tree in the center of the lot. The sky alive with clouds in hues of blue, gold, and pink, shifting as the sun sets. A flock of birds flying effortlessly in a perfect V-shape above the bustling traffic below.

When I stop to experience these moments, some of the strain is lifted from my being and I'm overwhelmed with gratitude for this opportunity.

I had a similar experience when I was working on one of the middle drafts of this book. As noted above, I find that a library can often be an enjoyable place to work. After hours of editing during one long weekend, I decided to take a walk outside and get some fresh air. Upon opening the door, I saw that it had been raining for some time. Everything was wet and reflected the small amount of light in the sky.

As I stood under an awning watching the rain come gently down, I became aware of a large puddle in front of me. When I shifted my focus to the puddle, I noticed how each raindrop caused circlets of water to surge out from the point of impact. The circles of water varied in size depending on the size of the droplet, and they would either dissipate or bump up against circles from other drops, blending together in a complex series of patterns. The entire display seemed alive and I lost awareness of everything else.

It was both a symphony and a dance. The rhythm of the drops hitting the puddle echoed off the concrete walls that surrounded me. I could see the reflection of each raindrop in the puddle prior to impact and then it was lost in the waves. Drops and waves randomly filled the dance floor that was the puddle. Sound and movement played together. It was a tremendous performance, one that could never happen exactly the same way again.

I became absorbed in this moment, this experience, and the world around me faded away. The details of the book, the bodily aches from sitting in a chair typing away for hours on end, the hunger I was feeling, it all went away. I don't know how long I stood there transfixed by this brilliant display. People often use the expression "it's as if time stood still" to describe these kinds of experiences. Here however, time wasn't even a concept, it didn't even exist. There was no sense of normal continuity. I was just held in this experience. What I did know for certain was the overwhelming sense of peace and gratitude I felt afterwards when the world found its way back in.

Prior to my exploration of mindfulness, I would have overlooked experiences like these altogether. During a break from work, I would have been too busy looking for some kind of feedback from the world. I would have created a story about how the rain affected me personally and how I would have to dress when I left and how difficult it could make driving home. Instead I got to experience magic—the world as it is, outside of our definitions, allowing me to take part in an aspect of its brilliance heretofore unknown to me. Giving me the opportunity to stop and experience and see what unfolded. These moments are here now. They are always here.

BEING IN MOTION

"When I climb, I feel an interior peace. You're obliged to concentrate on here and now, to concentrate totally. All of a sudden, you forget your problems, all the things that don't interest you."

- Climber Patrick Edlinger [xlvii]

If you were to ask any accomplished athlete what they were thinking about during moments of great accomplishment, more than likely they would tell you that they weren't thinking about anything. They were fully focused on what they were doing. In those situations, you can often see the focus and concentration clearly in their faces.

There is a beautiful scene in the movie *The Legend of Bagger Vance* [xlviii], in which an enlightened golf caddy is explaining to his protégé Rannulph Junuh, a young golfer attempting to make a comeback, the mental process of one of their competitors. He points out that the other golfer is taking a number of practice swings, not with the intent of trying to make something happen, but with an air of surrender. As if he understands that while he must focus on executing the most perfect swing he can, at the same time he has to "get out of the way" of the result. He encourages the protégé to try the same method.

Similarly, great performers who successfully pull off a particularly difficult piece are focused unwaveringly on their performance. When you observe them, they appear completely transfixed.

You might have experienced something like this yourself, for example in a yoga class. At the beginning of the class, if your mind is overly active, or you're anxious or upset about things that occurred during the day, it can be difficult to find your balance and hold the poses. However, as your mind starts to calm down and switches from these issues to focusing exclusively on the poses, you're soon able to balance and hold them with relative ease.

If you're going through a serious emotional upheaval, and are unable to calm your mind, you may be incapable of finding your balance throughout the entire class. At a time like this, I would recommend a good cardio workout, which will probably be of greater benefit to you. Cardiovascular exercise—such as running, swimming, or biking—has a wonderful ability to calm and quiet our minds.

TEXTING, SEXTING, NEXTING

Anyone with a smartphone is familiar with texting, which has become an increasingly common form of communication. Inevitably, sexuality came into the equation, giving rise to the trend of sending sexually explicit information, or "sexting." Playing off that terminology, I'd like to propose the concept of "nexting."

"Nexting" refers to living our lives in future mode, that is, constantly focusing on the next thing we feel that we need to do. It is a habit that is strongly reinforced by society. People are always asking: "Where are you going?" "What are you doing later?" "When are you going to get that finished?"

> You need to get to the store, you need to pick up a gift for Jimmy's birthday party this weekend, you need to get to the pharmacy to pick up that prescription, and you should go to a yoga class so you can feel more peace in your life! Then, after class, you need to finish that presentation at work so you can add taking on a new client to your already overloaded work duties. Don't forget you need to lose twenty pounds in time for Patricia's wedding in June. Later today you're going to... tonight you need to... you should... this week you've got to... you should... this weekend you should get around to... next week you'll do... next month you'd better... next year you'll become... Aaaaaaahhhhhhhhhh!!!!!!!!

In a way, nexting creates a sense of order in the world for us. Even while physically engaged in one activity, we're often thinking about and focusing on the next thing we need to do because this allows us to believe we have the current endeavor under control and the future is in order. The goal is in sight, or we are bored or frustrated, and we are ready to check off this current activity as being complete and move ahead with our day.

Ironically, we often complain that we are so overloaded with nexting and the stresses in life that we look forward to not having to do anything. We want the weekend to come or we want to go on vacation and get away from it all, to just sit back and relax. However, once the weekend comes or we arrive at our vacation destination, we still end up thinking about all of the things we're going to do even if we're planning to do nothing.

If we're not focused on the next thing, we may feel bored, uneasy, lost or empty. It's as if our lives are without structure. We look for something, anything, to fill up the time, to give us meaning and purpose, even if it's figuring out the next show we're going to watch on TV. For most of us, nexting has become our norm and a way of life. *(As a side note, while laws may vary by state, for your own safety and the safety of those around you, I highly encourage you to obey all traffic regulations and not engage in nexting while driving.)*

If we actually succeed in "not doing" for a period of time, do we experience feelings of guilt or discomfort? How long does our not doing last before we wonder where we're going to go to dinner or come up with something else to occupy our attention (such as focusing on the past or future)?

NEXT != (NOW + 1)

(That's tech talk for "Next is not the future." Hey, I'm trying to appeal to a broad audience here.)

This future-based focus creates a structure for how we approach our lives. Much of our lives involves the effort of reaching and achieving our personal goals, such as getting married and having children, obtaining the perfect job, or owning our own home. However, once we reach a goal, we almost immediately begin looking for the next goal, further manifestations of what's next. Putting them together creates the road map for our lives. Without a map, we feel lost.

We believe that we will arrive at a time when everything, including ourselves, will be complete. We may even reach that perceived time in life and realize that we are not complete, or as complete as we thought we'd be, that there's still more, leaving us feeling dismayed or distraught. We may find that the end point of completeness we believed in seemingly can't be achieved.

Do we believe we'll miss out on something if we don't know the next next? When, in actuality, we're constantly missing out on the only thing that matters. This moment, right here, right now.

Next...

YOUR "SHOULD" STINKS

In addition to always looking for the next thing, we also create and are fed expectations of how we *should* act. Often this sets up an unrealistic ideal, which can quickly lead to negative states of mind because we are not currently meeting that ideal.

We compare what we are doing to what we believe to be better, more productive, more acceptable, or more important. We believe our current behavior is not in alignment with some bigger plan or concept We then pass judgments on our own actions (or inactions) and, more often than not, wind up feeling bad about ourselves for not living up to these supposedly superior behaviors. We torture ourselves with feelings of guilt and shame, mercilessly flogging ourselves inwardly.

We also have the media, family, friends, and the voice—or voices—in our heads telling us what we *should* be doing and we often take what they are telling us as fact. We *should* go to the gym and exercise so we can look better, we *should* purchase *x*, *y*, and *z* products because they will make us complete, we *should* call our mothers more often, we *should* forgive our sister for her outburst at our party, we *should* settle down and start a family.

Should often creates conflicts in our addiction to nexting. We need or want to do *x*, but we *should* do *y*. If we do *x*, we may berate ourselves for our inability to do *y*, either because we just didn't have time to do both or because we lacked the self-control to follow through with the "better" option. Otherwise, if we do end up choosing *y*, we may trudge through that activity feeling resentful that we couldn't take the *x* road, the road we wanted.

Should comments often lead to feelings of inadequacy and are typically based on a perception that is itself flawed, i.e., that we are superhuman and can do *x*, *y*, and *z* simultaneously and perfectly. We have an irrational belief that others must have this ability and that there's just something wrong with us.

When others use this term, it implies that they know better than we do; if we believe them, we empower them to exert control over us. *(Oh look, you just got guilt all over you. Go ahead and clean yourself off, we'll wait.)* Of course, if it's someone whose opinion we trust and who exemplifies what they preach, it can be a word of power and something to pay attention to.

Next…

BREAKING HABITS: MINDFULNESS IN MOTION

Mindfulness, and the peaceful states of mind it can foster, is not something that is going to happen to us, as many people believe and are sometimes told or sold. More than likely, you're not going to wake up one morning and find it on the doorstep, delivered by overnight express. It requires that we continually remind ourselves to be present and engage our awareness in life as it unfolds, until it becomes a natural way of being. It's not standing around waiting for our ship to come in. It's definitely not acting like a zombie and zoning out, or drifting away, when we're not interested in or entertained by what's currently happening.

Mindfulness requires a shift—from allowing our thoughts to run free, unguarded and undisciplined (as reviewed at length in Section Two), to purposefully focusing on being present, regardless of the situation we find ourselves in and our judgments and perceptions about it. *(Like now... and now... and, yes... even now.)*

When we're mindful, we're continually striving to be ever more present, to experience this and every moment, "good" or "bad." There is something to be experienced in every moment, whether we like that something or not. (Please revisit Chapter Six: "Under the Influence," should you need a refresher on this concept.)

If you find that you become agitated by or frustrated with trying to be present, ask yourself why this is. Do you believe that certain things are just inherently boring and not worthy of your attention? Are some experiences beneath you? For example, do you see standing in line at the DMV office or waiting in line at the bank as a complete waste of time?

The fact is that, for some reason, you are required to be where you are in order to reach some objective, tedious as it may seem. And while you're there, you have a choice in how you are going to experience the situation. You can stand there and judge every person around you, focusing on all the other things you'd rather be doing or need to do (all the *nexts* and *shoulds*). In other words, you can choose to make yourself miserable and put yourself in a frustrated and stressful state of mind or not.

Notice that no one is forcing you into this state; you are willingly choosing to go there of your own accord. Or you can just accept that you are where you are and experience it without judging: the color of the paint on the walls, the voices of the people around you, the structure of the room you're in. Just observe them, try not to judge them.

And if you can't find anything to focus on that holds your attention, you can focus on your breathing or repeat a peaceful mantra or affirmation to yourself. You can practice just being still in the midst of everyday life and its many occurrences. You can have the humility to accept that the world and the situation you are in is as it is, and not how you may want it to be. Choices. *(There it is again. Damn!)*

THIS (THERE IS) ONLY THIS (MOMENT)

A powerful word that encapsulates the feeling of being present is "this." Focusing on this one word can bring us completely into the present moment… this moment, this situation, this experience.

(In case you were wondering, yes, this section ties into the title of the book.)

In fact, there are many words that can evoke this same feeling, and finding ones that resonate with you can be exceedingly helpful.

When we're presented with a situation that makes us unhappy, our minds tend to flare up, allowing our thoughts to run wild. We may be unhappy because we don't feel in control, or because we're bored, upset, scared, or tired and we want to be anywhere but where we are. A word like "this" can bring our minds back to the situation at hand, the situation as it is, this moment and this experience, accepting it as it is.

By recognizing your discomfort and repeating to yourself the word "this," or another similar word that resonates with you, you can remind yourself to be present, center yourself in the situation, and quiet the reactions of your mind.

Once you're refocused and able to look at the situation more objectively, take a step back and ask yourself why your mind was so active in that situation. Did you feel fear or frustration? A lack of control? If so, ask yourself why that caused you to react the way you did. Remember, we can control our reactions; other people and the world are beyond our control. *(With their darned free will and all.)*

"This" is a word that can be chanted all day long. When your mind starts jumping around to the past and the future, say "this," and allow it to center you in the moment, the experience, and the situation. Because there is only this. *(Ding! ding! ding! Title reference again.)*

In time, you may even come to see that this moment, each and every one, is always perfect, always complete as it is. It's your mind—how it behaves or misbehaves, acts and reacts to situations—that prevents you from finding and holding onto peace.

A clear mind will provide shelter and comfort even in the most chaotic situation, and not just for yourself. It can be of benefit to others around you as well. In the same way that soldiers are trained to maintain their clarity and perspective in hostile situations, you can train yourself to be a warrior in the battlefield of your own mind. What kind of mind would you want to be in charge of handling a difficult situation? One characterized by clarity, or one spinning with conflict and doubt?

BEING HERE

So just how do we engage in the act of being present? As we've seen, it's not some magical, New-Agey, secret technique; it's really quite simple and our success depends on how well we are able to keep our focus.

When we are mindlessly engaged in ambling and wandering daydreams, our focus, what we're giving our attention to, is our thoughts. To be present, we need to actively shift our focus to wherever we find ourselves at any given moment.

The easiest way to do this (and a method that's always available) is to pay attention to our senses. What are we seeing? Without judging, evaluating, or criticizing—just what are we seeing? What are the colors, shapes, movements, textures, and levels of brightness around us? What are we hearing, smelling, and tasting? What is our body experiencing? Do you feel the warmth of the sun or the coolness of the breeze? Do you notice any aches and pains in your body?

If you are walking down the street, or out in nature, what does the ground feel like underneath your feet? What is the terrain like? How is your body reacting to navigating the terrain? Are you stretching specific muscles to climb up stairs? Are you directing your feet or your hands to work together in a specific combination?

While this emphasis on your body and your surroundings may seem mundane, by taking your focus away from your rambling thoughts and shifting it to your environment, you learn to strengthen your will. You are building up willpower and the ability to focus—again, things that are rarely taught or valued in the world today. This strength of will is the strength to not engage in the constantly flowing stream of thought.

When you embark on a diet, you struggle with your habitual inclination to eat unhealthy foods. Gradually, you change your habits and build up the strength to resist temptation, ideally to the point where you no longer crave things that are unhealthy for you and realize the benefits of a healthy diet. In the same way, focusing on your senses is a way of resisting and overcoming injurious mental habits. As with any important change you attempt to make in your life, it is not without effort.

As mentioned earlier, there are varying degrees of being present. Eventually, in your practice, you may feel that you have become the experience itself. You are truly not doing anything or trying to make anything happen. It's as if there is no you, there is only the experience.

You may come to the point one day where you are so comfortable with your mind being quiet that you're able to let your attention rest in stillness itself, rather than living in the middle of thoughtless mind chatter. *(So get your will to the mental gym, which is everywhere and always available. Exercise it thoroughly, and it will become stronger.)*

(MOMENT)OUS OCCASION

To reiterate, these concepts of being versus doing and being present in the moment require a shift in the way you engage with your mind and, subsequently, with the world.

Most of us are under the control of our mind and thoughts, as if they're entities inseparable from ourselves that drive us to action, reaction, and inaction. The shift of which we're speaking involves telling yourself to see your mind and thoughts as something separate from who you are, as if there is another aspect to you, a higher aspect, if you will, that can build up the strength to gain control of the mind and use it as a tool when required.

EXERCISES: BRING YOURSELF BACK TO THE PRESENT

Try the following exercises to help reinforce the feeling of being present:

» At any moment, shift your focus from your thoughts to your breathing. It's something you're constantly engaged in, so why not focus on it? *(And if you're not breathing, hopefully you'll become aware of it fairly quickly and shift your focus to rectify that problem.)*

» Find specific powerful words or terms that resonate with you that you can chant throughout the day. Focus on repeating them continuously, over and over and over. Note how long you're actually able to repeat the chant. You may be shocked at how quickly your mind wanders away from this task and how much focus and concentration it takes to keep chanting, or to even remember to chant in the first place.

- You can choose just one word, like the word "this," or a multi-word phrase. Here are some others you might find helpful: "now," "be here," "be present," and "there is only this."

- Chanting affirmations can be extremely powerful when you are in a challenging state of mind. Repeating something with a positive focus can help you shift into a more peaceful state. For example, if you're feeling angry, you can repeat something like "I am at peace." Chant it repeatedly. In time you may find that you are actually beginning to feel peaceful.

- I don't recommend emphasizing the negative aspect of what you're experiencing, for example saying, "I am not in anger." That just serves to remind you of your anger.

- It's good to change the chant periodically. Once you become comfortable with a specific chant or word, you may become a bit lazy about repeating it, or think you're repeating it when you're actually not. Adding an additional word to the chant, or changing the chant completely, requires additional focus, a focus you may have believed you were already giving to the activity, but weren't.

KEY POINTS ABOUT MOMENTS

- The moments we remember stand out either because we willfully brought a particular focus to the experience, or because it was so outside the norm—possibly something that completely shattered our conception of the world— that we could not help but give it our full attention.

- We remember those moments so vividly because we brought an undivided awareness, interest, and intensity to the experience. We were, in fact, actively paying attention to and focused on what was happening because we were more interested in experiencing fully what was unfolding than being engaged by the distractions created by our minds. We willingly, willfully brought a sense of awareness to those moments.

- Unfortunately, even when our minds are not fantasizing about the future or dwelling in the past, we will often clutter them with countless other distracting activities.

As we've seen, we busy our minds by comparing ourselves to the people around us, evaluating the quality of our surroundings, judging whether things are of value to us, or creating a story around our role in the situation in which we find ourselves. With all of this activity going on, can we truly be in the moment? Are we present?

- We can experience our journey more powerfully by becoming aware of the moments we choose to focus on and the states of mind we indulge in along the way. And why not learn to focus on each and every moment? If we're in the moment and the moment is all there is, why not be there for it?

- When we are mindlessly engaged in daydreams, our focus, what we're giving our attention to, is our thoughts. To be present, we need to actively shift our focus to wherever we find ourselves at any given moment.

- A clear mind will provide shelter and comfort even in the most chaotic situation.

CHAPTER THIRTEEN: MEDITATION

The mind is its own place, and in itself
Can make a Heav'n of Hell, a Hell of Heav'n.

- John Milton, *Paradise Lost* [xlix]

QUIET TIME

As is the case with mindfulness, there are many beautiful and profound definitions of what constitutes meditation and many ways in which it can be comprehended.

Meditation is a practice based in Eastern spiritual traditions, and variations of this practice can be found in many cultures throughout the world. Like mindfulness, it can be of benefit to people who are seeking greater spiritual fulfillment, as well as those just looking for more peace and serenity in their lives.

In general, meditation involves setting aside a period of time in which to focus on keeping the mind quiet, to the best of one's ability, by not following thoughts. This is achieved through a variety of specific techniques.

If we were to stop and take fifteen minutes a day to practice formal meditation, that would still leave twenty-three hours and forty-five minutes for the mind to go and do whatever the heck it wants (and typically it will do just that, often resulting in mayhem and carnage, as described in detail throughout the book), which is why we love mindfulness practice so much.

A meditation practice can be a tremendously helpful addition to your mindfulness work, and it's one that I highly advocate. This book will not go deeply into the details of meditation, but will present a high-level overview that points out the benefits of employing the two practices together (because they're friends). If you would like more information on meditation, there are many resources available, including local yoga centers, classes in your community, a large variety of books and guides, and, of course, online.

Meditation is also one of the fastest ways to experience elevated states of attention. Not only can we see and experience magic manifest in the physical world, we can also experience worlds of light inwardly. In fact, I believe that the more you practice meditation, the more magic you'll come to see in your mindfulness practice.

YOU DESERVE A BREAK EVERY DAY

It's important to mention that, like a mindfulness practice, meditation can be very challenging when first starting out. This is said not to discourage you in the least, but only to help you be realistic. Almost everyone struggles when starting meditation practice, and continues to struggle to varying degrees as their practice evolves.

So if you find it incredibly difficult in the beginning, you're not alone. You're not broken and please don't believe that you can't do it. It is imperative to have patience and persevere. Don't expect to perform like a seasoned professional when first starting out.

To take a sports example, say you watch the Olympics and are blown away by the grace and acrobatic skill of the ice skaters. Deciding you want to flip and jump on the ice, you head out to the nearest rink, where you spend the next hour holding onto the rail and falling on your butt. Discouraged, you limp away, hand on butt, vowing never to return.

Olympic athletes have spent thousands of hours honing their craft, hidden away in sports facilities far from our curious eyes. Granted they sometimes have natural ability, but they work themselves to exhaustion training to be as perfect as they can be.

So when you see someone meditating in full lotus position with a giant smile on their face, remember that (a) they have probably spent years practicing yoga, (b) they may be naturally flexible, and (c) they likely have their bad days too, when it's a struggle just to sit in one place and keep their minds from racing a thousand miles an hour.

A MIND-LESS ORDINARY

In both mindfulness practice and in meditation practice, we are seeking stillness in the mind. To help us in this journey, various techniques are employed to quiet the mind.

A technique provides something for the mind to purposefully focus on so that it isn't randomly manufacturing and pursuing thoughts as it habitually does. In mindfulness practice, as we've seen, we do such things as shift our focus to our surroundings or our senses in order not to focus on thoughts.

In this state, you strive to keep your mind still, just quiet. You are not at war with it, judging yourself, others, or the world around you, nor do you perceive that they are judging you. You are not trying to accomplish anything or be anything. You are not trying to satisfy anyone. You let go of the idea of "you."

You are as you are, everything is as it is, and feelings of peace arise from that. You are the stillness and the stillness is every-thing. In these moments, it's all good, man.

Many people who meditate report that this stillness is quite profound. When the mind stops its constant churning, you begin to feel your Self—who you are, and not what the world or other people have told you that you are. Over time, that stillness can reach to depths that can't be easily described.

In short, the challenge in discussing and understanding the experience of "no mind" or "no thought" that arises through meditation is that there are no words that can do these feel-ings justice.

HEEL, BOY, HEEL!

As with mindfulness, it's essential in meditation to step back and separate yourself from your thoughts. You watch the activity (again, like watching a movie or watching the clouds pass over the clear blue sky), yet you see you are separate from it. As you build strength and focus, it is possible to quiet all of the mind's activity and chatter, or at least get to a place where it's not so loud and out of control.

Through mindfulness practice, you may have started to see that there are certain habits and trends in your thought processes.

Perhaps you spend a lot of time dreaming of fighting dinosaurs, or you're angry at the world because you feel like you have no control, or you frequently engage in sexual fantasy. *(Or perhaps your sexual fantasies involve intermittent fights with dinosaurs. Hey, if it saves time to combine them, more power to you.)* If typically you spend very little time being present, you will likely observe these same trends when you begin your meditation practice.

Unlike mindfulness, when you meditate you are not focused at all on the outside world, which is full of interesting things to focus on. Most meditation techniques involve solitariness, far from the busy world. In meditation, you become more acutely aware of your thoughts because you have little else to pay attention to.

As with mindfulness, when thoughts arise and you realize that your mind is engaged in chatter, you just bring yourself back to the technique you are utilizing. Catch and come back, catch and come back. This is something you will do often.

Imagine your thoughts are like a hyperactive chihuahua, continually running off to sniff some new exotic smell, and you're constantly having to reel it back in. Your thoughts actually may be more like a snappy greyhound or a slow basset hound, but you get the idea.

You may find that your mind goes off on a tangent for ten minutes before you even realize that it's wandering. This is perfectly normal. Again, once you realize what's happening, just drop what you're obsessing over and come back to the technique. *(Whistle for it to come back, if you must.)* There's nothing you need to do with that thought you were playing with; just drop it. *(Like a dog with a stick, drool and all.)* You owe it nothing.

Granted, thoughts that are tied to big emotional issues you are working through will sometimes be very strong, and it will be difficult to simply drop them. Those will take time. Sometimes just giving yourself permission to set them aside so that you can explore them in more depth later is required. And, if you're able to reach some level of stillness and quiet, you may come to see the issue in an entirely different light when you reflect on it afterwards.

In time, as you build up your abilities of focus and concentration, you may find that your tangents become shorter in duration. Instead of ten minutes, it now takes five minutes, three minutes, or one minute for you to realize that your mind is wandering. You can even get to the point where simply feeling the urge to think about something is enough to trigger a response.

RAINBOWS AND UNICORNS

As mentioned above, there are many meditation techniques to choose from and many forms of instruction through teachers, videos, audio recordings, and books. However, I think it's important to clarify what I mean by a meditation technique in order to distinguish it from a relaxation technique.

Some guided "meditations" feature written or spoken instructions that tell you to create a pleasant scenario in your mind, one that may even include unicorns and rainbows. The instructor is trying to guide you to your "happy place," for lack of a better phrase, a place where you are comfortable and can allow yourself to relax.

The contradiction here is that in visualizing these scenes, you are using your imagination—that is, creating thoughts—which is the opposite of what meditation is about.

There is nothing "wrong" with these techniques, but they are not meditation unless they bring you to a place of stillness, where you're not engaging your mind, but simply being. *(Honestly, for the record, I have nothing against rainbows and unicorns. But like most mature adults, I save them for tastefully displaying on my clothing.)*

QUIET, PLEASE

One popular technique you may come across is silent meditation. This technique involves focusing on the silence itself to the point where you become the silence. Silent meditation is extremely powerful; however, as a beginner, you may find it extremely difficult, if not overwhelming, at a time when you are just starting to learn to quiet your mind.

As the mind can be like a runaway train careening out of control, not having anything to focus on can be exhausting, and you may feel as if there is no way to escape the thoughts that are plaguing you. For this reason, many people practice other techniques for some time before embracing silent meditation.

Yet, in time, with this type of meditation, you can reach the point where you are the stillness, you are the silence, and there is no difference between it and you.

COULD YOU REPEAT THAT?

Another common technique is to chant, either silently or aloud, to yourself. The chanting is what we are telling the mind to do: focus exclusively on chanting to the exclusion of everything else. While this is also a technique we use in mindfulness, here you are not navigating your way through the world. Here you are alone, typically with your eyes closed, navigating through your thoughts en route to stillness, with only the chanting to hold on to.

One of the best-known and most beautiful chants is the Buddhist chant "Om Mani Padme Hum," which, very loosely translated, says that God/Eternity exists in all things and all things are God/Eternity. God/Eternity exists right now in your own heart and mind.

However, any chant or affirmation that brings you a sense of peace can be used—for example, "I am at peace," "I am love," or "inner peace."

By repeating these or other phrases over and over, to the exclusion of everything else, in time the mind can become still and peaceful, and can rest in that stillness.

If thoughts begin to arise, you simply return to the chant until the mind quiets down again.

WHILE YOU'RE AT IT

Focusing on your breath can also be a helpful technique. There are a number of variations, but in general the goal is simply to focus on your breathing... the breath in, and the breath out.

When practicing any meditation technique, you may find that your breathing becomes very shallow, which may cause concern. However, it's perfectly natural and there's no cause for alarm. The body will take care of itself.

Even if you're using another meditation technique, it can be helpful to begin by taking a few deep breaths and focusing on your breathing. You will find that this helps your body and mind to relax and slow down. While you are practicing another technique, it's not necessary to continue to focus on your breath; just allow the body to do what it does naturally.

BURNIN' DOWN THE HOUSE

Another meditation technique involves listening to music with your complete attention, locked in as if you are anticipating each note.

This is a good technique for beginners, as it allows you to focus on something outside of yourself. It's easier to let go and let the music pull you along. If your mind wanders, the music is there to pull you back; it can act as a continuing source of support. With this technique, you don't need to concern yourself with your breathing or with chanting.

To start, gentle New Age or instrumental music is recommended; then, over time, literally any kind of music that you find inspiring or that helps you to focus can work. Techno and trance music are among my favorites. *(And, just for clarification, that is not a sarcastic comment... it can be hard to tell sometimes, I know.)*

Music with lyrics may take time to get used to, since the mind wants to listen to what's being said, or even sing along. Yet, over time, lyrics can become just sound.

IT'S ALL ABOUT THE FIT

Happiness is like a butterfly; the more you chase it, the more it will elude you, but if you turn your attention to other things, it will come and sit softly on your shoulder.

- Henry David Thoreau (attrib.) [1]

Again, I recommend that you try out a number of techniques and find the one that works best for you. After a while, you may want to switch to another technique, which is perfectly fine; however, it's advisable to stick with one technique until you are able to hold your mind quiet for a significant amount of time and you become adept at catching it when it wanders.

It's important to remember that the technique is not going to make peace happen to you. You have to do the work to quiet the mind; the technique is a tool to help you in that effort.

EXERCISE: TIPS FOR STARTING A PRACTICE

» Choose a technique that resonates with you and try to practice it for ten to fifteen minutes, once or twice a day.

» To begin with, strive for fifteen minutes in the morning and/or fifteen minutes in the early evening. Otherwise, five or ten minutes is a good start! Even just two minutes (say, if you're running late) is enough to help establish a pattern.

» Try not to eat a heavy meal before meditating, nor should you starve yourself. Both will lead to discomfort and distraction during your meditation.

» Treat yourself to a special place for your meditations. Try to select a space that is out of the way and not in the middle of your daily home activities. You can also set up a "meditation table" where you can display items that inspire you and promote calmness.

» Keep a journal and write about your memorable meditation experiences. Writing about an experience helps to solidify it and can be a source of encouragement on days when you're having difficulty meditating. Don't write as if anyone will look at what you've written, just try and capture your experience as best you can.

» Keep a notepad and pen next to your meditation space so that those big "show-stopping" thoughts can be put somewhere safe while you continue with your meditation.

» Try to restrict distractions when you sit down to meditate. For example, turn off the ringer on your phone and put a "Do Not Disturb" sign on your door.

» Try not to turn your meditation time into a chore. Remember why you are interested in meditation in the first place. When you sit down, tell yourself that, for the next ten or fifteen minutes, there is nothing else you need to do. There is nowhere else you need to be and there is nothing you need to accomplish.

» Finally, try not to have any expectations prior to meditating or make judgments about the meditation afterwards.

KEY POINTS ABOUT MEDITATION

• Meditation is one of the most peaceful activities we can engage in. When we begin to quiet our minds and quell our thoughts, we find that much, if not all, of the pain and suffering we endure is created unnecessarily by us, through our thoughts.

• Like mindfulness practice, meditation can be very challenging when first starting out. This is said not to discourage you in the least, but only to help you be realistic. Almost everyone struggles when starting meditation practice, and continues to struggle at various points as their practice evolves.

- A technique provides something for the mind to focus on so that it isn't randomly manufacturing and pursuing thoughts as it usually does. This is similar to what we do in mindfulness when we shift our focus to our surroundings or our senses in order not to focus on thoughts. Here, however, we are not engaged with the world; it is us alone with ourselves. Choose a technique that works for you and do your best to set up a time every day for practicing that technique.

CONCLUSION

However mean your life is, meet it and live it; do not shun it and call it hard names. It is not so bad as you are. It looks poorest when you are richest. The fault-finder will find faults even in paradise. Love your life, poor as it is. You may perhaps have some pleasant, thrilling, glorious hours, even in a poorhouse. The setting sun is reflected from the windows of the almshouse as brightly as from the rich man's abode; the snow melts before its door as early in the spring. I do not see but a quiet mind may live as contentedly there, and have as cheering thoughts, as in a palace.

- Henry David Thoreau, *Walden* [li]

STRIKING A BALANCE

Now that we've spent time exploring in depth the two components that were laid out in Chapter One, "Paying Attention" and "Just Being," I wanted to spend some time revisiting the importance of striking a balance between the two. With this approach to mindfulness, it's important to become comfortable with both aspects, monitoring your thoughts and residing in mental stillness.

As a reminder, once you begin, you will find that you spend the majority of your time commenting on, categorizing and monitoring your thoughts and only a small amount of time actively experiencing stillness. As your practice evolves and you learn to actively influence and control your state of mind, thereby experiencing more stillness more often, then the proverbial pendulum will swing in the other direction. You are experiencing more stillness, being present, and there becomes less of a need to comment on, categorize, and monitor.

It's entirely possible to experience stillness and peace to the same extent that you now experience distressing and challenging states of mind. It's not as hard as you think it is. You will be amazed when you start to see the crossover effects that are possible, and how that helps you gain traction. Like our frustrated hiker in Chapter Five who was cut off by the cyclist, once you are able to identify a state of mind (in his case, feeling victimized), you can begin to see how it plays out in different ways in your life and, recognizing that it's unnecessary, eventually let go of it.

With practice, you can break the rigidity of inflexible states of mind and learn to become fluid, seeing the world, and yourself, from many different vantage points. Where you ultimately choose to take it is up to you. The landscape is wide open with possibilities.

BIG BUSINESS

There's a tool that's gained traction in the business world over the past few years that can also be applied to our personal lives. It's called "change management." The term refers to a strategic approach that businesses use to implement changes, which involves paying close attention to the manner in which the change is considered, applied and, ultimately, adopted.

In each section of this book, we've looked at how our current mode of operation can be problematic with regard to specific areas. Then we looked at how to recognize, and what can be done to change, our approach. We also discussed how difficult implementing change in our lives can be, and why we resist it to the extent we do. While it may appear easy to make individual small changes, looking at our lives as a whole can be overwhelming.

So, following the lead of big business, perhaps a strategy would benefit us as well. *(Besides, if it's helpful in the business world, then it must be valid and helpful in our personal lives as well... naturally.)*

A LITTLE HISTORY

With the advent of personal computer networks, data sharing over the Internet, and companies' shift from paper-based communication to digital workflow processes, employees have had to adapt to radically new methods of working.

No longer do we type up memos and distribute them around the office; instead we write emails (sometimes hundreds a day) and forward them to different people throughout our organization.

Additionally, with increased competition between companies, businesses face increasingly challenging conditions, including strong product competition, corporate takeovers, price wars, and constant technological innovations to keep up with. Companies must be agile and react quickly to changing conditions in order to stay alive.

However, what companies have found is that people generally don't react well to a rapidly changing work environment. While a few may thrive with constant change, most people are more comfortable and operate better when things are familiar.

They need to feel in control of their environment, knowing exactly what to expect and when things will happen. For them, novelty can be overwhelming, scary, intimidating, or confusing. And too much change too fast can backfire and lead to inefficiency.

To deal with the challenges that rapid change poses in the workplace, many forward-thinking businesses have adopted one of the numerous change management methodologies that have evolved over the years. These methodologies focus on gradual and methodical, proactively planned, realistic approaches to implementing change.

When executed successfully, workers gradually begin to see and reap the personal benefits of change in their day-to-day work lives, and they start to look for additional opportunities to make changes in the organization. In time, numerous people become advocates for change, which helps to create a culture in which change is more readily accepted and easily adopted.

Many of us also experience fear and resist making changes in our personal lives. Even when we're motivated to make an effort, we may worry about what going through that process will be like, how challenging and taxing, mentally and physically, it will really be.

Or we may assume it will be easy, and once we get into it, find it uncomfortable, difficult and frustrating. Subsequently we may lose our motivation, eventually reverting back to our old habits—a known quantity with which we have a level of comfort.

While it might be easy to start a diet, it's challenging to stay on one because we're frustrated and resentful about going from eating whatever we want whenever we want to a more limited and controlled regimen. We're motivated at the beginning of the year to start an exercise routine, and attack it full-force, only to encounter physical discomfort and limited results. We soon find reasons why we can no longer fit it into our busy schedules.

PRIMAL URGES

Change is difficult for the majority of us, pure and simple. Each of us deals with change at our own pace and with varying degrees of resistance.

Our lives, for the most part, are a known quantity over which we have some control, which helps us feel that we are in tune with the world. When we face change, we face the unknown. And facing the unknown, for most of us, means facing fear.

In its primal form, fear means to run and hide, take cover, get to safety—somewhere where we have a sense of control again. Once the threat has passed, we soon return to "some semblance of normalcy."

If, like the corporations that institute change management, we are able to take a more planned, realistic, and strategic approach to understanding our own operating systems, and be willing to make small internal shifts, such as the ones described in this book, we may begin to notice significant changes in our state of mind.

We can learn that, without having to change anything or anyone outside of ourselves, we can open up to ever-deepening levels of peace within us.

LONG-TERM CARE

So what does change look like from the perspective of mindfulness? Not to sound clichéd, but that really depends on you. How far do you want to take it? Some people are looking for tidbits of insight to help them feel a little more relaxed, calm, and centered when facing a stressful situation. Others may want the whole enchilada—mental clarity and peaceful states 24/7/365. Whatever your preference, either of these is possible, as is everything in between.

One of the most profound joys in practicing mindfulness is the ways in which these concepts will continue to expand for you over time, providing new ways of seeing things and ever-new levels of understanding. As I've mentioned throughout the book: it's a journey, not a destination.

If your expectation is that mindfulness will solve all of your problems (which it really can, maybe just not in the way you expect), or that it will be a "cure," try to think of it a little differently: you're your own cure. You don't need to look elsewhere for answers. You just need the right tools and the willingness to look. *(And now please go back and read Chapter Seven: "Expectations" again!)*

FINISH YOUR PEAS

As I've stated repeatedly throughout the book (*ad nauseam* for some of you), our greatest allies in this effort are patience, perseverance, and practice.

> **Patience:** It's best not to have the expectation that you will radically change overnight. Change takes time, at least for the majority of us, and especially when starting something new. Change will take as long as it takes. Generally, the bigger the issue, the longer it will take.
>
> However, once you begin to make small changes, your willingness to approach the larger issues will grow, along with your confidence.

Try not to beat yourself up when you struggle in your efforts, as this just makes things worse. Be compassionate with yourself and recognize that you're doing the best you can with what you have.

Perseverance: Just get up one more time than you've fallen down. That is the key, plain and simple.

Practice: Simply reading this book, or any book, is not going to solve your problems. You have to put the concepts into action.

So often in the self-help and New Age community, people believe that just reading a book on a particular subject will provide instant enlightenment on that subject. *("Oh, now I get it. Got it! Done! Next.")*

Reading a book about martial arts will not enable you to walk into a dojo and walk out an hour later with a black belt. Until, like Neo in *The Matrix*, we are able to obtain an instant download of jujitsu, we're going to have to put in the hours.

ARISE, GO FORTH AND CONQUER (YOURSELF)

Following are some final tips for approaching and maintaining your mindfulness practice, for your personal Change Management Plan:

- However you perceive your personal limitations with regard to making changes, these perceptions can change as well; nothing is set in stone.

Believing that this practice, or anything, is "too difficult" or "too hard" for you is also a perception, and it can be challenged and potentially changed.

- There is no end point in self-discovery. There are only deeper and greater realizations and levels of peace to experience within yourself. There is no graduation ceremony, internally or externally.

  And if you're looking for the world to reflect back to you how peaceful and insightful you've become from your practice of mindfulness, then that's something to examine as well.

- You will still encounter difficult, challenging, and trying times and experiences. The world will not change, wars will not end; but your perceptions and interactions with people and the world can.

- When facing difficult times, you may focus so much on the difficulties in your life that you start to believe that you will never see another bright day, that nothing good will happen to you, ever again. You will perpetually live in a state of darkness.

  We tend to forget that we have gone through challenging times before and we have gotten through them. We went on to experience brighter days and moments.

  During those dark times, we may have believed that life should be something other than what we were experiencing. But if we had just experienced those moments in the moment, knowing that they would eventually change (because everything is always changing), they would not have seemed so overwhelming while we were going through them.

- You may have noticed that the topics of compassion and gratitude were mentioned liberally throughout the book. It's for good reason. I cannot stress enough the importance of these two tools. More than anything, they will help you get yourself out of the way. Keep them in the forefront of your practice and review them frequently.

- Approach your practice as a game, not a chore. A game to help you discover greater peace, serenity, and beauty in life.

  If you find yourself becoming frustrated with your practice, try to refocus on the successes and realizations you've experienced. As mentioned earlier, reviewing your journal during challenging times can help revitalize your practice.

  Strive to find fun ways of incorporating mindfulness strategies into your daily life.

- Laugh often and with abandon. Purposefully seek out things that make you laugh. Whether it's silly videos on the Internet, ridiculous cartoons, or clips from your favorite funny movies, do whatever you need to do to get yourself to a happier state.

  Laughter is one of the most powerful tools we have for shifting our state of mind when things get heavy.

  Often we get accustomed to low states of mind and don't even recognize when we're in them for long periods of time. Laughter can help shake us out of them.

- Constantly be on the lookout for references to mindfulness in the world, whether in literature, art, movies, or even in social or business situations. They manifest in an unlimited number of forms and can open you up to new insights. You may have noticed that some of the quotes in this book took on a different meaning when presented in the context of mindfulness.

  By doing this, you allow Life and Eternity to be among your teachers.

- Continue to explore the world of mindfulness by reading other books on the subject, referring to spiritual texts, and/or taking classes and workshops.

  This is your personal journey and there is not a one-size-fits-all approach. You are unique (just like everyone else); so too should be your journey.

  Remember, the journey is the destination... so you've already arrived.

DON'T FORGET TO ORDER A SIDE OF MAGIC

To conclude, I would like to present a couple of personal stories from people who participated in my workshops and who continue to actively work on their mindfulness practice. It was participants like these who inspired me to create this book. Through their efforts, I have been privileged to witness radical transformations in others.

For me, like being enchanted by raindrops dancing in puddles, just observing the changes that mindfulness can bring is a large part of the magic. It helps me see, gratefully, that there is no end to what is possible.

Through many hours of practicing meditation and mindfulness, I have found the beauty in life that I missed for so many years. I know every day will not be perfect, that crap will still happen, but I can now deal with it differently.

People in my life have commented on how much I have changed. Some of the comments were brutally honest and made me wonder what kind of person I used to be. I see that I was a rather nasty person, I was angry all the time, judgmental, hurtful, mean, and selfish. That is an ugly realization that crushed my ego, but I'm so thankful for being shown a way to end or lessen these personal traits.

My way of thinking has changed. How I see others has changed. How I deal with things has changed. I know now that if I want something, I can achieve it by myself through diligence and personal power, instead of hoping for or relying on something or someone else, as had been my pattern in the past.

-Sandy

Mindfulness to me is noticing the stillness that is always present.

This stillness seems to hold every moment when you take the time to notice it. I recall one brisk fall night: I was walking through a parking lot to my car and noticed a calm about me that was absolutely effortless. In fact, it would have required effort to leave it, and why the heck would I!? It was peaceful and at the same time energizing.

I looked up at a tree framed in the yellow glow from a lamppost. The tree was round in shape with green leaves and looked like it belonged in a storybook. It was as if the tree was standing still in time. There was a crisp breeze about, but it seemed that the tree was motionless, as if the leaves weren't moving in the wind.

That was a beautiful moment.

-Billy

AUTHOR'S NOTES

First and foremost, I offer my sincere gratitude to my Teacher for all that he has done and continues to do for me and for his students everywhere. My greatest hope is that I may adequately represent a fraction of his grace in my work. Through his immense patience and wisdom, he was able to open a heart which had been trapped in fear for a very long time.

To Ms. Nicole Grace and Mr. Scott Wilson: your patience, humor, and ability to inspire can never be overstated. The graciousness and generosity you display in your lives knows no end. I am constantly amazed by all that you do and the extent to which you give of yourselves. It is a tremendous gift to be able to bear witness to those actions. I pray never to take for granted my good fortune in continuing to learn from you. I know that words will never do justice to the gratitude I feel for all that you have done for me.

To those who have studied alongside me, I am eternally appreciative of the laughter, tears, and adventures we have been able to share together. Your willingness to reach out a hand and help raise me up when I faltered during many difficult times has not gone unnoticed.

It is thanks to all of these teachers and the grace of Eternity that I was able to complete this book.

My parents and family have always supported and accepted me and my endeavors without question, and I don't think anyone could ask for more. While not completely understanding many of my interests and choices, they have nonetheless always been supportive. I realize how fortunate I am to have this foundation in my life and I am extremely grateful.

I am sincerely grateful to my editors, Jon Hofferman and Catherine Elliott Escobedo, for your patience in working with this new writer. Your enthusiasm and professionalism have eased many a furrowed brow and look of confusion when I was feeling overwhelmed by this endeavor. I believe anyone who has the opportunity to work with you will be the better for doing so.

Finally, to the many amazing and colorful workshop participants I have had the honor of standing in front of over the years, you are an ongoing source of inspiration and joy for me. Some of the most profound moments and experiences in my life, for which I am most grateful, have occurred in those classes with you. Your willingness to ask questions, share your stories of tragedy and humor, and listen to and actually try out the practices I set forth, humbles me. You have been the source of many private (and a few public) tears of gratitude.

ABOUT THE AUTHOR

Michael Brooks is the founder of ZenWhim, Inc., a company dedicated to sharing the teachings of mindfulness in an approachable and humorous format. His attraction to meditation and mindfulness arose out of his own spiritual seeking at a young age. Since 2004 he has been teaching meditation and mindfulness classes and workshops in both Northern and Southern California to a wide-ranging audience—from stressed company executives to enthusiastic soccer moms.

Additionally, Michael has worked for over twenty years in the field of computer technology. During that time he has progressed through every role involved in creating and managing computer software, from programmer to program and portfolio manager. He has worked in diverse environments, from Wall Street financial companies and regulated medical device companies, to small dot.com startups. As a result, he has a strong understanding of what it means to live and work in the world, and what it's like to cope with stressful office and personal politics.

His writing comes out of his personal experience using mindfulness to navigate his own challenging states of mind, as well as the transformations he has been privileged to observe in others. This book grew out of his deep desire to make the teachings of mindfulness accessible to a wider audience in a logical and approachable format.

NOTES AND FURTHER READING

FRONT MATTER

[i] Henry David Thoreau. *The Journal of Henry David Thoreau*, April 24, 1859.

INTRODUCTION

[ii] This quote is usually attributed to Henry Ford. http://www. goodreads.com/author/quotes/203714.Henry_Ford, accessed May 24, 2013.

[iii] GoodReads.com. http://www.goodreads.com/author/ quotes/2742325.Omar_Khayy_m, accessed May 24, 2013.

SECTION ONE

iv Laozi, *Tao Te Ching*. Wikiquote.org. http://en.wikiquote. org/wiki/Laozi, accessed September 2, 2013.

CHAPTER ONE: WHAT IS MINDFULNESS

v Internet Meme. Author Unknown.

vi Jon Kabat-Zinn. *Full Catastrophe Living: Using the Wisdom of Your Body and Mind to Face Stress, Pain, and Illness.* New York: Dell Publishing, 1990.

vii Henry David Thoreau. *Walden.* Public Domain Books, 2006. Kindle edition.

CHAPTER TWO: GETTING STARTED

viii This quote is often attributed to Kahil Gibran. http://www. goodreads.com/author/quotes/6466154.Kahlil_Gibran, accessed September 14, 2013.

ix Lewis Carroll. *Alice's Adventures in Wonderland.* Public Domain Books, 1997. Kindle edition.

CHAPTER THREE: THE ONLY THING CONSTANT

x This quote is often attributed to Albert Einstein. http:// en.wikiquote.org/wiki/Albert_Einstein, accessed September 14, 2013.

xi *The Matrix.* Directed by Andy Wachowski and Lana Wachowski. With Keanu Reeves and Laurence Fishburne. Warner Bros. Pictures, 1999.

[xii] William Shakespeare. *Othello*, II, iii, lines 369-370.

SECTION TWO: ROOT CAUSE ANALYSIS

[xiii] *The Wordsworth Dictionary of Quotations* edited by Connie Robertson. London: Bibliophile Books, 1998.

CHAPTER FOUR: UNDERSTANDING THE PLAYING FIELD

[xiv] Leo Tolstoy. "Three Methods Of Reform" in *Pamphlets*. Translated by Aylmer Maude. http://en.wikiquote.org/wiki/Leo_Tolstoy, accessed September 14, 2013.

[xv] J.K. Rowling. *Harry Potter and the Goblet of Fire*. New York: Scholastic, 2000.

[xvi] Lewis Carroll. *Alice's Adventures in Wonderland*. Public Domain Books, 1997. Kindle edition.

[xvii] This quote is often attributed to Mohandas K. Gandhi. http://thinkexist.com/quotes/mahatma_gandhi, accessed September 14, 2013.

[xviii] This quote is often attributed to Confucious. http://www.goodreads.com/author/quotes/15321.Confucius, accessed September 14, 2013.

[xix] Oscar Wilde. *The Importance of Being Earnest*. New Jersey: Barnes and Noble Classics, 2003.

[xx] Lewis Carroll. *Alice's Adventures in Wonderland*. Public Domain Books, 1997. Kindle edition.

CHAPTER FIVE: PERCEPTIONS

xxi Marcus Aurelius, *Meditations*. Public Domain Books, 2012. Kindle edition.

xxii Marcus Aurelius, *Meditations*. Wikipedia.com. http://en.wikipedia.org/wiki/Meditations, accessed May 24, 2012.

xxiii John Watson. *The Homely Virtues*. London: Hodder & Stoughton, 1903.

xxiv GoodReads.com. http://www.goodreads.com/author/quotes/47790.Martha_Graham, accessed November 23, 2012.

CHAPTER SIX: UNDER THE INFLUENCE

xxv William Shakespeare. *Hamlet*, II, ii, line 259.

xxvi Marcus Aurelius, *Meditations*. Wikipedia.com. http://en.wikipedia.org/wiki/Meditations, accessed May 24, 2012.

xxvii Dale Carnegie. *How to Win Friends & Influence People*. New York: Simon & Schuster Adult Publishing Group, 1982.

xxviii BrainyQuote.com. http://www.brainyquote.com/quotes/quotes/w/waltwhitma146892.html, accessed November 23, 2012.

CHAPTER SEVEN: EXPECTATIONS

xxix GoodReads.com. http://www.goodreads.com/author/quotes/884168.Russell_Brand, accessed November 23, 2012.

xxx While this quote is often attributed to Albert Einstein or novelist Rita Mae Brown, the most likely source is the Narcotics Anonymous "Basic Text," released in 1981.

CHAPTER EIGHT: AUTOBIOGRAPHY

[xxxi] Mohandas K. Gandhi. *Ethical Religion*. Madras: S Ganesan, 1922.

[xxxii] Thomas Byrom. "Choices." In *Dhammapada: The Sayings of the Buddha*. Boston: Shambala Publications, 1976.

[xxxiii] This quote is often attributed to Harvey Fierstein. http://www.goodreads.com/author/quotes/4775.Harvey_Fierstein, accessed November 23, 2012..

[xxxiv] Diamond Dallas Page. *Never, Ever Give Up. Arthur's Inspirational Transformation!* Retrieved from https://www.youtube.com/watch?v=qX9FSZJu448.

CHAPTER NINE: PROJECTIONS AND REFLECTIONS

[xxxv] Plato. *Apology*. Translated by Benjamin Jowett. http://classics.mit.edu/Plato/apology.html, accessed June 29, 2013.

[xxxvi] GoodReads.com. http://www.goodreads.com/author/quotes/57108.Gloria_Steinem, accessed November 23, 2012.

CHAPTER TEN: CLARITY

[xxxvii] http://www.abrahamlincolnonline.org/lincoln/speeches/persevere.htm, accessed September 14, 2013.

[xxxviii] This quote is often attributed to Thales. http://en.wikipedia.org/wiki/Know_thyself, accessed September 14, 2013.

CHAPTER ELEVEN: HAPPINESS AND GRATITUDE

xxxix Cicero. *Oratio Pro Cnæo Plancio, XXXIII.*

xl This quote is often attributed to Abraham Lincoln. http://www.quotationspage.com/quotes/Abraham_Lincoln, accessed November 23, 2012..

xli Abraham Lincoln. "Address Before the Wisconsin State Agricultural Society, Milwaukee, Wisconsin" (September 30, 1859). *The Collected Works of Abraham Lincoln.* Edited by Roy P. Basler. Vol. 3. Ann Arbor: University of Michigan Digital Library Production.

xlii William Blake. "Auguries of Innocence." http://www.public-domain-poetry.com/william-blake/auguries-of-innocence-9210, accessed September 14, 2013.

SECTION THREE: BE... SIMPLY BE

xliii Robert A. Heinlein. *Stranger in a Strange Land.* New York: The Berkeley Publishing Group, 1991.

CHAPTER TWELVE: NOW IS THE TIME

xliv Matthew 6:34.

xlv Jon Kabat-Zinn. *Full Catastrophe Living: Using the Wisdom of Your Body and Mind to Face Stress, Pain, and Illness.* New York: Dell Publishing, 1990.

xlvi Swami Prabhavananda and Christopher Isherwood, trans. *How to Know God: The Yoga Aphorisms of Patanjali.* Hollywood: Vedanta Society of Southern California, 1953.

xlvii William Yardley, "Patrick Edlinger, a Trendsetter for Sports Climbing, Dies at 52," *New York Times*, November 26, 2012, accessed on November 29, 2012, http://www.nytimes.com/2012/11/27/sports/patrick-edlinger-a-trendsetter-for-sport-climbing-dies-at-52.html.

xlviii *The Legend of Bagger Vance*. Directed by Robert Redford. With Matt Damon, Will Smith and Charlize Theron. Twentieth Century Fox Film Corporation, 2000.

CHAPTER THIRTEEN: MEDITATION

xlix John Milton. *Paradise Lost*. London: E. Stock, 1877.

l This quote is often attributed to Henry David Thoreau. http://www.goodreads.com/author/quotes/10264.Henry_David_Thoreau, accessed November 23, 2012.

CONCLUSION

li Henry David Thoreau. *Walden*. http://en.wikiquote.org/wiki/Walden, accessed September 14, 2013.

CPSIA information can be obtained at www.ICGtesting.com
Printed in the USA
LVOW06s1032220414

382719LV00001B/123/P